Not unto Us

A Celebration of the Ministry of Kurt J. Eggert

William H. Braun and Victor H. Prange
Compiling Editors

Northwestern Publishing House
Milwaukee, Wisconsin

This book is offered not merely as a tribute to a gifted man but in grateful acknowledgment to the Lord of the church for the blessings he has bestowed on his people through the ministry of Kurt Eggert. It is therefore only fitting to offer the book under the title of one of his own hymns: "Not unto us, not unto us be glory, Lord; Not unto us but to your name be praise" (CW 392).

All Scripture quotations, unless indicated, are taken from the HOLY BIBLE, NEW INTERNATIONAL VERSION®. Copyright © 1973, 1978, 1984 by International Bible Society. Used by permission of Zondervan Publishing House. All rights reserved.

The "NIV" and "New International Version" trademarks are registered in the United States Patent and Trademark Office by International Bible Society. Use of either trademark requires the permission of International Bible Society.

All rights reserved. No part of this publication may be reproduced, stored in a retrieval system, or transmitted in any form or by any means—electronic, mechanical, photocopying, recording, or otherwise—except for brief quotations in reviews, without prior permission from the publisher.

Library of Congress Control Number: 00136659
Northwestern Publishing House
1250 N. 113th St., Milwaukee, WI 53226-3284
http://www.nph.net
© 2001 Northwestern Publishing House
Published 2001
Printed in the United States of America
ISBN 0-8100-1328-2

Contents

Foreword 5
   Carl H. Mischke

Selected Essays on Worship and Music by Kurt Eggert 7
   Compiled by William H. Braun

Texts, Tunes, and Compositions by Kurt Eggert 79
   Compiled by William H. Braun

The Life of Kurt John Eggert 91
   Ruth Eggert

The Lutheran Chorale of Milwaukee and
Kurt Eggert's Music Leadership 105
   Mary Prange and Peggy Henning

The Kurt J. Eggert Hymnological and
Liturgical Memorial Collection 113
   Arnold O. Lehmann

Recollections of *Viva Vox*, 1955–1961 115
   Ralph D. Gehrke

Hymnody and the Proclamation of the Gospel 129
   Carl F. Schalk

The Formation and Flow of Worship Attitudes in
the Wisconsin Evangelical Lutheran Synod 141
   James P. Tiefel

The Shaping of *Christian Worship: A Lutheran Hymnal* 167
   Victor H. Prange

Foreword

Kurt John Eggert was my college and seminary classmate for seven years, four at Northwestern College in Watertown, Wisconsin, and another three at Wisconsin Lutheran Seminary in Thiensville (now Mequon), Wisconsin.

Whenever someone was needed to play the organ or piano or direct a choral group, Kurt was never far away. I enjoyed singing with him and under his direction in a male chorus, a mixed chorus, an octet, and a quartet. At one point during our college days, he even succeeded in recruiting 16 of us (no small feat) for a somewhat informal singing group that came to be known on campus as the Gleemen. Since we were a purely volunteer, self-appointed organization without official standing, we had to rehearse during our free time, usually at some odd hour. Fortunately we did not have to compete with television sets and computers. Word soon got around, and eventually we were even permitted to sing in public at some of the regularly scheduled concerts of the college.

It was readily apparent to all of us that a career in music awaited Kurt somewhere. But where? Without a doubt he could have used his considerable musical talent in positions outside of the church and been well compensated for it. But the Lord led him to use it in the service of our Wisconsin Synod; and we are much richer for it.

Unlike most accomplished musicians, it is especially noteworthy that only four years of Kurt's public ministry were spent in the academic community: at the former Milwaukee Lutheran Teachers' College in Milwaukee. Thirty-two of them were spent as a pastor, serving God's people in the parish, where the real life of the church takes place. His experience as a parish pastor prepared and equipped him, as few other things could have, for the final assignment of his ministry.

When our synod resolved in 1983 to begin work on a new/revised hymnal and authorized the Conference of Presidents to call a full-time project director for this major undertaking, we were led rather easily and naturally to the name of Kurt Eggert. The Lord led him to accept the call. The rest is history. *Christian Worship: A Lutheran Hymnal* is without question his finest legacy to the synod he loved and in whose public ministry he served faithfully for 45 years.

The plan was that Pastor Eggert would formally present the first copy of the new hymnal to the synod through its president at our August

1993 convention in Saginaw. But the Lord in his wisdom had other plans. Because of Eggert's failing health, a factor that made his work extremely difficult during the last months of the hymnal project, I had the privilege of presenting the first copy to him personally in his hospital bed prior to the convention, on June 17, 1993. Five days later the Lord called him home.

May this volume serve as a fitting tribute to the dedication of a man. But above all, may it serve as an incentive to praise and thank our gracious God for giving this man to us "for such a time as this."

Carl H. Mischke

Selected Essays on Worship and Music by Kurt Eggert

Compiled by William H. Braun

Viva Vox
    Dear Fred (Imaginary Letters to a New Choir Director)
    Integrating Organ and Choir Music with the Hymn of the Week

Church Music
    The Case for the Propers in Liturgical Worship
    Canticles for the Congregation

Symposium: Meeting Contemporary Needs in Christian Worship
    Accent on Contemporary
    Accent on Balance

Focus on Worship
    Focus on the Wedding
    Focus on the Wedding Music—The Solo

"Grace Notes"
    Michaelmas
    A Quiz for Church Organists
    Try Unison Music
    Ye Good Olde Summertime
    Practice Makes . . .
    Keys to Choir Success: No. 1
    Neglected to Death

Northwestern Lutheran
    The New Hymnal: A Blue Book
    Our Changing Worship Language
    Pressing On to the Future and Holding On to Our Past

Wisconsin Lutheran Quarterly
    Gospel Hymns and Lutheran Worship

Kurt Eggert wrote a great deal throughout his life on the subject of worship and music. These writings took various forms, ranging from the short "food for thought" paragraphs of "Grace Notes" in *Focus on Worship* to larger formal essays published as articles in the important Lutheran publications of his day such as *Church Music*. The following essays are a small representative sampling of what Eggert wrote over the years as found in the different publications to which he contributed or in the presentations he made for various conferences on worship. For a complete chronological listing of the essays and articles, see the Appendix on page 84.

From *Viva Vox*

In 1954 Eggert, along with Ralph Gehrke, began publishing a quarterly circular entitled *Viva Vox*, which was designed to print the essays and discussions that came out of the seminars that were held for pastors and church musicians in the Watertown area. While the scope of the publication extended far beyond the Watertown area, its basic aim remained "to stimulate improvements of the music in our church services." The following two articles taken from *Viva Vox* are as pertinent today as when they were first written in the late 1950s.

Dear Fred (Imaginary Letters to a New Choir Director)
Viva Vox, 1958 (Vol. IV, No. 1, pp. 7-9)

Dear Fred,
  . . . It is good news that you have been asked to take over the choir at Immanuel's. Yes, I know you've had no special training and that you feel that lack keenly, but you do have the desire to do something to improve the worship in your midst, and in the long run that desire and your Christian common sense will solve more problems than mere formal training is ever able to solve.

Now as to "some suggestions on how to proceed"! One of the things that should be clear from the outset is this: (I) *what you sing must fit into the Order of Common Service.* The choir is not to add any new elements to the service but is, as the musically trained part of the congregation, to aid the rest of the congregation in its worship by either singing those parts of the service that are too difficult for all or that call for special interpretation. The choir should, therefore, participate only when it is "substituting" for the rest of the congregation in one of the regular parts of the service. For instance, it can sing the Gradual (which is too difficult for the congregation as such); it can sing other settings of the *Kyrie*, for instance, to help the congregation understand the meaning and nature of the *Kyrie* it sings every Sunday. The choir should, however, never add songs merely "in order to beautify the service," as if the congregation could be treated as a sort of listening concert-audience. Too many present-day choirs suffer from "anthemitis," the "disease" of now and then adding concertlike special musical contributions to the service; such anthems, pleasant and helpful as they may otherwise be, usually undermine the real work of a genuine church choir and in the long run serve to dampen rather than incite congregational worship.

You will do much better, therefore, to limit yourself, for the beginning at least, to (1) singing alternate stanzas of the Hymn of the Week (according to the suggestions in our Workshop Planning Booklet or *Viva Vox*; this can be done at first even in unison, then in the harmony of the hymnal, and finally in special settings of our church-music composers) and (2) singing in unison the Graduals (use Buszin, *The Graduals for the Church Year*; later, as you gain experience, you can add *Introits for the Church Year*, which are a bit more difficult). Later on, as your choir gains more experience and confidence, you can "graduate" to other settings of the *Kyrie, Gloria, Sanctus,* etc., and to simple motets and anthems for special services and special seasons; but even then this music dare only substitute for parts of the regular service (a motet on Psalm 23, for instance, substituting for the Gradual on Good Shepherd Sunday); it must contribute to, and not detract from the unity of the service.

Another cardinal point (which is in a way included in the point I made above) is this: (II) *what you sing must fit the church year*. Our Planning Booklet enables you to understand the theme and basic unity of each Sunday or festival and conveniently sets before you all the various propers of the day, so that you may plan your choir work far in advance in keeping with the church year. Pastor Miller will, I am sure, be happy to cooperate with you if you submit a list of the Hymns of the Week which you want to use as the basis for your musical program; and, if he wishes to deviate from that order at some time, he can let you know plenty of time in advance. Using the Order of Common Service and the church year as the two points from which to begin your planning will be most helpful and rewarding.

The most valuable all-around book on church music I know is the little one by Henry E. Horn called *O Sing unto the Lord* (Muhlenberg Press, 90¢). It is available from our publishing house and will give you much more background on the things I've referred to than this letter is able to do. But in any case, God bless your choir work so that the gospel is proclaimed and celebrated in your midst in living worship!

Yours in our Lord,
Thomas James

Dear Fred,

. . . It was good to hear the report on your choir's progress. Few letters have given me such joy. Your continued self-criticism pleases me, because without that you cannot continue to progress. But what pleases me most is that you and your choir seem to be experiencing that exhilaration that comes from vital participation in genuine worship-participation every Sunday. I'm so happy that you began as a genuine church choir and not as a parish concert choir. Starting with the Gradual and with alternate singing of the Hymn of the Week seems to me to be the best way of getting that across to choir members and the congregation. That the people are beginning to sing these great hymns with joy and understanding is something that I expected. I also thought Organist Weller would revise his initial negative opinion about alternate singing once he really got to know what it can do. But you be sure now to strengthen the cooperation between yourself, him, and your pastor by continuing to submit to them your music plans for each quarter (especially those for alternate singing). If you institute quarterly or semiannual planning meetings, you can take up other common problems and keep in close contact.

Now you ask for suggestions of easy choir music that is in keeping with what you are doing. Well, the suggested choir selections which the workshop planning leaders worked out for the Planning Booklet will be a good place to begin. As far as basic collections of choral music are concerned, I'd suggest you get only one or two such collections now: perhaps *The Parish Choir Book* (CPH, four-part) and/or *The Morning Star Choir Book* (CPH, unison and two-part). That will suffice for the time being. But at the same time you ought to get music catalogs from both Northwestern Publishing House and Concordia Publishing House, and when you are near, you ought to make a special visit to the publishing house's music display to examine what they have there personally. More than that, write to Professor M. Albrecht at New Ulm for information on the Doctor Martin Luther College Series, and ask Concordia Publishing House to send you exam-packs of new and old choral music (you can keep the packs ten days, pick out what suits you, and return the rest). In that way you will be able to build up your own tailor-made music library.

But above all, you will have to keep the great worship goal of your choir work in view, and you can do that only by realizing again and again in faith what great events take place in the divine service in which you sing. For there God graciously comes to us sinners with his greatest gifts, his Word and sacrament! By taking that coming seriously, you and your choir will be enabled to do what a genuine church choir is called to do.

Yours in our Lord,
Thomas James

Integrating Organ and Choir Music with the Hymn of the Week
Viva Vox, 1959 (Vol. V, No. 2, pp. 3-5)

Regular readers of *Viva Vox* will recognize the term *Hymn of the Week*. The Hymn of the Week, or Hymn of the Day, as it is also called, is the hymn (or a hymn) which reflects the general theme or content of the particular Sunday or festival service. For example, most all of our congregations expect to see No. 262, "A Mighty Fortress," on their hymn boards on Reformation Sunday. Without a doubt, this has become the hymn which we want to sing on that day. Likewise, days like Good Friday, Easter, Ascension have their own particular theme or event of salvation to be celebrated, and there are hymns which are particularly appropriate for these days.

Each Sunday of the church year unique

Actually, however, not only festivals like those mentioned above but every Sunday of the church year has its own character and content as reflected by the Scripture readings and other propers appointed for the day. There are also, in most cases, excellent hymns which fit especially well on these particular Sundays. For example, what hymn would be more fitting and natural on the last Sunday of the church year than "Wake, Awake," based as it is on the Gospel for the Day—the parable of the wise and foolish virgins? After reading the text just once, you would surely sing "Ye Sons and Daughters of the King" (No. 208) on the First Sunday after Easter. Or how about "Dear Christians, One and All,

Rejoice" for Cantate Sunday, or "Salvation Unto Us Has Come" for Septuagesima (wages and grace)?

Lutheran heritage lost

During the years when the church year was more fully observed in the Lutheran church than it is today, there was a fairly strong traditional use of particular hymns for particular Sundays. There was developed a list of principal hymns for the church year much like the series of Gospel and Epistle readings we use Sunday after Sunday. However, by the time the extravagances of Pietism and the sterile negativism of Rationalism had done their work in the Lutheran countries of Europe, the observance of the church year had largely disappeared, and with it the use of the Hymns of the Week and other Lutheran liturgical traditions. In our own land, Reformed ideals and practices have influenced our church more than is generally appreciated. We have to a degree now begun to recapture the Gospel-centered observance of the church year. We might do well to establish or reestablish now the use of the Hymns of the Week.

Use them or lose them

A principal benefit to be derived from establishing the use of a Hymn of the Week series would be the preservation of the solid core of the better hymns of our Reformation heritage. The only way to keep good hymns is to sing them. Nothing else can do it. Merely having them in the hymnal, or lecturing about their worth, or doing noble lip service to them is labor lost unless we actually sing them. The repetition of certain hymns year after year will do much to give them a place in the hearts and worship life of our people.

Hymn of the Week series available

A suggested Hymn of the Week plan has been drawn up by Professor R. Gehrke based largely on the modern German series and has been appearing in connection with the Hymn Studies and Service Guides for the Church Year published in this or previous issues of *Viva Vox*. Since the series is drawn from the historic hymn series that developed in the golden age of Lutheran church music, the Hymns of the Week are, of course, mostly German chorales. Some adaptation and substitution, however, has resulted in the inclusion of certain treasures from English, Greek, Latin, and Scandinavian hymnody.

Too "heavy"?

If the series appears "heavy," it might be noted that the Hymn of the Week only provides for the "middle hymn" of the service. This gives room for the use of other types of hymns if desired. Also, it should be remembered that it is these German chorales of ours which to a large extent carry the emphasis of the church year and can, therefore, be fitted to the specific Sundays and festivals. Finally, the present series is of course not a law for anyone. Use will have to determine whether modifications or substitutions should be made in the future, and nothing prevents any congregation from making its own adaptation of the plan.

A unique opportunity

Many readers of this article, perhaps, are utilizing the present series of Sunday bulletins published by Northwestern Publishing House in their various congregations. This series of bulletins features an illustration of the Hymn of the Week on the cover and includes a short commentary on the hymn on the back cover. If your church is using these bulletins, now would be the natural and ideal time to introduce the use of these hymns.

If the Hymn of the Week plan is worth introducing in your congregation, it is also perhaps worth emphasizing. More can be done than simply to have the congregation sing the Hymn of the Week each Sunday. Why not build your organ and choir music around the Hymn of the Week each Sunday? First of all, this would help you to integrate the whole service, since these hymns reflect the central thoughts and content of each Sunday's celebration. Secondly, the organist, choirs, and school children can all make an effective contribution toward helping the rest of the congregation to learn to sing and to enjoy the singing of the Hymn of the Week.

Sing antiphonally

Why not sing the Hymn of the Week antiphonally each Sunday? Let the choir and/or the day school or Sunday school children alternate in singing the stanzas with the congregation. The advantages of antiphonal singing have been dealt with in other articles of *Viva Vox,* but we might simply state again that antiphonal singing certainly does stimulate and provide welcome variety and interest for the congregation's singing. In addition, it is a distinct help to the congregation in learning to sing the hymn if it is at all difficult.

Use the choir

Have your choir sing alternately with the congregation. It might sing its particular stanzas in unison with the organ accompanying, or a cappella in a simple four-part setting, or two-part with organ accompaniment, etc. It can be as simple or elaborate as you desire. If the hymn is long, the choir might sing its various stanzas in several ways. The congregation not only has a chance to catch its breath while the choir is singing, but it is afforded a good opportunity to listen to the melody if it is somewhat unfamiliar. More than that, experience has shown that antiphonal singing tends to bring the individual worshiper to pay more attention to the words of the hymn than singing all the stanzas in the regular way.

Why not the children?

Here is a golden opportunity to accomplish two things with the children: (1) Teach them the best of their Lutheran hymns and (2) involve them frequently in the worship service of the congregation. Certainly these are both important goals and can be accomplished at one and the same time more or less automatically with the Hymn of the Week. Day school children, especially in the upper grades, can easily learn the melody and something about the text and background of two Hymns of the Week per month. Every other week or once a month the children can participate in the singing of several stanzas of the Hymn of the Week. This will not only help to bring the children to church but will give them a place in the framework of the congregational worship. They are made to feel part of the whole congregation rather than a "guest choir" brought in for the day. Children may sing in parts if desired, but much is achieved by unison singing, and this may be done with a real minimum of effort. The Sunday school pupils should not be overlooked either. They may only be able to sing once during a particular season of the church year (e.g., Advent), especially if they memorize the texts, but they should by all means be included. This should be done even where there is a Christian day school.

What about the organist?

The organist can also do much in making the singing of the Hymn of the Week a stimulating spiritual experience for the congregation. If you are the organist in your church, you might consider building your principal organ music around the Hymn of the Week: Play only a very brief prelude at the beginning of the service (a Bach harmonization or perhaps a contemporary setting of the opening hymn melody, or the like) and then play music based on or inspired by the Hymn of the Week as a prelude to that hymn. Generally speaking, more good music based on Hymn of the Week melodies is available than for the tunes often chosen for the opening of the service. Beside this, it is a question worth considering whether people are not more receptive and ready to listen to the organist at the time of the second hymn than at the very beginning of the service.... The emphasis of the organ would be on that hymn which reflects and echoes the central theme and tone of that particular Sunday. This would not often be the case with the prelude at the beginning of the service, since the opening hymn is so often a general hymn of praise or hymn of invocation.

Another way the organist can possibly help in highlighting the Hymn of the Week for the congregation is by the use of occasional *variant accompaniments to the hymn singing*. Organists might be interested in examining the hymn accompaniments by Helmut Bornefeld, for instance. These are not, first of all, preludes (although they may be used that way also), but they are designed as accompaniments to the congregational singing. (Bornefeld's accompaniments appear in a number of small volumes available from either Northwestern Publishing House or Concordia Publishing House.) The use of an accompaniment different from the hymnal version in an occasional stanza of the hymn can be stimulating. It should be pointed out, of course, that the accompaniments must be done rightly, in such a way that the general flow of the hymn is not disturbed. This would be true also of stanzas sung in harmony by the choir. All contributions by the organist and choir must be (and can be) done in such a way that everything stays within the framework of "the congregational hymn singing." Used rightly, variant accompaniments to the hymn singing will not interfere with but rather "give a lift" to the singing of the whole congregation.

From *Church Music*

Church Music, one of the important liturgical music journals of the 1960s and 1970s, was edited by various faculty members of Concordia Teachers College, River Forest, and published by Concordia Publishing House. Eggert regularly attended the "Lectures in Church Music" given by the college every fall and was invited to make several presentations at this conference, as well as submit articles for publication in the semi-annual journal.

The Case for the Propers in Liturgical Worship
Church Music, 69.1, pp. 19-26

Ask a liturgical expert his opinion of the propers and you may well be treated to an articulate, even eloquent defense of the propers as a noble heritage of devotional literature, rooted in the Scriptures, shaped by the faith and needs of the church through the ages, and bequeathed to us today as substantially relevant for the worship of today's faithful. Ask a parish pastor what he thinks of the propers, and you will likely get a mixture of cautious approval and pointed criticism. Ask the man in the pew for his reaction to the Sunday propers, and the chances are you will get a blank look that calls to the mind the Ephesians Christians' reply to the apostle Paul regarding the Holy Ghost: "We have not so much as heard whether there *be* any. . . ."

Probably no conclusions should be drawn from such a spectrum of offhand comment. Scholars, though usually strong defenders of liturgical worship and of the propers, are well aware of the many problems connected with them. Most laymen, though they may be unaware of the technicalities of the structure and function of the propers, are by no means unaware of their *content*. They know which texts speak to their hearts' need and enable them to express their hearts' response. They know, and in too many instances, I believe, they are disappointed in the propers.

This article attempts to present a case *for* the propers. In doing so, we mean to distinguish between the idea of propers in liturgical worship and the *form* and *content* of the propers as we have them today. An attempt will be made to establish two points: the value of retaining the idea of propers for liturgical worship; the necessity for revision and improvement in their form and content.

The propers and their function

In general, the propers are those parts of the liturgy which *vary* in text according to the Sunday, festival, or season of the church year. They contrast with the "ordinary," or *invariable* parts, whose texts are the same Sunday for Sunday. The propers for the service as we have them today in *The Lutheran Hymnal* and the *Service Book and Hymnal* include, first of all, the Introit, Collect, Lections, and Gradual, which vary for each Sunday or festival day. Then there is the Sentence for the Season (Gradual for the Season) and the Proper Preface, both of which vary according to the seasons rather than the Sundays of the church year. Finally, there are those parts of the service which are not formally appointed or always thought of as propers but which function strongly as such: the sermon, hymns, and appropriate choral music. (It should be added in connection with the Lessons that the *Service Book and Hymnal* allows also for the reading of a Lesson from the Old Testament, to be followed by the singing of a psalm or hymn version of a psalm.)

The minor services, Matins and Vespers, exhibit a wealth of variable material: the Invitatories (responsive antiphons), which precede the singing of the *Venite* (Psalm 95) at Matins and vary with the season; the Psalms, together with their proper antiphons; the Lessons and their Seasonal Responsories; the Office Hymns and the canticles; the Collects for the Day and other collects; and the versicles and antiphons proper to the various collects and canticles.

The idea of proper

Because the texts of the propers change as we move through the church year, they bring to the liturgy a kind of "inevitable" variety. They "flesh out" the skeleton of the ordinary and give particular face and feature to the various services. From an artistic point of view, this variety provided by the propers is an important complement to the sense of unity brought to the service by the unvarying ordinary. Thus the propers supply our worship with a dimension which a liturgy like that of the Eastern Church, which never adopted the use of the propers, does not possess.

Variety for its own sake, however, is neither the original purpose nor basic function of the propers. The idea behind the propers, as the name itself implies, is that of something appropriate or fitting. In a general way, of course, all the parts of the liturgy are appropriate-proper, that is, to the nature of Christian worship. Each of the texts of the ordinary too is appropriate for its individual function and place in the service. The chief purpose of the propers, however, is to tell us what time it is on the calendar of the Christian year. They point us to the particular event commemorated or the special truth or teaching that is to be unfolded and relate it to our worship by providing appropriate words of petition, praise, trust, etc., for our response. They provide a point of view, a frame of reference, for the whole liturgy, each one distinctive and appropriate for a particular festival, Sunday, or season of the church year. The great value in the idea of the propers is this, that through these appropriately selected readings, psalms, and prayers, the events of our Lord's life and saving work are unfolded and related to our own time and life. The health of the church in every age is dependent upon such gospel confrontation.

How the propers developed

It is worth noting that the propers began very simply and naturally, with no thought of developing a liturgical system or logical scheme for worship. The story of the origin and growth of the propers is really the story of the development of the church year, that calendar by which the church divides and devotes its God-given time to an annual recollection of the life and work of Christ and their significance for the Christian life. The full story of the development of the church year is beyond the scope of this article and may be traced in the excellent study by Edward T. Horn III. The point worth emphasizing, however, is that the development of the church year, and along with it the content of the propers, grew out of the desire of the early church continually to recall and relate to itself the life of its Lord.

As the major festivals and commemoration of specific events was established by the Christian community, the need for appropriate worship materials was met by turning to the Psalms and selected readings from Scripture. Both were used in the synagogue services and so were familiar, at least to the Jewish Christians. At first the readings from the "Memoirs of the Apostles" and other parts of Scripture were consecutive, the reader picking up in one service where he had left off in the previous service *(lectio continua)*, but the idea of selections appropriate to the commemoration of certain events soon resulted in the use of pericopes for all the Sundays and special days of the year. Since the *Gospel* not only brought the figure of Christ and his words directly before the worshipers but was also the most explicit account of the event being commemorated, it is easy to see why the Gospel became the chief or controlling proper in the service. The *Psalms* also were a natural resource for "proper" materials, partly because they were already there, but especially because their wide variety of devotional expression-confession, praise, exhortation, trust, etc., made them ideal

---

[1] Edward T. Horn III, The Christian Year (Muhlenberg Press, 1957).

for relating the historical event or teaching of the day's Gospel to the hearts and lives of the congregation. Both of the principal propers of the Sunday service, the Introit and the Gradual, draw the bulk of their content from the Psalms, although we have today only selected verses instead of the entire psalms originally sung.

How the propers function in worship

In order to see how the texts of the propers function in the service and to evaluate the extent to which they still realize their ancient idea and ideal, consider the propers for the first Sunday of the church year:

THE INTROIT
V. Unto Thee, O Lord, do I lift up my soul; O My god, I trust in Thee. Let me not be ashamed; let not mine enemies triumph over me. Yea, let none that wait on Thee be ashamed.
V. Show me Thy way, O Lord; teach me Thy paths.

THE COLLECT
Stir up, we beseech Thee, Thy power, O Lord, and come, that by Thy protection we may be rescued from the threatening perils of our sins and saved by Thy mighty deliverance, who livest and reignest with the Father and the Holy Ghost, ever one God, world without end. Amen.

THE GRADUAL
All they that wait on Thee shall not be ashamed, O Lord.
V. Show me Thy ways, O Lord; teach me Thy paths. Alleluia! Alleluia!
V. Show us Thy mercy, O Lord, and grant us Thy salvation.

If we attempt to generalize the function of the propers on the basis of the fairly typical sample, we might say something like this: the Gospel brings us the Christ-event, or central truth, for the day; the Introit sets the tone of the day (joyful, penitential, contemplative, etc.) and voices the timely truth which relates past events to present worship; the Collect voices a specific petition based on the Gospel, or seasonal theme, or related to the Epistle itself, and usually adds a practical application or doctrinal exposition suggested by the day's or season's themes (sometimes it provides the central theme for the Sunday); the Gradual is a response of petition or praise, harking back to the Epistle or anticipating the Gospel or sometimes both; the Proper Preface establishes a point of view for the celebration of Holy Communion.

The harmony of the propers

It can be readily shown that seldom do *all* the propers function in a clear and "proper" harmony on a given day. Sometimes, especially in the nonfestival half of the year, hardly any harmony or governing principle is discernible. On the other hand, *harmony* in the propers does not mean the repetition of a specific theme throughout all of the service. If we superimpose such a straitjacket on the propers, we will constantly be disappointed. Harmony does not mean that every note of the C-major chord is C. Rather, the propers serve to point out the various *implications* of the general truth or event recalled by the Gospel. Each has its own assigned place and function in the service, its particular emphasis, its individual content. The propers relate to each other as different but harmonious tones of a chord, and to the central theme of the day as descants do to a melody or counterpoint to a cantus firmus. Each proper contributes something to the service—explanation, application, variation, intensification, etc.—so that when the service is finished, there emerges a sense of wholeness and unity together with uniqueness of content, tone, and significance that sets that particular service apart from any other. When harmony of the propers is viewed in this way, I believe that the propers for the first Sunday in Advent, for example, reflect a substantial and satisfying harmony.

The value of the propers

Should the use of the propers be retained as an organizing principle of Lutheran worship? There are many who would just as soon let them go as try to make them go in the service! This writer is firmly of the opinion, however, that the idea of propers in our liturgical worship ought by no means be discarded. Where the various propers as we have them in our service books are truly communicative and edifying for the congregation, they should be retained and used. Where they do not function effectively, we should be bold enough to attempt a careful revision or refashioning. A number of reasons for retaining the idea of the propers stand out.

The propers turn the wheel of the church year, keeping our eyes focused on Christ and orienting our worship and life constantly to his saving life and work of salvation. If we understand and value the church year not only as a formal and schematic device for worship but also as a means of rooting us constantly in the deep foundations of the

Christian faith, we will better appreciate the propers which are so intimately connected with the church year.

The intent of the propers is to make past objective events timely. They point out the present reality and significance of salvation history and help us relate the events to our own lives.

Viewed aesthetically as well as devotionally, the propers provide a welcome and valuable variety to complement the unvarying ordinary of the service. If the ordinary is the fundamentum of each service, the propers supply the overtones which lend color, mood, and interest. By establishing a more or less definite theme or frame of reference, they help to give each celebration a distinctive character, while at the same time binding up the service into a unified whole. From the larger perspective of the whole year, they supply our worship with an overall unity which revolves around the life of Christ and the Christian life.

They assure an annually balanced fare of law and gospel. Comparison with the Catechism will reveal that there is virtually none of the chief teachings of Scripture which does not receive an accent in the appointed pericopes and other propers.

The use of the church year and the propers enables an orderly planning and preparation of appropriate choral and organ music. This point is also of importance for the production of musical materials.

The propers and their problems

If the points mentioned above have any validity or persuasiveness at all, it is fair to ask why it is that the propers receive such unenthusiastic reception in so many Lutheran churches. A casual notice of the frequency with which the propers are ignored by the choirs, read rather mechanically by the pastor, "stood through" resignedly by the congregation, or omitted entirely should be warning enough that all is not well with the propers. The causes are neither few nor hard to find. They may perhaps be grouped conveniently under three headings: (1) poor propers, (2) poor performance, (3) poorly prepared participants.

Let us consider the last one first. Sometimes the propers are ineffective simply because the worshiper is not ready to worship. Unless a person comes to the service spiritually hungry, ready to receive from God and respond to him, he is not likely to get much from the propers. A brimming cup cannot be filled. There is, however, another kind of unready worshiper. Some people are not edified by the propers, especially the Introit and Gradual, simply because they are so poor in knowledge and understanding of Scripture. The Bible imagery, historical allusions, symbolic terms, and typical references are simply beyond them. For such people the value of the propers is sharply reduced. Sometimes brief hints and helps in the Sunday bulletin or other preservice preparation can aid, especially where the propers are particularly obscure. The best answer, however, is the ongoing liturgical preparation accomplished by the pastor who preaches Sunday after Sunday in tune with the church year. The preacher who himself lives in the framework of the liturgical year, studies the propers carefully, and selects sermon texts appropriate to the day will find himself almost inevitably alluding to the various propers and expressions from them. Regular liturgical preaching gradually builds up the theological and scriptural vocabulary and understanding necessary for a wholesome use of the propers.

The second general cause of discontent with the propers is poor presentation. Poor reading and poor singing are both markedly successful in obscuring the content of the propers or making them sound unimportant. For several reasons it is desirable to have the Introits and Graduals sung rather than read, provided they are sung well. First of all, these are, historically, musical forms with a definite structure. This structure is best realized when sung. For example, singing allows the Alleluias of the Gradual (which were originally a form separate from the Gradual) to be given a kind of emphasis that is awkward in reading. Besides this, the somewhat slower presentation of the sung proper gives the rather compressed content of these propers a better chance of being understood. Also, the reading of the Gradual between the Lections interrupts the give-and-take nature of the liturgy. The reading of the Epistle seems to call for a major response of the people at this point (either by the congregation or a section of it, the choir). When the pastor reads the Epistle, then supplies the response himself, something is lost. It must be admitted, however, that good reading is better than bad singing. Poor singing of the propers can obliterate the whole content.

Another factor responsible for poor presentation of the sung propers is the attitude of many choirs towards the propers in general and the musical settings in particular. They find the music for the propers dull and uninteresting and so give the propers insufficient rehearsal in their eagerness to get to the "real music" of the anthem. Some also find unison music beneath the dignity of an adult choir. With such attitudes the predictable result is poor performance. It is true that most settings of the propers, particularly those using a musical formula which serves many texts, are not dramatic or interpretative music. Rather, the music is designed essentially to carry the text and bring it to the congregation with clarity and grace. This makes it necessary for the choir to study the meaning and speech rhythms of the text. Where this is carefully done, the result will be a kind of beauty and satisfaction well worth experiencing. If the choir has a right attitude regarding its place as part of the congregation, whose responsibility and privilege it is to sing those parts of the service beyond the ability of the whole congregation, then the singing of the propers will edify both choir and congregation.

The third and probably most important reason for the negative attitude largely held toward the propers concerns the content and to an extent also the form of the propers themselves. Poor propers are not edifying, even when the listeners are ready to be edified and the propers are well performed. The really significant problem that exists with the propers, especially with the Introit and Gradual, lies in the area of intelligibility. There are some times, however, when the congregation simply cannot make any sense out of one or more of the propers. How, for example, can the congregation join in the prayer uttered by the choir or pastor in a section of the Gradual for Trinity 10: "Let my sentence come forth from Thy presence: let Thine eyes behold the things that are equal!" If the propers are ever to capture the devotional imagination of Lutheran congregations and realize their ancient idea and ideal, then they must be intelligible not only to the liturgical scholars and pastors, who have studied them thoroughly, but also to the man in the pew, who only hears them once in the service! Propers that fail to communicate are poor propers.

Why the propers sometimes fail

Sometimes the *thought* expressed in a proper is so difficult that it fails to communicate either its meaning or relationship to the day, for instance, the Gradual for Christmas Day:

> Thy people shall be willing in the day of Thy power: in the beauties of holiness from the womb of the morning.
> V. The Lord said unto my Lord, sit Thou at My right hand: until I make Thine enemies Thy footstool. Alleluia! Alleluia!
> V. The Lord said unto Me, Thou art My Son; this day have I begotten Thee. Alleluia!

A major hindrance to communication is the archaic *language* of the propers. This is especially true of the Introit and Gradual, which draw so heavily on the Psalms. Even phrases which are familiar because of repeated use in the propers are often not understood or are misunderstood. Some samples: "Let me not be ashamed"; "Judge me by Thy strength"; "Have respect, O Lord, unto Thy covenant"; "Unto Thee shall the vow be performed"; "Thou hast brought back the captivity of Jacob"; "Thine enemies roar in the midst of Thy congregations: they set up their ensigns for signs"; etc. Not all of these phrases are totally unintelligible, of course; but their effectiveness is dulled by the remoteness of expression.

The *form* of the Introit and Gradual is also a problem for communication. Since the several verses are only fragments of original whole psalms or major parts of psalms, it is difficult for the worshiper to get a concerted thought from the single hearing. This is especially true when the antiphon and psalm verse of the Introit, for example, seem to take off in different directions. Consider this sample from Trinity 1:

> Antiphon: O Lord, I have trusted in Thy mercy: my heart shall rejoice in Thy salvation. I will sing unto the Lord: because He hath dealt bountifully with me.
> Psalm: How long wilt Thou forget me, O Lord? How long wilt Thou hide Thy face from me?

Even though the propers often do not function in an ideal and completely satisfying way, they should not be viewed as a lost cause or unworthy of careful preparation and presentation. The devotional richness of many individual propers along with the generally satisfactory harmony on dozens of days of the church year ought to promote a positive attitude. Even if no change at all is made in the present form or content, the case for the propers would be greatly strengthened in every congregation if pastor, church musician, choir, and people would undertake to do all they could to make the propers work. Careful planning of the service by pastor and church musician can result in sermon, hymns, and choral and organ music which is in tune with the day. If the same amount of effort and creative thinking were expended on worship as is given to programs of the congregation in the areas of stewardship, missions, education, and the like, there would be a marked increase on the part of the people in active participation in the Sunday worship. At the same time, however, it is true that there are problems with the service in general and the propers in particular which are a continuing source of disappointment and irritation. Here careful study by commissions on liturgy and other qualified persons ought to result in definite steps for change and improvement. We hope that such improvement, at least in the *language* of the propers, will come soon.

Toward improvement

Each of the propers has certain problems, some more serious than others. The chief problem propers are the Introit, Gradual, Alleluia, and Tract. Even the Lections, however, which enjoy a general approval, and the Collects for the Day, which in spite of their beauty and perfection of form are not popular with congregations, should be looked at with an open-minded aim towards improvement. In some cases, an updating of language will probably be enough. In others, more radical revision or replacement of an individual proper might be indicated. Even the replacement of a whole series of propers, such as a new series of Introits, should not be beyond our vision.

There are four principles which can serve us in evaluating our present propers and also in determining a sense of direction and manner of procedure as we contemplate the improvement of the propers. They are the following:

- Lutheran worship is *scriptural* in content and gospel-orientated.
- Lutheran worship is *congregational* in nature, involving the whole body of worshipers as active participants.
- Lutheran worship is *liturgical* in form, retaining the historic liturgies of the Western Church and the organizing principle of the church year.
- Lutheran worship is *artistic* in expression, utilizing all the resources of the arts in interpreting and illuminating the content of the worship.

These principles are not the exclusive property of the Lutheran church, of course, since they are based on the nature and entire development of Christian worship as well as on the specific history and worship practice of Lutheranism. However, the special strength and almost unique characteristic of Lutheran worship has been the effecting of a healthy *balance* between them. There is a certain priority for these principles, but Lutheran worship is at its best when *each* of these principles is allowed proper expression. History teaches us that this balance can be rather easily upset. Each age must wage its own struggle to retain it. For the last three quarters of a century, scholars have been working to restore to us the content and forms of the church's liturgies, including the propers, which had been nearly lost in the grand discard of Christian faith in the age of Rationalism. We owe these men a notable debt for the restoration of this liturgical heritage. The challenge that faces us today, however, is that of making the forms and expressions of the liturgy fit the needs and pressures of modern life and worship. We need to make sure that forms like the Introit and Gradual communicate meaningfully in bringing God's Word to the congregation, and in providing for the response of faith. We need to keep the *congregational principle* in the forefront of our thinking as we look toward improvement of the propers.

New Introits

If there is any one proper that deserves the name of problem-proper, it is most likely the Introit. Its original practical function as an entrance song sung during the procession of the clergy into the church or sanctuary has disappeared. Its size has shrunk from that of an entire psalm or good portion thereof to a single verse and an antiphon whose relation to the psalm verse quoted is not always apparent. In general, the Introit does not often enough fulfill the promise in the familiar claim that "the Introit sounds the keynote, or theme, of the day."

As one uses the Introits year after year, the feeling grows that what is wrong with the Introit is more than updating of language or even replacement of whole sentences or sections can repair. Perhaps the time has come to undertake a whole new series of Introits. One comes slowly to this conclusion not only out of a sense of respect for the material of such ancient origin and persistent use in the church, but also because the writing of really good liturgical material is difficult. If it is true that the Introits too often fail to fulfill their intended liturgical function and also on occasion fail to communicate any really meaningful content to the worshiper, then it is time to recall Christ's words about the Sabbath and insist that man was not made for the liturgy but the liturgy for man.

A good proper ought to do three things: (1) say something scripturally important and meaningful for today's worship, (2) communicate it clearly to the serious worshiper, (3) relate itself recognizably to the content and/or tone of the service or season of the church year.

Beyond these requirements, there are a number of features which would seem desirable in any new Introit to be fashioned: (1) a prelude-type of proper, one which would give us an overview of the day's celebration and a clear imitation of what is coming; (2) propers which would have a New Testament accent, rather than one based on the Old Testament psalms; (3) propers which would be both objective and responsive, allowing for both a Word of God and a "word of man based on a Word of God" (ideally this would express both the general subject and the mood or tone of the day); (4) propers which would have the same scheme or form each Sunday and would bring the arrangement of the content in the same order (contrasted with the present Introit in which the psalm verse sometimes brings the Word and sometimes voices the response).

The new Introits:

EASTER I
A. Peace be unto you. Alleluia
   Blessed are they that have not seen and yet have believed. Alleluia! Alleluia!
V. Reach hither thy hand, and behold the print of the nails, and be not faithless, but believing.

EASTER II
A. The Good Shepherd hath risen. Alleluia.
   Who hath given His life for His sheep. Alleluia! Alleluia!
V. My sheep hear My voice, and I know them and they follow Me.

are not presented as any sort of finished product, but rather to see what kind of thing might be done, and thereby hopefully to stimulate others to take up the task of providing new Introit texts. Although material for new Introits could be drawn directly from Scriptures and so provide wholly new selections and content, the alternative of utilizing existing liturgical materials (including the present Introits) is here adopted. The *Communion,* or *Communion Verse,* a historical proper rooted basically in the gospel, commends itself as an excellent source for new Introits. I believe that it can serve us better in making the Introit a "mountaintop proper" than in a possible restoration of its use in the service follows singing the *Agnus Dei.*

A final word: edify

Whether or not these sample Introits provide any kind of useful direction for improvement in this proper is not for the writer to judge. But we hope, at least, that the deficiencies in this and other of the propers may somehow be remedied, and that without much delay. The need for something a little less sophisticated than much of the present proper material is pressing. If the worshiper does not understand *what* is being said in the service, he cannot logically conclude *why* it needs saying, and he certainly cannot help *say* it with either heart or voice. If we are reluctant to revise or replace present materials out of too great a sense of respect for the past, we might remember that much of that material originated in a time when the church was sadly unconcerned about the congregation's participation.

If the propers are worth retaining, then they are worth improving if possible. If the idea and ideal of the proper is worth having (and no other has served the church nearly as well in all the history of Christian worship), then all of our liturgical knowledge, skill, and dedication ought to be devoted to the realizing of the full potential of that idea for worship.

Our ultimate concern in working with and on the propers is well stated in that biblical word *edification*. The case for retaining the propers rests finally here, and so does the case for improving them where they do not edify. Where men are truly edified, that is, built up into the same stature of the fullness of Christ, there God will also be glorified. And where God is truly glorified, there man will also be edified. We can ask no more of the propers, and we should be satisfied with no less.

Canticles for the Congregation
Church Music, 75.2, pp. 10-13

It's too bad about Carrie Canticle. Everybody knows she and Willie Worshiper would make a wonderful pair—everybody except Will, that is. But you know Willie . . . heart of gold but not exactly the type that will climb to the top of the highest mountain in pursuit of his ladylove! Goodness knows, Carrie's more than willing, and what a wonderful girl she is! Fine family, lots of character, wholesome—one of those beautiful people who keep growing on you as you get to know them better. If only Willie could really get to know her! Some of her musical friends have been trying to get them together for quite a while. Even Pastor Johnny Luther tried to play Cupid a few times behind the scenes and arranged a couple of dates, but it didn't click. I think Willie's really kind of interested in Carrie, but I think she sort of scares him. I don't really think it's her accent that bothers him (Carrie's from the old country, you know), but I do think those outlandish clothes her friends keep urging her to wear make Willie awfully uncomfortable. I mean, they're beautiful and all that, and her friends think she looks very elegant and proper, but they seem to make Willie feel like he's taking out Queen Victoria! So . . . looks like Carrie is going to keep on being a wallflower unless one of the boys in the choir gets interested. There were a few of her friends in the choir, you know, who were interested in Carrie for a while, but that was before that curvy blonde, Carol Anthem, joined the choir. Now all the guys are buzzing around her, goggle-eyed, and poor Carrie's back in the corner. It's really a shame! Maybe if Pastor would really make an effort to talk to Willie and tell him what he's missing . . . or maybe if Carrie would get herself a new wardrobe and change that odd hairdo of hers, Willie might take a fresh look and, well, who knows, maybe they still might make beautiful music together. . . . It's too bad, but how long can a girl go on hoping?

Thus far, dear reader, the sad saga of Carrie Canticle, who is at this moment alive but obviously not too well, pining away in silent solitude at her appointed station in the Matins and Vespers and more remote regions of *The Lutheran Hymnal* and the *Service Book and Hymnal*, unsung, unloved, and unwed. Whether her future prospects appear less melancholy than her past and present situation—that is the intended subject of this article.

The canticles

Although the canticles could fairly be described as "the unsung songs of the liturgy" or, in the even less elegant description of one worshiper, as "the pages we skip in Matins and Vespers," there is a more proper definition: the canticles are passages of Scripture (not psalms) of a rather exalted content and poetic form, deemed useful for corporate worship and historically a part of the Divine Office, or Hour Services.

The major canticles, as they have been accorded the place by use in Roman Catholic, Lutheran, and Anglican tradition, are four: the *Benedictus, Magnificat,* and *Nunc Dimittis* (all from the gospel of St. Luke) and the *Te Deum Laudamus*, which together with another canticle, *Benedicite,* is unique in that its text is not directly from the pages of the Bible. These four are included, with music, in the Matin and Vesper liturgies of *The Lutheran Hymnal* and *Service Book and Hymnal*. The *Te Deum* is appointed for Matins, with the *Benedictus* as alternate; the *Magnificat* for Vespers, with the *Nunc Dimittis* as alternate.

In addition to these four, the *Service Book and Hymnal* (p. 125) provides eight additional canticle texts, and *The Lutheran Hymnal* (p. 120), nine. All of these are without music. *Contemporary Worship 5: Services of the Word*, prepared for provisional use by the Inter-Lutheran Commission on Worship, provides a total of nine for use with the six services. All have newly composed music. Besides the major canticles *(Te Deum, Magnificat, and Benedictus),* the list includes "The Beatitudes," the *Gloria in Excelsis* (borrowed from the Eucharist), and four new texts in the nature of scriptural paraphrases: "Worthy Is Christ" and "Listen! You Nations" by John Arthur, and "Rise and Shine Forth" and "If We Die with the Lord" by Lucien Deiss. Among all these available texts, "The Beatitudes," "Rise and Shine Forth" (based on Isaiah 60), and "Worthy Is Christ" (based on Revelation 5) seem especially worthy of use as canticles.

Of the past

The use of portions of the Scriptures such as psalms and canticles is rooted in the morning and evening sacrifices in the temple, a custom which the early Jewish Christians continued in their daily gatherings for worship. By the fourth century, when Christianity was finally free to order its public worship, public services were held daily, at least in many places, for which a rather fully developed set of worship resources was available, including the canticles. It is monastic communities, however, with their seven daily hours of prayer, that expanded the use of canticles and gave them a fully structured use in worship. The canticle became one of the principal features in the offices, along with psalmody, hymnody, Scripture readings, the Responsory, and prayer. The Lutheran Reformation, though concentrating its chief efforts on revisions of the Holy Communion, retained the use of Matins and Vespers in a simplified form and urged attendance of the people at the weekday and Sunday services and also at other supplementary services where these orders were used. The canticles—*Te Deum* and *Benedictus* for Matins and *Magnificat* and *Nunc Dimittis* for Vespers—were used with their Latin texts and plainsong melodies, although Luther did translate the *Te Deum* into German in 1529.

The Church of England followed the lead of the continental reformers, and the beautiful translations of the canticles were adapted by John Merbecke in 1550 to the traditional plainsong melodies. These in turn were shortly given a wealth of polyphonic settings for the choir by various English composers. Though the Morning Prayer and Evensong liturgies were popular and actually became the chief congregational services in the Anglican Church, the parts of the services, including the canticles, were mostly spoken rather than sung in the parishes. The place of the canticles was changed in the Anglican service. In the Lutheran orders the canticle functions as a kind of summary response of praise after the Lessons, Responsory, and Sermon. In the Anglican prayer books the canticles serve as Responsories between the Lessons.

The Matins and Vespers were almost totally lost to Lutheran congregations in the general disintegration of Lutheran theology and liturgy during the two centuries of Pietism and Rationalism. Although the spiritual reconstruction which began in the second half of the 19th century eventually restored the content and liturgical forms of 16th-century Lutheranism to congregations here in America (the Common Service, 1888), the need for English texts and for music to go with them prompted the choice of Anglican chant for the congregational canticles. The Lutheran church in Germany, however, retained the use of the plainsong melodies.

Of the present

We can be grateful that the orders of Matins and Vespers, with their rich potential for praise, prayer, and growth in the Word, have been restored for our use. Our present challenge, however, comes from the wide nonuse of these services, and when they are used, from the frequent omission of such important features as the canticles and even the psalmody. What is the real future of these services? We are pleased to see that *Contemporary Worship 5: Services of the Word* makes large use of the canticles. But we are concerned that present and future liturgical planning should, with regard to the canticles, consider several important questions in the light of contemporary worship: *Should* the canticles be sung by the congregation? *Can* they be sung by the congregation? *Will* the canticles be sung by the congregation?

Should *the canticles be sung by the congregation?*

The answer to this question should be a resounding YES! The reasons are not primarily historical, liturgical, or even musical. They are theological. Our ultimate aim should be to bring into the knowledge and affection of the congregation the content and power of these great Christian songs and make them available as expressions of faith and praise to God. How they are sung, at what place in the liturgy, by whom, and indeed whether they are *sung* at all—these are not really the key considerations. The important thing is that they are *known* and *used* by the whole community of believers. The compelling reason is the fact that the canticles, particularly the three gospel canticles and the *Te Deum*, focus squarely on Christ and salvation through him. We need to remember again and again that it is the power of this gospel that creates and nourishes faith and is the real stimulation for the expression of thanks and praise to God. This is the reason why canticles should be studied by our school children; interpreted from our pulpits; sung by our choirs; and best of all, sung (or at least spoken) by the whole congregation at worship. It is because the canticles are such faith-stirring proclamations and celebrations of God's grace toward us sinners that it is painful for us to admit that, of the four major canticles, only the *Nunc Dimittis,* which has found its place in the Eucharist, is heart, mind, and lips the assured possession of the average Lutheran worshiper. And the *Te Deum,* which can fairly lay claim to being the greatest hymn of praise ever produced by the Christian church, carries only a nodding acquaintance with the majority of Lutheran congregations.

A second, related reason why the canticles should be a frequent part of congregational worship lies in their *ideal suitability for corporate use.* Every worshiper finds a place in these songs. The three gospel canticles bring to our minds the intensely dramatic personal experience of the New Testament singers. These songs, which celebrate the incarnation, belong to every Christian, not only to Zechariah, Mary, and Simeon. Their inspired praise of that event and its implications can be echoed by the heart and lips of every believer in every place and every age. They bind together Christian with Christian as they bind together promise and fulfillment, Old Testament and New.

A third reason for full use of the canticles by the congregation relates to artistic considerations, or rather to Christian and specifically Lutheran attitudes toward the arts. If it is indeed a truly Lutheran point of view that the arts are God's good gift to us, to be received with thanks, valued highly, and placed into his service, then it seems strange that we can get so excited about publishing, promoting, and singing pop "creations" that say next to nothing, while at the same time consigning songs like the canticles to the worship museum through our nonuse! These hymns, particularly the *Te Deum,* must rank, even apart from their spiritual content, among the great literary creations of the world, certainly among the finest in the world of Christian prose and poetry.

Perhaps we have not really answered the specific question, should the canticles be sung by the congregation? The answer again has to be yes.

That is simply because of the power of music—if it is indeed the right kind of music—to illuminate and emotionalize the words and phrases of the text and to heighten the joy of the worshiper. If it is not possible to sing the text, however, the canticles should still be used. We have not really explored the power or variety inherent in choral speaking. With the *Te Deum*, at least, speaking the canticle together can generate real excitement. It needs to be printed in the worship folder in a fashion that makes its structure and the sense of the text clear to all worshipers. The power and elegance of the rhythmic prose will do the rest.

Can *the canticles be sung by the congregation?*

Yes, but not very well! The music that is provided for the canticles in both *The Lutheran Hymnal* and the *Service Book and Hymnal* is in the style of Anglican chant. This style is rooted in an English adaptation and harmonization of the old plainsong melodies and employs a *reciting note* to which varying numbers of syllables can be sung, plus the formal punctuation supplied by cadences. Because phrases of varying length, such as we have in psalms and canticles, can be sung on the reciting tone, and because these melodically simple formulas are repeated verse after verse, one might expect this chant form to be easy and practical for the congregation. The opposite is the case. Congregations generally find the chants used for canticles hard to read and follow, awkward to sing, and rather monotonous in longer songs such as this.

The reason for these difficulties is rooted in the clash between the desire and inclination of worshipers to follow an invariable metrical beat in the chant and the original nature and intent of chanting itself, which followed the rhythms and accents of the words. Much of the blame for neglecting the singing of canticles must rest with the music supplied for these chants, with its basic difficulties that the congregation cannot seem to overcome. As sung by choirs that are sensitive to the word rhythms of the English language, these chants can be very beautiful. But consider what usually happens when the congregation is asked to chant. The worshiper sings the chant in exactly the same way a race driver urges his car around the track—wide open on the straightaways and braking sharply for the curves. He rushes through the reciting note sections of the chant and brakes sharply at the cadences. The important music question is, *Why* does he sing the chant this way? The worshiper is only following his rhythmic instincts! Conditioned by all the music he hears around him day after day, he expects a regular pulse in his chant. When he chants, the reciting note provides the initial pulse. But where is the next one? He perceives it to be the first note of the cadence, so he rushes toward it, spilling syllables as he goes. When he arrives at the more familiar terrain of what seems to him to be good, normal half notes, he establishes the pulse happily and firmly (and quite slowly) and tops off the final notes of the cadence with a solid accent. The total effect is, of course, unmusical and also unsatisfying for the singer. Anglican chants are simply not useful vehicles for the congregation's part in worship.

If we are to have music for the canticles that avoids the difficulties inherent in Anglican chant, it would seem that we must have music that is *through-composed,* with melodies that incorporate a *regular rhythmic pulse* to which the congregation can relate and which follow the natural word-accents of the English language.

If the canticles are to become truly the people's song, then the composer will need to meet the needs of the singer as well as the demands of the text itself. If the man in the pew were more articulate about matters of this sort, what would he say to the composer of music for worship? I think he might ask him to consider something like the following qualities:

1. Music that is *simple* enough to learn and to sing with confidence.
2. Music that is *melodically and rhythmically appealing* enough to invite his hearty participation.
3. Music that will make the text "come alive"; music that will help him sense that when he is singing the *Te Deum,* for example, he is not just singing an appointed part in the liturgy. Rather, as he moves through the canticle, he is personally praising the high and holy God together with the angels, proclaiming the mighty works of God's grace in Christ, and committing himself to God's care in firm faith and triumphant hope.
4. Music that does not sound exactly like what he hears all around him everyday, but that is not also totally different from it.

Will *the canticles be sung by the congregation?*

The canticle texts are themselves the best answer to the question of whether or not they *should* be sung by the congregation. The question as to whether the congregation *can* sing them must, at this point, be left up to the talented and dedicated church composers of our day. But the question as to whether the congregation actually *will* sing them will ultimately depend on the pastors and worship leaders of each parish. If God would grant us the gift in our time of a really fitting and inspiring musical mate for the *Te Deum,* that would be an event itself worthy of a *Te Deum*! But past experience teaches that even such a gift might well be lost simply by lack of concern at the parish level. We do not really need any more "hidden" treasures in our hymnals and liturgies; we have enough of them now. What we *do* need is a time of *discovery* for our congregations.

Musical settings for hymns and liturgies are being produced rather rapidly. Probably the ideal music for the *Te Deum* is yet to be written. But some of the music for the canticles and especially also for the responses, recently published in *Contemporary Worship 5: Services of the Word,* give substantial hope that perhaps truly worthy and eminently singable music for Lutheran worship may be on the way, music that will enable the congregation to sing also the canticles with joy and high delight. If and when that comes about, it will take as much patient effort and dedicated concern to bring these to the congregation as is being presently asked of the poets and composers who are producing them. But in this whole area, they do not serve well who "only stand and wait." There is too much that can be done immediately with the canticles in the congregation, with or without the new music. The starting point, at least, is for each pastor to study the traditional scriptural songs anew, ponder them, let them work in the heart. When this is done, these marvelous words of God will themselves create a desire and determination to share them with the congregation, to plan their use in the worship, to write about them in bulletins and newsletters, to encourage their singing by the choirs, and so begin to recapture for the congregation itself something of the exalting experience of singing the great canticles of the church.

From the Symposium:
Meeting Contemporary Needs in Christian Worship

The following two essays were the result of the Christian Worship Seminar held at Dr. Martin Luther College, New Ulm, Minnesota, in April 1971. These essays were published in a volume entitled "Meeting Contemporary Needs in Christian Worship." The symposium consisted of five parts: (1) Accent on Contemporary, (2) Accent on Congregation, (3) Accent on Variety, (4) Accent on Music, (5) Accent on Balance. Kurt Eggert wrote the first and last essays in this collection.

Part One: Accent on Contemporary

We need to cultivate a sense of the contemporary in our worship. By that we mean to say that we need to emphasize a sense of now and a sense of reality and relationship to life.

A sense of now

There is much about our Sunday service that is old. The basic structure of the liturgy has been around for almost fifteen hundred years, and the form in which we have it harks back to the Common Service of 1888. Nearly all of the 660 hymns of *The Lutheran Hymnal* were written in centuries other than our own. The bulk of the organ and choir music still heard in our churches is patterned after the tired style of 19th-century "church music" and does not sound very much like either the serious music or the pop and folk music of our day. In addition, the language of the readings, propers, and ordinary of the liturgy is that of the King James Version of the Bible. This is the way that English-speaking people talked in the 16th century but don't talk now. With all this in mind, it is really no wonder that many worshipers find our Lutheran service rather quaint and archaic-sounding.

Obviously, however, "old" cannot simply be equated with "worn out." We do not propose forthwith to dispatch all that we have to the trash can. The point is, however, that the archaic sound and feel of our service can be a real obstacle to worship, especially for the young, the liturgically uneducated, and the "new" members of our churches. It may contribute a feeling that the Lutheran service is literally "out of this world" and not of vital import to the "now" generation of the 1970s.

What can we do to give our worship a more contemporary feel? Where "old" also includes "unintelligible," we can begin by getting serious about educating for worship. That which is old or archaic-sounding is much less objectionable if it is thoroughly understood. We have been rather thorough in our synod in educating in doctrine. We have also done a good deal to make the language of the KJV familiar, although this remains a knotty problem and is being dealt with separately in our seminar. Our efforts at educating in the what and how of worship, however, have been spectacularly feeble. We have not been sold, apparently, on either the need or importance of this kind of education. We have relied on osmosis, but that process is inadequate to the need. A "crash" program on liturgy is not the answer either. What we need is rather a persistent, on-going program of education in which we gradually lead members into an understanding of the structure and "shape" of the liturgy, its dialogue character and rhythmic back-and-forth motion, the significance and function of each section, etc. "Why are we singing this?" "What is happening now in the service?" "What is this part supposed to do in the service?" The asking and answering of such questions will help people realize that something important is "going on" in the liturgy and will make it easier for them to get personally involved in it.

In the area of hymns it would be good for our worship if our heritage hymns could be supplemented by hymns which reflect contemporary life in their subject matter, phraseology, metaphors, and allusions. Good contemporary hymns will not materialize on command, but something can be done by way of stimulation of interest and encouragement of budding poetic and musical talent.

In the matter of music for the propers and ordinary of the liturgy, we have a difficult problem for which no single, easy solution seems to be at hand. We can, however, do something about our organ and choir music. We can gradually but steadily permit some of the works of our contemporary church composers to be heard. The fresher harmonies and accent on rhythmic interest can help build a bridge to the present and lessen the "dated" sound of our church music. An increasing number of people today are used to playing or at least hearing music of considerable harmonic and rhythmic complexity, and their ears do not need a sustained dominant seventh chord to effect a "modulation" from C to G! Careful selection of text for our choral music also can help to bring a sense of now into our worship. People today like to hear texts which speak in a very direct, down-to-earth way about spiritual things. We should avoid the ambiguous texts made to sell to all faiths and communions generally that are characterized by tired phrases of religious cliché and use of pictures and allusions which are vague and uncertain in meaning. Search out serious, straight-forward, unmistakably Christian texts, especially those which include metaphors and allusions drawn from 20th-century life.

Without doubt the preacher has the best opportunity to bring a sense of now in the worship. It is truly the most difficult part of the preacher's art to apply the truths of Scripture to the contemporary life-situations of his hearers, but there is nothing in the service that does more to make people realize that the service is related to their life. Examples from today's daily life—allusions and applications to present situations—these more than anything else give the worship a contemporary feel. There are certainly a number of problems and pressures in our society which are unique to our own time. The population explosion; the "pill"; the problem of identity in a nation of huge corporations and computerized operations; the rootlessness of people who move often, make few friends, and are strangers in their own congregations; small family units which no longer include grandparents and aunts and uncles, and where children do not easily learn the art of communicating with other ages and generations; mixed marriages; the obsession with sex; the success-oriented goals of the American establishment and the reverse philosophies of the counterculture—these are only a few of the situations and problems which are somewhat unique to our own society. Modern man has the same basic sinfulness and need as people in Paul's day, but the temptations and sins are different, and the problems and anxieties are different. The pointed application of law and gospel to our own time will be a powerful factor in instilling a sense of now into the worship hour.

A sense of reality and relationship to life

But we need to do more than try to avoid the impression that our service is an anachronism. We must also take some steps to insure a sense of reality and vital relationship to life in our worship.
Some church members harbor strange notions about worship. Here is a man who says, "I can be just as good a Christian without going to church!" When he does attend worship, it must be with only the vaguest notion of why he is there. He will likely spend the hour as a noninvolved observer. Another man views worship as "something for the soul," and therefore somehow unconnected with his body, mind, and "real life." He takes his soul to church much as a man might take his car to the garage to have it serviced. He is concerned about it, but it is not a personal experience. He sits with patient detachment through the worship hour, waiting for his soul to be recharged, and then returns home with the conviction that it is once again in good running condition. A third type of worshiper is the Walter Mitty individual who sort of turns into his "other self" on Sunday mornings and looks to the worship hour as a temporary escape from the painful realities of everyday

life. At the close of the service, he turns reluctantly back to the "other world" where life is real and earnest and full of trouble and routine, and where God seems very remote.

Such worship attitudes represent distortions which are, I think, rooted in a misunderstanding of the nature of Christian life. Jesus said it best when he said that we are in the world but not of the world. By this Jesus did not mean to say that we are somehow to divide our life into two segments—into real and unreal, or into spiritual and physical, or into body and soul. A Christian does indeed lead a kind of double life, but it is a totally unique kind of life.

A Christian is not of this world. We live a "hidden life." The influences which motivate, guide, and sustain us are not apparent to non-Christians around us. Our essential life is lived "by faith in the Son of God, who loved us and gave himself for us." We are not an organization of people, but members of the body of Christ. (This is not a picture or metaphor, but a mystic reality!) We are one with saints above and saints below, and we await momentarily the glorious appearing of our Lord Jesus Christ.

All of this gives to our whole life, and especially to our corporate worship, a unique and heavenly dimension. In a sense, it is a spaceless and timeless dimension. Yet since we share this situation in the here and now, it is a perfectly contemporary dimension. It is in our gathered worship, perhaps, that we become most deeply aware of this heavenly dimension. There are those exalted moments when we feel ourselves already "seated together with Christ in the heavenly place," when we lift up our voices "with angels and archangels and with all the company of heaven" and sing, "Holy, holy, holy is the Lord God of Sabaoth." This is the unique glory of Christian worship, made wholly real for us by our oneness in Christ.

At the same time, we are very much in this world. We may sing with the angels, but we do not sing as the angels. We cannot disengage our body from our soul. We neither live nor worship as disembodied spirits. We are flesh and blood, placed here in time and space. We share the sinfulness of the sinful and unbelieving world around us. We likewise share the common human burdens of trouble and suffering and sickness and death. Of this we are painfully aware in our everyday living. On Sunday morning, however, it is possible to become escape artists and to use the worship hour to disengage ourselves from the realities of our earthly life. We are not, however, to use our faith as an escape from the world but to "overcome the world." The heavenly dimension of our worship dare not be viewed as some kind of God-approved drug which will permit us to trip into fantasy so that we can forget for a bit our troubles and cares. The opposite is true. The spiritual treasures of our faith are not fantasy but reality. Precisely here—in the reality of Christ's atoning death and resurrection, in the reality of the Spirit's presence and power in our midst, in the reality of our status as children and heirs of God—lies the victorious answer to our sin and guilt, the power to combat temptations, and the strength to carry our everyday burdens and cares. It is vital that the power of our faith impinge directly on our life problems in the here and now. It is unfortunate that for some Christians, Christian life and worship seem to have only two dimensions: what God did for us in the past and what God will do for us in the future. When we confess, "Christ redeemed me . . . that I might be his own and live under him in his kingdom," this does not begin when we die or at the judgment, but right here and now.

The implications of all this for our worship are that the realities of both sides of our Christian life ought to be fully reflected. On the one hand, we will want our preaching, praying, liturgy, hymns, and choir music to illuminate the reality of our spiritual treasures. We want to be made fully aware that we are actually God's holy people and that the Christ of history is with us now. What he said to his disciples then is spoken to us now. What he instituted on that first Maundy Thursday he shares with us now. On the other hand, however, the sermon and songs and prayers need also to remind us that we are sinners, poor human beings in need of constant rescue. We are the weak, lukewarm, self-satisfied, rebellious, besieged, bedeviled, and altogether needy sinners to whom the Lord is talking and beckoning in the Scriptures.

This is our contemporary situation. This is how it "really is" with us Christians: We are at once saints and sinners. We are citizens of heaven, possessing the glorious and eternal treasures of God, and yet we are frail mortals who carry these treasures in earthen vessels. These are the side-by-side realities of our Christian life, and any worship forms worthy to be called "contemporary" must take these realities into full account and build on them. If we prepare our sermons, write our prayers, choose our hymns and music with this perspective, then our worship will, despite any other imperfections, be "contemporary" in the truest sense of the word. It will be real and related to life, and will meet the most basic needs of every "now" generation.

Part Five: Accent on Balance

So far in this symposium we have focused on four "Accents" or key words which seem to be important in meeting contemporary needs in worship:

1. Accent on CONTEMPORARY
2. Accent on CONGREGATION
3. Accent on VARIETY
4. Accent on MUSIC

In this final segment of our panel presentation, we propose the adding of a fifth key word to the four listed above. That word is *balance*. First of all, we need a sense of balance between Sunday morning and the rest of the week, between our congregational worship service and the larger service of our whole Christian life. Secondly, we need to cultivate a sense of balance in viewing the Sunday service itself.

I. The Sunday service and our Christian life

Some in the avant-garde of liturgical reform today seem ready not only to scrap the established forms of liturgical worship but also to dispense more or less completely with preaching and the congregational service itself. They would do this in favor of social action of various kinds, informal dialogue, small and informal group meetings, etc. Surely this course of action can lead only to loss of God's full truth, fragmentation of the church, and ultimate frustration for most of those involved. However, I do not think that such proposals pose a real danger for us. I see no inclination in our own synod to follow such a course.

The danger for us, I think, lies in the other extreme. We are inclined to define worship in terms of one hour on Sunday morning. We tend to think of the congregational service as our "worship" and the rest of the week as a sort of gray and desert area through which we make our way until the next Sunday oasis. On Sunday morning we are the "gathered church" and very conscious of the fact that we are God's people, sheep of his flock, Christ's disciples and Christ's ambassadors. During the week we are the "scattered church," and the danger is that we slip back into thinking of ourselves simply as people instead of God's people, as workers rather than God's workers, as churchgoers rather than witnesses. This distorted perspective cripples our discipleship and does not add up to a "Christian life."

This is by no means to imply that our congregation at worship is not indeed the center, the very heartbeat, of our Christian life and worship. It is truly all of this, precisely because on Sunday morning we are the gathered people of God, gathered around his Word and sacrament. Here our concern with God, and his with us, comes to a sharp focus and intensity that it does not have during the week. Here is the well and lifespring of our life in Christ. Here he speaks to us and comes to us and works in us and blesses us. Here we acknowledge our sins and confess our faith and bring our sacrifice of prayer and thanksgiving, of money and praise. But this is not the whole of it. Our liturgy—our service—dare not end here. The Lord sends us forth to live out the sermon and the service during the week.

Our problem is, of course, that we do not do this very well. The more distressing thing is that we are often hardly aware of this lack and imbalance! Our strong and legitimate stress on church-going has unfortunately fostered the notion that if a man is faithful in attending the worship and is regular at the Lord's Table, he is pretty much leading a "good Christian life." But there are some things which the Sunday service hour does not and cannot take care of. Our Savior has told us to be a light and a salt. We are to demonstrate a loving concern for others. We are to build each other up, to be concerned over the erring one, to admonish and to strengthen and to comfort and to heal and to mend in the name of the Savior, by his Spirit. And we are to witness, by our life and also by our personal testimony, so that others are brought to faith in him. All this is part of our service, our worship. And beyond these specific acts of Christian love, concern, and witness, there is the whole fabric of our regular, everyday, hum-drum life. The way we view and discharge our everyday vocation as husbands, wives, students, citizens, factory and office workers, druggists, teachers, truck drivers, or whatever; the way we talk to each other and about each other; our personal Bible study and prayer activity—whatever we think and do out of faith, in cheerful and thankful obedience to his will—all this is our service, our worship. "Whatever you do, whether in word or deed, do it all in the name of the Lord Jesus" (Colossians 3:17).

The point about all of this is not simply that we need to know this, but that we be more conscious of it. The more conscious we are that our whole life-activity, body and spirit, is to be a living sacrifice to the Lord (Romans 12:1), the more natural and inviting will the Sunday worship hour become for us. The right kind of involvement and participation in the

Sunday worship must begin during the week! As the Sunday service is to prepare and strengthen us for the coming week, so also our life from Monday through Saturday must prepare us for Sunday morning! Our worship life is one thing! We are ever and always both in the world and not of the world. On Sunday morning we need to be especially conscious of the fact that we are still in the world; during the week we need to remind ourselves constantly that we are not of the world. But both are part of one worship life. The more we think of our weekly life as part of our worship, the more Sunday morning will seem the culmination and climax of the week. Our Sunday worship has some entirely unique dimensions, but if we step into that worship as into a totally "other" world, disconnected from our weekly activity, then not even the best liturgical forms, most expressive pipe organ, choicest selection of hymns, and best-prepared organ and choir music can be expected to bring us to a sincere and hearty involvement and participation in the worship service.

As pastors and church musicians, we have some unique opportunities to cultivate an awareness of our weekly activity as worship. Let our preparation for the Sunday service itself be a worshipful activity, done "as unto the Lord." Our professional calling leads us necessarily into the study of God's Word, into contact with the forms of our liturgical heritage, into personal contact with our hymns, into the making of prayers, into analysis and rehearsal of choir and organ music. In this we have a blessing and advantage which is not enjoyed by the rest of the congregation. However, that does not insure that our study and preparation will automatically be the worshipful activity it ought to be. There is always the temptation to become "professional" in our attitude. We need always to approach our preparation with the prayer that the Spirit would move and enable us to give nothing less than the very best with the talent and ability he has given us. Secondly, we should make our various preparations for the Sunday worship with a loving concern for what will edify the whole congregation. The pastor's prayerful struggle to apply the content of the sermon text to the various needs and life-situations of the members as he becomes aware of them; the organist's devoted hunt for music which will not only reflect the particular tone and emphasis of the coming service but will also speak to the hearts of the worshipers; the choir rehearsal that is not only a more or less enjoyable battle with notes, rhythms, and harmony but also a concern with the meaning of the texts and a concern for what can be brought to the listeners on Sunday morning—all such attitudes and activity in preparation for Sunday can be and should be truly a part of our worship. The making of special prayers, the arranging of flowers and care of paraments, the preparations of a service banner, the rehearsing of a new hymn by the congregation in preparation for a festival—all these can be perfunctory tasks or they can be worship activities, growing out of a desire to serve and edify each other and to present gratefully to the Lord something as beautiful and meaningful as we can. The more that we and the other members of the congregation approach our weekly life and specifically our preparation for Sunday morning in this way, the more our gathered worship on Sunday morning will become a joyful and hearty celebration.

II. Balance in the Sunday service

The second area in which we need to be concerned about a sense of balance is in the forms and suggested reforms of the Sunday service itself. We have urged that the service be recognizably contemporary, that there be an increased emphasis on congregational participation, that we strive for variety as we move through the church year, and that we exploit more fully the unique power and function of music in the congregational worship. In urging these various "accents," however, a sense of balance must be preserved. Liturgical forms and reforms in Christian worship must always be viewed in perspective with the agreed functions and purpose of worship.

Contemporary

Does the structure and/or content of our Sunday service need to be replaced, radically revised, moderately revised, or not revised at all? Before we can answer that question, we need to ask ourselves the other question: Do we still want to do the same sort of things in our worship that we have been concerned with in the past?

Do we still want to come together to demonstrate and express, physically and spiritually, our fellowship in the faith? Do we still want to share the Lord's Supper? Do we still want to receive the Lord's counsel and comfort, admonition and warning, inspiration and strength by the hearing of his Word? Do we still want to confess our sins to him and hear his assurance of forgiveness? Do we still want to bring to him our thanks and praise, prayers, intercessions, and offerings? Do we still want to come together to encourage and strengthen and support each other by confessing and singing and praying and listening and partaking of the Sacrament with each other? If these are still the things we want to do, then our present liturgy is, in a functional sense, an up-to-date and contemporary vehicle for worship. It does give us ample room and opportunity for this rather wide spectrum of worship activity. So then, if we urge an "accent on the contemporary" for our Sunday service, this does not mean that because our liturgy is old, for instance, we need to replace it in its entirety with something altogether new in order to be contemporary. There is no question but that there are deficiencies and problems with our order of service, but throwing out the baby with the bath has always been a somewhat unbalanced course of action. It is possible to make a really radical revision of our present liturgy, or even to construct a totally new order of worship. This has, in fact, been done, and some of these experimental liturgies have some excellent features. However, any new liturgy that is intended to replace our present order must be at least as "tied to the Word" in its content and as wide and flexible in its function as our present order.

In our panel presentation, we have also espoused an emphasis on congregational participation, on variety, and on music. Each of these needs to be viewed with a sense of balance and an evaluation of what our present liturgy offers in these areas.

Congregational participation

In urging greater congregational participation in the service, a sense of balance will help us avoid several traps. One is to expect too much of the liturgy. As was mentioned before, the best liturgical forms cannot insure hearty participation from worshipers who are not ready to worship. Each must bring to the service some eagerness to receive, some willingness to give, some openness to learn. In addition, there is the necessity for compromise. In corporate worship there are apt to be rather wide differences in taste, education, cultural and religious background, and in levels of artistic appreciation. This makes compromise necessary; it is an unavoidable price that must be paid for worshiping together. If there is to be a high level of congregational participation, the only alternative to a constant settling for the lowest common denominator is a willingness on the part of the congregation to "grow into" the agreed liturgical forms.

Another trap to avoid in talking about congregational participation is the idea that "everyone must do everything." This is as bad as having the service become a choir concert or a pastoral monologue. The idea surfaces sometimes in opposition to antiphonal singing of hymns. The cry goes up, "You're taking the hymns away from the people!" But congregational participation does not mean that the whole congregation must sing everything any more than it means that the congregation must speak all the prayers. Listening can also be participation. What is necessary is that, to the greatest extent possible, the various parts of the service be intelligible and meaningful, and on a level that will enable the congregation to share in some way in everything that is done, including the solo music of the organist, the singing of the choir, and the readings and prayers of the pastor. The structure of the Lutheran liturgy insures ample opportunity for the congregation to participate actively in the worship, if only we make the most of the opportunities it presents.

Variety

In pressing the need for variety and change in our worship, we ought not overlook the flexibility and opportunities for variety already built into our present liturgy. There is a rather nice balance in our liturgy between the ordinary and the propers, between the parts which are ever the same and those which are constantly changing. This insures something in each service that is familiar and something that is at least somewhat different. If everything in the service except the sermon, let us say, were always the same, it would be monotonous and "a horrible thing for the Sabbath." On the other hand, if everything or nearly everything were different each week, it would be frustrating for most worshipers. The common complaint, however, is that our worship does not have enough variety. In the Lutheran liturgy, the propers (Introits, Graduals, Collects, and readings), together with the hymns and sermon, must provide the variety. This they do by "turning the wheel of the church year," bringing into sharp focus each Sunday a new event or truth for emphasis. Except for the Scripture readings, the propers have apparently been rather unsuccessful in bringing an intended brightness and distinctive variety to our worship. Doubtless the structure, content, and especially the language of many of the propers can be faulted and charged with this failure. On the other hand, how hard have we tried to make the propers or even let the propers speak tellingly to us? We ought to make every effort to retain the idea of the propers, because the church year focuses our attention on the foundation of our faith, on the life and work of our Savior. If the Introits and Graduals need substantial revision or replacement with new kinds of propers, let us be bold enough to do so. But beyond this, more options are open to us without dropping the idea of the church year or disturbing the general structure of our liturgy. We can read other series of pericopes; we can substitute seasonal hymn stanzas by the congregation or a seasonal sentence by the choir for the regular Graduals; we can use other forms of the General Prayers; we can sing the Creed on occasion; we can sing the propers and vary the series of musical settings from time to time; we can learn new hymns and sing them in different ways; we can utilize instruments in the service if we have them available. In short, we could effect a good variety in our worship by being more imaginative and adventuresome in the way we do things. It is not always necessary to change the *what* of the service, only the *how*.

Music

Finally, in our attitude toward music and its use, we need to keep our sense of balance. We are speaking here especially about the solo music of the organ and the "inspirational song" of the choirs. We need to cultivate a discriminating taste for music that is truly good and edifying for worship. Not all good music is good for worship, and not all music written for worship is good. We should cling to the treasures of our heritage, and the only way to do this is by actually singing and playing them. And we should also welcome the potential treasures of today and tomorrow and be ready to give them a fair hearing. The mysterious, God-given power of music is not restricted to any one supposed "sacred style" or any one era. Let us look for music that moves us Godward, that stirs our faith and emotions, that sets up thought-associations, that has precious texts, that lights up and gives wings to a Word of God. The bane of our worship services today is the vast amount of music that is not really bad, but not really good either. It is simply a kind of "nothing" music, gray, formless, neutral. It may be well-crafted and carry a good text. Yet it does not "speak" to us. Such music may be old or new, a plainsong chant or a contemporary motet. The labor of love in searching out "good" music is the first vital step in making music meaningful in our worship.

Last night Professor Meyer played a short piece of the kind that "said something," at least to me. It was the prelude of Paul Manz based on the old chorale melody "God the Father, Be Our Stay." This is an old and serious hymn that betakes itself to the big issues. The chorale melody brought to mind the large petitions of this hymn, enlisting God's power in our struggle against the evil one. Attached to the chorale melody, however, was this rather carefree, almost saucy, obbligato. I don't know what was in the mind of the composer, but to me this carefree accompaniment said that a child of God doesn't need to worry and fear. We can count on our God. He sets our table in the presence of our enemies. In spite of Satan, we can "go dancing down the aisles, three cheers for our Savior!" I thought that was a good piece of music. It added another dimension to the old chorale.

There are many in our church who are itching to leave the "old" music behind, especially the old chorale tunes. We ought to be very slow about this, because many of the chorales, though certainly not all, have much to offer us today. On the other hand, there are probably many more in our church who resist contemporary music with a passion. This is somewhat strange, because until recent times, the church has constantly produced "new" music and welcomed it. We ought to keep an open mind and make the effort to "grow up to and into" the new expressions. Who knows how far the boundaries of music may be stretched in the future in earnest and edifying expressions of the Christian faith? It is probable that the jazz idiom, for instance, will not be useful for the church, especially because of its necessary dependence on the creativity and improvisation of the individual performer. On the other hand, when you listen to a motet of Heinz Werner Zimmermann, who combines a sturdy chorale melody with the basic fabric of a 16th-century motet; adds a kind of improvisational, almost ecstatic soprano descant; sets it all into the syncopated rhythm so characteristic of jazz; and undergirds it with the strict discipline of the jazz beat in the bass, then one must ask himself seriously, "Does this kind of music have a possible fruitful use in Christian worship?" Who knows but that the world of mixed media, where color, speech, choral and instrumental music, and the sounds of taped and electronically composed "music" all combine, may someday, under the hand of dedicated Christian composers, give the church worthwhile expressions of the faith. Let us look with an open mind, testing, trying, judging, and ultimately using what appears to be edifying. The church will necessarily never be on the "cutting edge" of the new, but ought to be careful not to "snip off the new buds," just as it should not "cut off the roots." Let us reach out for and hold fast to the good. Let this search and adventure be our ongoing worship as church musicians! With a sense of balance, we will remain true to the ideals of Lutheran worship and, under God's blessing, edify the church of God with music both old and new.

From *Focus on Worship*

The Commission on Worship began publishing a small journal in 1971 entitled *Focus on Worship*, which was to replace the annual church music workshops. Eggert was the editor of this publication from 1971 to 1987. The following two essays deal with the worship and music of the wedding service.

Focus on the Wedding
Focus on Worship, Trinity 1976 (No. 1)

The marriage rite, as commonly performed in the Lutheran church and specifically in our own church body, is almost unique in the long list of service rites and ceremonies. What other rite tries to combine a secular and civil ceremony with spiritual worship, ecclesiastical traditions with secular customs, deeply personal concerns with broadly congregational ones, romantic love and affection with Spirit-born Christian love? And all this within the framework of the Lutheran service at which members of the wedding party and assembly may often represent widely different religious convictions, customs, and traditions.

It should not surprise us, then, that the marriage rite is also unique in the amount of tension, conflict, and plain confusion it generates. It is fair to say that no other rite or service of the church gives pastors and church musicians so many headaches. Church members who normally accord pastors and organists the responsibility of arranging the content and form of the worship—a function for which they have been trained and called—become instant experts on liturgy, music, and ceremony. Attitudes are evidenced, requests are made, and liberties are indulged which church members, at least, would not dream of in connection with any other service. Things happen in the wedding service which would be almost unthinkable at any other worship of the congregation.

The real problem

The underlying problem, not always recognized, lies in the attempt to combine secular and spiritual concerns in one tightly knit framework of worship. Both have traditions, customs, and concerns that seek expression in connection with the marriage ceremony. But they run on different wavelengths. The one is usually emphasized at the expense of the other. Sometimes they tend almost to cancel each other out.

The secular and the spiritual compared

On the one hand, marriage is really a secular institution, ordained by God for all men, not only for Christians. Even apart from faith, God blesses this estate when husbands and wives live faithfully in this union. Neither the church nor the state really marries a couple. They marry each other by agreeing to live with each other as husband and wife in the marriage union. Therefore, the exchange of marriage vows is the essential element in the marriage ceremony, whether civil or ecclesiastical.

On the other hand, marriage has deep spiritual implications for Christians. The marriage relationship, as every part of life, is to be controlled and motivated by the faith-relationship to Christ. The Christian is moved and prompted by the Holy Spirit, working through the Word and sacrament, and marriage too is given a new *dimension elevation* when viewed from the perspective of Christian faith and love.

Why a church ceremony?

The state, which has an interest in marriage for the good order in society, extends the right to ordained clergy to perform legal marriages. Although marriage is not a sacrament or means of grace, and the church has no directive to marry, Lutheran pastors welcome the opportunity to focus the minds and hearts of Christian couples on the spiritual implications of their marriage vows. The church does this through a marriage rite that consists basically of normal ingredients of worship: Scripture and its application, prayer, and praise.

Most Christian couples today want to have a church wedding, but probably not always for the right reasons. If the average couple is asked, "Why do you want to have a church wedding?" their first reaction will probably be, "Why not? Isn't that the normal thing?" It's true that the church wedding is part of the classic American wedding tradition. It is also convenient, affording invited guests and relatives adequate and fairly comfortable seating, and often providing a beautiful and inspiring setting for the ceremony. Besides all this, the price is right! Though understandable, these are not very spiritual reasons for choosing a church ceremony.

Most Christian couples do have a concern for the spiritual implications of marriage and do tend to value the kind of service the church provides, but a large percentage of them do not seem to have thought very deeply about it. Occasionally a couple requests a church wedding whose appreciation for the value of the church service seems to be summed up neatly in the sentence, "Get me to the church on time, and get me out as fast as possible!" On the other hand, one thoughtful couple stated the following reasons for wanting a church wedding:

> Since God is the one who has created marriage and blesses it, we want to begin our marriage before the altar in our church. We want to thank God and praise him for bringing us together, for our love for each other, and for the joys he has placed into marriage. We want to be reminded of what God says to us about marriage and have his counsel and guidance as we begin our life together. We want to pray for the Lord's help and blessing on our marriage, and we want our friends and fellow Christians to share our joy and add their prayers for us.

Couples who have such a spiritual concern will appreciate the Lutheran marriage rite which provides for just such concern. They will also readily sense the overriding worship character of such a ceremony and will without much difficulty avoid anything which might tend to dilute the mood of worship or dilute the Christ-centered character of the service.

Some problems and suggestions

Simply said, the Lutheran marriage rite is a worship service. Its content is spiritual, and the mood is serious, even in the context of wedding joy, simply because things like Scripture and praising God and beseeching him in prayer are serious. At the same time, it needs to be said that the wedding service is not a normal Sunday service. Certain customs, traditions, and special concerns are legitimate or unavoidable and need to be accommodated. Others may need to be eliminated. Let us consider a few such situations:

1. There is a natural spotlight on the bride and groom. It is their wedding and their day; nobody else in the congregation is exchanging marriage vows. On the other hand, when all kinds of demands are made on the basis that "it's our wedding and why can't we have what we want at our wedding," then it needs to be remembered that it is also a Lutheran service. The pastor is still the servant of the whole congregation. Also, this is the only time some people at the wedding may have any contact with a Lutheran service. Let it represent Lutheran teaching and liturgical tradition as nearly as possible.

2. Weddings obviously need some kind of processional. However, the romantic "bride-cult" tradition encourages brides to view the processional as an ego trip, a sort of combination triumphal procession, fashion parade, and film festival. The total preoccupation with the bride does not accord very well with the God-given role of husband and wife

in the marriage relationship. It also makes everyone tend to forget that the couple is on the way to the altar to exchange solemn vows and to engage in prayer and praise. The wedding day calls quite naturally for physical adornment, festive decorations, joyful music. However, some restraint needs to be employed with the processional. A sung processional tends to help keep a devotional attitude and atmosphere. On the other hand, for some processionals we have witnessed, the singing of "Jesus, Lead Thou On" would be ridiculous! One bride summed up the present-day attitude pretty well when she said in innocent frankness, "I don't want any solo for my wedding, just the parade music in and the parade music out." One alternate to the present kind of processional which is gaining some popularity is having the bride and groom walk in together, followed by the wedding party and parents.

3. The solo music requested for weddings is probably the source of more heated arguments than any other single item in the service. This topic will be treated separately in the next issue of *Focus on Worship*.

What it takes is a clear understanding of Christian marriage itself and the nature and purpose of the wedding rite; spiritual concern and sensitivity; and a lot of calm, evangelical discussion. All of us need a willingness to expend much more thought and effort to achieve that goal. It will be worth it!

Focus on the Wedding Music—The Solo
Focus on Worship, Epiphany 1977 (No. 1)

The wedding so-low

Not infrequently, the vocal solo marks the distinct low point of the service. Also not infrequently, the premarriage discussion of the solo music marks the low point of the pastor/couple relations! Consider a typical situation of this sort. The couple has entered the pastor's study to "settle" the matter of the wedding solo on which they have set heart and mind. The pastor, however, feels that the solo is one which he should not or cannot approve. The discussion is joined with apprehension on both sides. Neither is sure how the matter will turn out. The old limerick comes to mind:

> There was a young lady of Niger
> Who smiled as she rode on a tiger.
> They returned from the ride
> With the lady inside
> And the smile on the face of the tiger.

Who wins and who loses? Who gets swallowed and who gets to smile? Well, of course, if there is no real meeting of the minds, nobody gets to smile. If the pastor is adamant, the couple goes off muttering and shaking their heads at the "stubbornness" of the minister. If the pastor gives in, he feels that he has compromised his integrity and glumly contemplates the prospect of standing tight-lipped and inwardly squirming through the singing of the solo. He also knows that as surely as spring follows winter (except in Milwaukee), there will be other couples at the wedding who will shortly appear in his study with the request for the same song. And both pastor and couple know that the trump card in that discussion will be the line, "But pastor, you let So-and-So have it for their wedding!"

Why

Why should a "little" thing like a wedding song become a source of serious friction? And why are differences not resolved more easily and amicably? The answer may be rooted in the fact that pastor and couple are likely looking at the wedding and its music from quite different points of view. They are running on different tracks, and never the twain shall meet! The pastor is moved by theological and liturgical considerations; the couple is motivated by wedding traditions and their personal feelings.

Track number 1

The pastor looks at the wedding as a ceremony within the general framework of Lutheran worship. He considers his function as officiant to be that of a Lutheran pastor, representing the congregation and responsible to it for all that is said or sung in the service. He does not want or expect anything in the ceremony to be joltingly different from the normal standards of Lutheran worship. He feels that musical texts should have the same focus on God and Christ as the songs generally sung in the Sunday service, and he expects the music to be stylistically within the general bounds of normal congregational worship experience. He wants the solos to reflect Christian truth and serve in building up Christian faith.

Track number 2

The pastor may be surprised to know that the couple is looking at the wedding in much less spiritual (and certainly less congregational) terms. To them the wedding ceremony is a personal ceremony to which they have invited relatives and friends as witnesses. It is, simply stated, "their" wedding, and they feel personally responsible for the planning of every detail (with the possible exception of the words spoken by the minister). Given this basic point of view, it seems perfectly normal for them to choose whatever music they might personally like for the wedding. They really do not understand the concern of the pastor and tend to interpret any objections as unwarranted interference with "their" wedding.

But why do couples sometimes come up with music that is completely outside the realm of Lutheran worship or even without any spiritual connotations at all? The pastor may react to a request with private amazement and ask himself: "Where on earth did they find that? They certainly never heard anything like that in our services!" Their answer is that they are not looking to the church service for ideas in planning their wedding! The pastor may well ask, "Why don't they just normally pick music from the hymnal or from traditional service music?" That may seem normal to the pastor, but couples are guided in planning their wedding by *wedding traditions.*

In nearly every aspect of the wedding—invitations, the reception, gifts, dress, flowers, pictures, and all the rest—the couple is conditioned by tradition. Every bride dreams of a "beautiful" wedding. That really means a "traditional" wedding. And what constitutes a beautiful and traditional wedding is decided for the couple by what they have seen and heard about weddings from friends, magazines, movies, TV, newspaper articles, and especially other weddings they have witnessed. These weddings are not necessarily restricted to Lutheran weddings. Thus ideas for planning the wedding and the ceremony itself, including the music, may come from many sources.

Furthermore, wedding music may be chosen for sentimental or romantic reasons. Couples, being "in love," tend to expect that the wedding solo will express in some way their love for each other. A particular song may have strong personal associations for the couple. How beautiful it would be, they think, to have "their song" sung at the wedding! So, influenced by their own feelings and the pull of American wedding traditions, the couple selects wedding music which perplexes the pastor but seems entirely reasonable to them.

Bridging the gap

There are two ways in which pastors and organists commonly resolve serious differences about wedding solos or other music. The one is the "let there be peace" approach. The other may be summed up in two short words: "No. PERIOD!" In the first case, the pastor has come to the conclusion that no piece of music is worth friction between pastor and couple or their parents. He often finds it convenient to pass on potential problems to the organist. The organist, though he or she may be concerned, may also be encouraged to think, "If the pastor is not taking a stand on this music, why should I become the sacrificial lamb?" The problem with this "peace at (almost) any cost" approach is that it becomes increasingly difficult to "draw the line," and unedifying music tends to perpetuate itself in the congregation's wedding practice.

The second method of avoiding protracted argument is simply to inform the couple that the wedding solo requested will not be sung in the service! This is often bolstered by an appeal to a congregational resolution indicating that the pastor and organist will make all decisions regarding music for weddings or detailing what may be sung or played at weddings in the parish. Used rightly, such resolutions may be helpful, but the temptation is to appeal to them in a legalistic way. Ceremonial laws about liturgy and church music do not reflect truly evangelical and Lutheran practice.

There may be times when one or the other of the above procedures may be a pastor's only option. One cannot provide couples with an instant course in music appreciation. Also, if the spirituality of the couple is such that they will need the wedding rehearsal to refresh their memories as to the precise location of the altar in the church, anything more than the above will probably be a lost cause! With most couples, however, there is a better way.

A more excellent way

The more excellent way involves a truly pastoral concern for the feelings of the couple, for the ideals and norms of Lutheran worship, and for the edification of those in attendance at the wedding. It takes time and effort, but the gentle art of persuasion is still worth pursuing. If the pastor will take the trouble to explain the nature of the wedding service, the function of the music, and his own responsibility as pastor, the result will generally be the choice of acceptable music.

The function of the wedding solo

Pastors may find difficulty in articulating the function of solo music in the service, and a few words may be helpful. The couple comes before the altar that their marriage may be "sanctified by the Word of God and prayer." At least that ought to be their intent. The Lutheran marriage service as we have it leads a couple to view their marriage as God's institution. It instructs them on the nature of marriage as he has designed it, provides the exchange of their vows of lifelong fidelity "in the sight of God," and implores God in prayer for his blessing and guidance. The wedding solo should have the same high purpose and should function in the same way! Let the solo also be God-centered! What higher function can the solo music aspire to than to praise God for the joy and blessing of marriage, or to bring an instructive Word from God for the marriage, or to pray for God's blessing upon the couple?

By its very nature, solo music has considerable "impact" in the service. The right kind of words and music can be very meaningful and edifying. But wedding solos that are less than truly spiritual are an interruption in the service! Texts that are only incidentally religious or that focus on romantic love, and music that is overly sentimental or betrays its commercial origin tend to depress and deflate the spiritual tone of the service and draw the minds of those who listen away from God.

Getting practical

Pastors and organists need practical suggestions of good music to offer couples. Experience teaches that it is easier to persuade people about the value of good music than to convince them of the inadequacy of poor music. The last issue of *Focus on Worship* offered some suggestions for solo music. A few personal recommendations are offered below. One does not really need a long list. Although one does not like to use the same music over and over, yet as far as the couple and wedding guests are concerned, it is (hopefully) a one-time ceremony and each wedding congregation is largely different from the next.

Compile your list

Pastors and especially organists should gradually compile a list of suggestions for vocal solos which they can recommend with confidence. This, of course, takes time and some outlay of money by the individual or parish. The Northwestern Publishing House music catalog lists some suggestions. Concordia and Augsburg have special brochures on wedding music and vocal selections. Also available from the various publishers is the kit "Music for the Marriage Service" ($9.95), which includes a 60-minute cassette with recorded organ and vocal selections.

Practically speaking, the problem is to find selections that not only have worthy texts and music but are also appealing to the average couple. In recent years a fairly large number of vocal solos have been published. In this writer's limited experience, many of these carry scriptural texts and are musically well-crafted, but they do not appeal to couples because the solos are a bit too sophisticated musically. Try to find a happy medium.

Recommended

Here are a few personal favorites:

> "O Love That Casts Out Fear"—Bach
> "Jesu, Joy of Man's Desiring"—Bach
> "Come, Follow Me, the Savior Spake"—Karg-Elert
> "Love Divine, All Love Excelling"—arr. Bunjes
> "O Jesu, Joy of Loving Hearts"—Brahms

All of the above are appealing and relatively easy for both organist and soloist. They are all included in that book which ought to be in the library of every parish, organist, and soloist: *Wedding Blessings,* edited by Paul Bunjes (Concordia, $3.00).

Hymns should not be overlooked. They are the simplest and most accessible wedding music. One of the happier developments on the contemporary wedding scene is the growing use of congregational hymn singing. This gives the guests real participation and relates the whole ceremony more closely to normal worship. Such hymns can be general hymns of praise and joy. They do not always need to be tied to the marriage theme, just as hymns for the Communion distribution do not always need to be about the Sacrament itself. Hymns such as "Now Thank We All Our God" or "Praise to the Lord, the Almighty" are well-known and suitable. Hymns may also, of course, be used as solo music; for example, hymn settings of the 23rd psalm (TLH 426, 436, 431). Especially nice is "The King of Love My Shepherd Is" sung to the tune ST. COLUMBA. This version is included in *The Children's Hymnal.* There is also a setting for unison and three-part voices by David Johnson which is in an SAB collection of anthems called *Gloria Deo* (Augsburg). This same volume includes another excellent version of Psalm 23: "My Shepherd Will Supply My Need," set to a folk tune from southern Appalachia (optional flute descant included). Other usable hymns are "O Perfect Love," "O Blest the House" (vv. 1,2,5), and "O Happy Home."

This article has assumed the presence of the vocal solo as a usual feature of the church wedding. Obviously, many weddings have no solo music, nor need they. But if vocal music is to be sung in the service, let it be spiritually uplifting, textually and musically. Hopefully we can all think a little deeper, raise our sights a little higher, and work a little harder toward the improvement of music for the wedding. *It's your move.*

From "Grace Notes"

Inside each *Focus on Worship,* Eggert (editor of this publication) submitted short bylines entitled "Choirloft," "Console," and "Grace Notes." These short essays, many of which are only a paragraph or two in length, are little informative tidbits to keep church musicians aware of the opportunities and responsibilities involved in their call. Sometimes these bylines consist of an announcement, a direction to a new publication to be read, or an encouragement to a choir director to attend an upcoming workshop. More often, however, they are simply little thought- and action-provoking propositions which are appropriate reminders about the many facets of a church musician's profession. The following entries are a sampling of the varied issues covered in this format.

Michaelmas

Michaelmas, or St. Michael's and All Angels' Day, as it is called in our hymnal, is a festival largely overlooked in our church year calendar. The day is always September 29, but it may be celebrated on the following Sunday. The general observation of this day in our congregations would be a wholesome thing. The amazing and comforting things which the Scriptures tell us about the angels should receive some regular emphasis in our worship. Many people really know very little about angels, and from time to time various strange notions surface in our congregations. Aside from this, however, all of us should be more aware of their powerful influence in our midst, remembering that they are "*ministering* spirits, sent forth to minister for them who shall be heirs of salvation." We need to pray more with the simple, childlike trust of Luther: "Let thy holy angel be with me, that the wicked foe may have no power over me."

A Quiz for Church Organists

A good, smooth playing of the liturgy and hymns is much more important to most worshipers than prelude, offering music, and postlude. True or false? True. (Sorry.) Good solo music, well-performed, can add much to the worship. But nothing you do in the service will be more appreciated than what you do to help the worshipers with *their* part in the service.

It is good to forget to switch on the tremolo sometimes. True. It is very good. In fact, it is very good to forget to switch it on nearly all of the time. At any rate, thou shalt absolutely not use the tremolo for hymn accompaniment!

The shorter the hymn, the faster you play it. False. A general rule is to give the short, four-line hymns a more stately tempo and the longer chorales a little more verve than is usually accorded them.

It is good to use a variant harmonization for some stanzas of a hymn. True and false—the jury is still out on this one. It depends on the harmonization and how it is played. Sometimes it inspires the congregation and gives the singing a lift; sometimes it depresses the singing noticeably. If the worshipers stop singing in order to listen to what you are doing (or to *wonder* what you are doing), this should be a clue! If the harmonization is not too far out, and if it is smoothly played, and if (this is the most important) it does not disturb the rhythmic *pulse* of the hymn, then it can be a plus for the service.

Worshipers do not need to breathe except at the end of stanzas. In spite of apparent contrary opinion, this must be termed false.

In accompanying children's voices, it is a good idea to omit the pedal. True. Children's voices need judicious accompaniment. Heavy registration and the 16' pitch levels of the pedal are not good.

It is always good to play the hymn tune all the way through before the congregation sings. False. An interesting hymn prelude or intonation is fine. But if the intonation has established the tune, key, and tempo, why play the tune again in the hymnal harmonization? And who needs a longer familiar hymn played all the way through at the end of the service or for a closing stanza after the Benediction? A line or two will give the worshipers time to find the hymn and provide the necessary musical clues. Who wants to stand and listen to a band play "The Star-Spangled Banner" all the way through before he gets a chance to sing it?

Try Unison Music

More and more unison music for choirs is being published these days, and more and more choirs (not only beginner groups and children's choirs, but also larger and more capable groups) are finding it engaging and useful. Fresh and rhythmically interesting melodies, coupled with imaginative accompaniments for organ and other instruments, are reasons for growing acceptance. Don't overlook unison music in planning your choir program for the coming season!

Ye Good Olde Summertime

Behold, the summer is come, and thou mayest rest thy weary bones, enjoy the goodly sunshine and cool waters, and indulge thyself reasonably in that which is charcoal-broiled. But remember, O man, that soon again the schedule resumeth and the ice-time cometh. Wherefore it behooveth thee to do wise planning this faire season, lest the fall come upon thee unaware and thou find thyself in a dither.

Summon forth, therefore, from ye olde publishers of musick a goodly assortment of exam-packs and that which cometh on approval and sort out that which is good. Take care to order only that which is worthy and doth excite and rouse up thine own spirit, for verily much junke is published and indeed advertised with large letters. Beware also that thou order not single copies only for thy duplication machine, lest the composers of musick starve or thou be sued (as indeed it hath already happened in one kirk of Olde Milwaukee).

Now, if thou doest all these things anon, thy choir members shall rejoice and marvel greatly that all things are so in readiness, and thy heart shall swell within thee and happy shalt thou be. So shall it be with him that planneth wisely in ye good olde summertime!

Practice Makes . . .

Practice makes perfect? Maybe not, but it sure makes better organists! Are you what people refer to as a "miserable" organist? Take heart. With practice you can become "tolerable." (Don't laugh—the difference may be critical.) Are you at present a "tolerable" organist? You can become "capable." And if you are already an "excellent" player, you may with practice become "super," "really great," or even "inspiring." Set yourself the serious goal of moving one step up the ladder.

No, practice may not make perfect organists, but it does make for happier worshipers. And isn't that what the Christian calling is all about—serving, helping, edifying the body of Christ? If you can help your congregation to sing a little bit better or to participate a little more fully and joyfully in the worship, isn't it worth the effort?

Keys to Choir Success: No. 1

The single most important factor in a successful choir program is the choice of good, interesting *music*. Somehow or other, the choir director must make personal contact with music that moves and excites—*himself* first of all! If *you* find a piece dull, why should your choir or congregation find it to be otherwise? And there is no excuse for programming dull music in the worship!

Unfortunately, the price that must be paid by the director is hours of looking through and playing through stacks of music (most of which will be quickly discarded). But if you are willing to pay the price, you will have taken the giant step toward building a vital and successful choir program.

Neglected to Death

Some hymns live and some die. But those that die are never "sung to death." They are usually "neglected to death." Use or lose is the way it works. Each new hymnal sees hymns dropped and hymns added. Most of those dropped were tried and tested by congregations and found wanting in text or tune. Like the characters in *The Mikado*, "they never will be missed."

But there is a small handful of "big" chorales in our hymnal which have stood the test of time but have not really been tested by our generation. They are probably doomed to extinction because they are being "neglected to death." They are "God the Father, Be Our Stay" (TLH 247), "Kyrie, God Father" (TLH 6), "We Now Implore God the Holy Ghost" (TLH 231), and "Christ Is Arisen" (TLH 187).

Why are they neglected? Basically because they are not as immediately accessible as "Glory Be to Jesus." They need to be *known* to be appreciated, but they need to be sung more than once in a while to be known! Only when they are known, when they can be sung comfortably, will they reveal their power and spiritual richness.

How can we rescue these "big" hymns? *Use them for a season at a time as responses after the Epistle:* for example, No. 6 during Lent; No. 187 during the Easter season; No. 231 during the last part of Trinity (from Michaelmas [September 29] till Advent); No. 231 the first five Sundays of Trinity. Join SOC (Save Our Chorales)! No dues, no meetings, bumper stickers on request.

From the *Northwestern Lutheran*

Eggert contributed a large number of articles to the *Northwestern Lutheran*, as can be seen in the Appendix on page 84, which lists the titles of his articles from the 1950s through the 1990s. Shortly after being appointed project director for *Christian Worship: A Lutheran Hymnal*, Eggert saw the need for educating and informing both clergy and laypersons of the changes as well as the progress that was being made on the new hymnal. He undertook this dual mission in part by regularly submitting articles which dealt with many of these issues. The three following articles are a sampling of the numerous essays he wrote and delivered in this endeavor. These three essays come respectively from the beginning, middle, and end of the nearly nine-year period he served as the hymnal project director.

The New Hymnal: A Blue Book
Northwestern Lutheran, February 15, 1985 (Vol. 72, No. 4, pp. 56,57)

Sunday morning . . . the church bells ring, the organ sounds, and we all . . . reach for our hymnal. In that book we have all that we need to follow the path of our worship—the liturgical songs and responses, the prayers we will pray, the Scripture we will hear, the hymns we will sing. We need only to turn to the right page and join in.

But what if our hymnals suddenly vanished? Supposing that all of our hymnals were confiscated and we were forbidden to replace them. Such things have happened to Christians at various times and places. What would we do? Well, one thing that we would not do is to stop worshiping.

But imagine trying to reconstruct our worship from memory. How many of our 660 hymns could be recalled? How much of our liturgical material beyond the pages 5 and 15 liturgy? How we would suddenly appreciate those who had memorized large numbers of hymns. Or the organist who could play remembered melodies without a hymnal.

But doubtless we would lose many of the gems which have been collected for us in our hymnal from the whole history of Christian worship. Our worship would go on, but one thing is sure: We would appreciate as never before what a treasure we had in our hymnal.

The synod approves new/revised hymnal

Fortunately, our hymnals are resting safely in their pew racks. We do not need to try to reconstruct our worship or replace lost hymns. But we are doing something else to demonstrate concern for our worship and appreciation for our hymnal. At its last convention the synod decided to continue the Lutheran tradition of periodically updating and improving its hymnals. It resolved that work should begin on the publication of a "new/revised" hymnal for the synod.

Although the convention had indicated a high priority for the new hymnal, lack of available funding threatened to delay the project. However, Northwestern Publishing House offered to underwrite a sizable portion of the cost by funding the expenses of a full-time director for the work, who began his duties on June 1. He will work closely with the worship commission and assisting committees to bring the project to completion.

Hymnal Committee appointed

The Conference of Presidents recently appointed a group of 12 persons to serve as the Hymnal Committee: Pastors James Fricke, Mark Jeske, Iver Johnson, Harlyn Kuschel, Victor Prange, and James Tiefel; and Professors Bruce Backer, Richard Buss, Theodore Hartwig, Arnold Lehmann, Kermit Moldenhauer, and David Valleskey. To facilitate the work, this group will divide itself into a Hymn Committee, to be chaired by Pastor James Fricke, and a Liturgy Committee, headed by Professor David Valleskey.

There will be others, however, who will be involved in the hymnal project. A larger group of men and women, to be called the Hymnal Task Force, will shortly be appointed. This group will reflect a good cross section of the synod's worship needs and desires and provide a wider spectrum of talent and expertise for special tasks. With the selection of this group, the first phase of the hymnal project, preliminary planning and organization, will be completed.

The second and major phase of the work will be the actual production of materials and manuscripts. Ultimately, as materials are readied for field-testing, the congregations of the synod will be directly involved in the project. The third phase of the work will be the publishing process, which may take up to two years and includes the professional scribing of words and music, preparation of a full paste-up of the book, and printing and binding.

The last step is the introduction of the hymnal to the congregation. This will involve synod-wide workshops and the preparation of various printed and audio materials to insure a comfortable initial acquaintance with the new book.

The task ahead

The production of a new hymnal promises to be a challenging and somewhat intimidating task. The hymnal needs to serve all the members of the congregation and all the congregations of the synod. Members of a congregation normally differ not only in age, but in education, musical tastes, cultural or religious background, and personal worship preferences. And the congregations of our synod also exhibit a wide difference in characteristics and worship needs.

They are large and small, rural and urban, mission churches and old-line Lutheran. Some are racially mixed or have a large number of members coming from churches with nonliturgical traditions of worship. Some have small musical resources and others are richly endowed. And some congregations are accustomed to little or no change in their worship patterns, while others seek worship options and find such variety stimulating.

What kind of hymnal?

What kind of hymnal do we need and want? What kind of hymnal would you like to see in your church? The synod has provided a general guideline in purposefully calling the new book a "new/revised" hymnal. This somewhat unusual description indicates that neither a clone of *The Lutheran Hymnal* nor a radically new kind of book is desired. The synod has provided additional guidelines describing the hymnal as (1) scripturally sound, (2) in harmony with the character and heritage of our synod, (3) reflective of the larger mainstream and perspective of the worship of the Christian church, and (4) judged to be highly satisfactory by the majority of our members.

Another source of direction for the committees is a list of needed changes or desirable improvements. One such would be the lowering of the pitches in a number of hymns and portions of the liturgies to provide more comfortable participation by the congregations. Another relates to the need for new harmonizations for certain types of hymns. Two high-priority items which will need to be addressed are the needed liturgical changes and improvements in our Sunday liturgy and the change in worship language.

Our synod is already in the midst of a language change. But that is not reflected in the present hymnal. Our pastors are increasingly praying in today's English, and our children are learning their Bible stories and catechism in the words of the New International Version and the recently published contemporary *Luther's Catechism.* It seems inevitable that such use will increase. The real challenge here will be to provide new worship language with the dignity, rhythm, and grace that befits the nature of our worship. Worship in today's English does not have to be trendy, awkward, flat, or irreverent. Those at work on the hymnal will surely make every effort to avoid that.

The second high-priority need is to accommodate the liturgical changes which are already strongly in use in our congregational worship. The widespread adoption of the new church year calendar and three-year series of Scripture readings is not reflected in the printed pages of *The Lutheran Hymnal.* And improvements in the present propers (Introits, Collects, Graduals) were requested already a number of years ago by the synod.

Retaining the best

Since we are presently only at the beginning of a six- or seven-year project, specific solutions and decisions regarding the above and other needs all lie in the future. The blueprint for the hymnal is not yet drawn. But in the most general terms, we can expect that our new hymnal will retain the best of what we already have and incorporate the best of new hymns and liturgical materials.

Almost every bride anticipating her wedding day plans to wear "something old, something new, something borrowed, and something blue." In a sense, that applies to the hymnal. Our new book will be full of the old. We have a rich heritage of words and music, hymns and liturgy that span almost 20 centuries of Christian worship. It would be foolish and arrogant to ignore that.

But we expect that our new hymnal will also include much that is new. The last 40 years have been unusually productive in the creation of excellent new hymns and liturgical resources appropriate to our own times and worship needs. We can enrich our worship by a judicious selection of these new things, including perhaps some hymns or liturgies produced in our own synod.

Our hymnal will also contain much that is borrowed. New hymnals normally build on hymnals of the past. The hymnal committees will need to study all sorts of hymnals, especially the recently published Lutheran hymnals, as they search for worthy items for inclusion in our book. There is much of potential value for our hymnal already at hand. Something blue?

Most important, we want and expect our hymnal to be blue! Its cover may or may not be that color, but the word describes the overall spirit and content of our hymnal. In the language of church symbolism, the color blue represents hope. Blue is the new and increasingly popular liturgical color for Advent because of the hope and anticipation that characterizes that season.

Let our hymnal be filled from cover to cover with the blue of Christian hope, proclaiming "Christ in us the hope of glory" and calling us to our mission of sharing with everyone the "reason for the hope that is in us." Let it breathe the joyful spirit of the gospel, which inspires our worship and moves us to glorify the name of our Lord and Savior Jesus Christ. With God's blessing we will have such a new blue hymnal!

Our Changing Worship Language
Northwestern Lutheran, October 15, 1987 (Vol. 74, No. 18, pp. 346-348)

Without a doubt, the most common criticism of the *Sampler* liturgy revisions has been the use of the pronouns *you* and *your* in place of the traditional *thou, thee, thy,* and *thine* when referring to God. The chief objection was that addressing God as "you" was "demeaning the deity," "profaning God's name," "dragging God down to our level," "making God common," and was "irreverent" and "disrespectful."

Is addressing God as "you" instead of "thou" disrespectful, demeaning, etc.? Let's take a calm look at some of the factors involved:

1. Historically the pronouns *thou* and *you* carried no connotations of respect or disrespect. It was simply that *thou* was singular and *you* was plural. At the time of the publication of the King James Version of the Bible in 1611, a number of second-person pronouns were in use: thou, thee, thy, thine, ye, you, and your. If you were addressing one person, you said "thou." If speaking to a number of people, you said "you."

There was no particular formality of politeness or respect associated with *thou,* for example. The use of *thou* and *thine* was not restricted to God. Any kind of person or object could be addressed as "thou"—child or adult, prince or peasant, friend or foe, angel or demon, bird or animal, wind, cloud or sea.

2. Language changes. Gradually the use of the pronouns was streamlined and simplified. The distinction between *thou* and *you* fell away, and *you* was used for both singular and plural. In America at the time of the Revolutionary War, nobody used *thou* and *thee* in normal conversation except the Quakers. For a long time now, English has had only one second-person pronoun, *you,* for both singular and plural.

3. Why, then, have we been using *thou*? Because when the simple use of *you* was adopted by everybody, Christians continued to use *thee* and *thou* in their worship and prayer. Why? Because that was the language of the Bible in use, the King James Version. In order to read and understand the King James language, it was necessary to study it. Some say, "Certainly everyone can understand the meaning of *thou, thee*, and *thine*." True.

However, when you use the pronoun *thou*, there is a whole set of verb forms that must go with it. You cannot say, "Thou are God." You must say, "Thou art God." Likewise with *wouldst, shouldst, hast, wast, didst*, etc. And other verb forms need *est* endings: "Thou openest thy hand and satisfiest the desire of every living thing."

4. As long as we were using the King James Version of the Bible, it was normal and natural to reflect that speech in our worship. Pastors prayed in the "King James," children memorized their Bible passages from that Bible, liturgies were modeled after the sonorous English of the *Book of Common Prayer* (written largely by Bishop Cramer about 1550). Gradually the language of the King James Bible became a sort of "religious language" used by most Christian churches. Numberless prayers and thousands of hymns and other religious literature have been written in that style.

5. Perhaps this long usage has led some to feel that the liturgies in our hymnal cannot be altered, that the Lord prefers the King James language to modern English and, specifically, that the Lord prefers to be addressed as "Thou" instead of "You" or "you." God is the author of all languages, and there are about 1,500 languages or dialects into which the Bible has been translated. He has expressed no preference. He has given us no rules or ceremonial laws governing our worship.

What God looks for in us are hearts filled with faith, humility, repentance, gratitude. He bids us worship him "in spirit and in truth," that is, with sincerity and according to his revealed truth. God has given us freedom as far as the form of our liturgies and worship is concerned. And that included pronouns. It is true that the German language has two forms of pronouns, formal and informal. The German *sie* is the formal or polite form of the second-person pronoun. *Du* is the more informal or intimate pronoun.

But the amazing thing is that Luther's German Bible used the intimate pronoun *(du)* to address God! Just the opposite of what some would do with *thou* and *you*. The usual version of the German Lord's Prayer begins with the words, "Vater unser, der DU bist im Himmel." Though we surely want to approach God with awe and reverence, yet

God because of Christ calls us his children and invites us to pray to him "as dear children ask their dear father." We remember also that hundreds of German hymns all address God with the intimate pronoun *du* and not the stiff and formal pronoun *sie.*

6. An extraordinary thing has happened in the last 25 years. The language of worship, based on the KJV for 350 years, is changing rapidly. What has brought this about? New translations of the Bible in today's English. Until we had English translations which were at least as accurate and generally acceptable as the KJV, the King James Version was our normal Bible.

We now have accurate translations in today's English. And the accuracy of these translations is matched by the way they transmit the sense of the Bible passage clearly and often at first reading. This is not true of the KJV, where normally in Bible classes and children's confirmation classes, a good bit of time is taken up just in explaining the KJV words and sentence structures.

7. Our synod has no "official" Bible translation. But for its publications the synod has chosen to use the New International Version, and it is in strong use throughout the synod. The large majority of our congregations are hearing the Scripture lessons in the NIV language. Most of the children in our Lutheran elementary schools are memorizing Bible passages in the NIV. And most of our pastors are praying in today's English in the services.

About 18 months ago a survey of pastors revealed that of a total of 485 responding, 431 were using the NIV for the Scripture readings! This is amazing when one remembers that the complete NIV was published in 1978—just ten years ago. Surely the popularity of the NIV is attributable to its successful communication of the meaning of the text. No translation is going to be perfect, but the NIV appears to be a better tool for bringing God's Word to both churched and unchurched than the KJV.

Compare the following examples from a new book *The NIV—The Making of a Contemporary Translation* by Kenneth L. Barker (Zondervan, 1986). Read each example of the KJV first; then check the corresponding NIV translation.

KJV	NIV
Genesis 26:31 "And they rose up betimes in the morning."	Genesis 26:31 "Early the next morning"

KJV	NIV
2 Chronicles 2:7 "a man . . . that can skill to grave with the cunning men that are with me in Judah and in Jerusalem"	2 Chronicles 2:7 "a man . . . experienced in the art of engraving, to work in Judah and Jerusalem with my skilled craftsmen"
Psalm 119:147 "I prevented the dawning of the morning."	Psalm 119:147 "I rise before dawn."
Matthew 26:27 "Drink ye all of it."	Matthew 26:27 "Drink from it, all of you."
Luke 23:15 In the KJV Pilate says of Jesus: "and, lo, nothing worthy of death is done unto him"	Luke 23:15 "as you can see, he has done nothing to deserve death"
Acts 27:21 "Sirs, ye should have hearkened unto me, and not have loosed from Crete, and to have gained this harm and loss."	Acts 27:21 "Men, you should have taken my advice not to sail from Crete; then you would have spared yourselves this damage and loss."
1 Corinthians 5:3-5 "For I verily, as absent in body, but present in spirit, have judged already, as though I were present, concerning him that hath so done this deed, in the name of our Lord Jesus Christ, when ye are gathered together, and my spirit, with the power of our Lord Jesus Christ, to deliver such a one unto Satan for the destruction of the flesh, that the spirit may be saved in the day of the Lord Jesus."	1 Corinthians 5:3-5 "Even though I am not physically present, I am with you in spirit. And I have already passed judgment on the one who did this, just as if I were present. When you are assembled in the name of our Lord Jesus and I am with you in spirit, and the power of our Lord Jesus is present, hand this man over to Satan, so that the sinful nature may be destroyed and his spirit saved on the day of the Lord."

KJV	NIV
2 Corinthians 5:21 "For he hath made him to be sin for us, who knew no sin."	2 Corinthians 5:21 "God made him who had no sin to be sin for us."
Philippians 4:14 "Notwithstanding ye have well done, that ye did communicate with my affliction."	Philippians 4:14 "Yet it was good of you to share in my troubles."
Hebrews 7:18 "For there is verily a disannulling of the commandment going before for the weakness and unprofitableness thereof."	Hebrews 7:18 "The former regulation is set aside because it was weak and useless."

Many more examples are cited by the author, but these may be sufficient to remind ourselves that although the KJV is often eloquent, rhythmic, and graceful, it is also frequently obscure, misleading, and awkward.

The bottom line in all of this is the fact that we are in the midst of a change from the use of the King James Bible to the New International Version. Actually, that transition in our synod is almost complete. And as the NIV gains in use and familiarity, more and more worship materials—liturgies, prayers, catechisms, instructional materials for Sunday schools and day schools, etc.—will be printed in today's English with Scripture references from the NIV.

As we look to the publication of a new hymnal with a number of liturgies, a decision must be made regarding the language. The "language question" is not a matter of a couple of pronouns. It is a basic question of whether we are going to bring our worship forms into conformity with today's English or whether we cling to the King James language. If the question were to be decided today and for today's worshipers, it might be easy and popular to retain the KJV.

Looking ahead 20, 30, 40 or more years, that would seem to be a mistake. Consider the foreseeable future: Each succeeding year the KJV Bible will be less heard, less read, less studied. Children are not likely to be taught the archaic words and sentence structure of the KJV because there will be little need for it. We may deplore this, but when undertaking long-range publications like a hymnal, we need to consider the future.

Worship materials written in the KJV style, especially hymns, will be with us for a long time, and the traditional version of the Lord's Prayer may continue indefinitely as the favorite version of the WELS. Nevertheless, a basic decision needs to be made and a direction established for a smooth transition into the future. At some point one generation of worshipers will need to make a sacrifice and the effort to learn the new and forsake the old. It would be a favor to those who follow in our footsteps if we would be willing to be that "one generation."

Pressing On to the Future and Holding On to Our Past
Northwestern Lutheran, August 1993 (Vol. 80, No. 8, pp. 262,263)

The story of *Christian Worship: A Lutheran Hymnal* actually began in 1953 when the Lutheran Church—Missouri Synod (LCMS) initiated work on a revision of *The Lutheran Hymnal* (1941), the hymnal shared by the synods constituting the Synodical Conference. In 1959 the Wisconsin Evangelical Lutheran Synod (WELS) accepted the invitation to participate in the revision work. In 1965, however, the LCMS abandoned the project in favor of a new pan-Lutheran hymnal, leading to the publication of *Lutheran Book of Worship* (1978) and *Lutheran Worship* (1982).

After studying various options, the WELS in its 1983 convention resolved, "That the synod now begin work on a new/revised hymnal of its own, one that under the blessings of God will be scripturally sound and edifying, welcomed and judged to be highly satisfactory by a majority of our members, in harmony with the character and heritage of our church body, and reflecting the larger perspective and mainstream of the worship of the Christian church."

In 1984 the Conference of Presidents called a full-time project director and appointed working committees. The Liturgy Committee, Hymn Committee, and Commission on Worship formed the Joint Hymnal Committee. Later in the project a full-time music editor was called. The hymnal group worked steadily for seven years to finish the hymnal manuscript, followed by a year and a half of layout, design, and promotion. In 1993, the completed hymnal is being introduced along with *Christian Worship: Accompaniment for Liturgy and Psalms* and *Christian Worship: Manual.*

The phrase "new/revised" in the synodical resolution was interpreted to mean a hymnal which preserved the Christian and Lutheran heritage of liturgy and hymns from *The Lutheran Hymnal* and at the same time improved and expanded it.

Liturgy

Much of the familiar content of *The Lutheran Hymnal* has been preserved. The three historic liturgies—the Common Service, Matins, and Vespers—are retained with some revision. Two new liturgies are included, the Service of Word and Sacrament and the Service of the Word, following the structure of historic Lutheran liturgy, but with new or revised texts and with newly composed music. These liturgies were added to provide some of the liturgical variety sought by many congregations and individuals.

Also included in the book are rites for the Sacrament of Holy Baptism, Christian marriage, and Christian funeral. Three brief liturgies, Morning Praise, Evening Prayer, and General Devotion are designed for use in schools, conferences, and congregational organizations.

The regular use of psalms is a new liturgical feature. In addition to its traditional use in Morning Praise and Evening Prayer (Matins and Vespers), the Psalm serves as a response to the First Lesson in the Common Service, Service of Word and Sacrament, and Service of the Word. The most important and most familiar psalms were selected and arranged for liturgical use by carefully shortening them to six or seven verses. All the psalms or psalm sections are responsorial and have been furnished with easy and attractive congregational refrains. Sixteen melodies have been provided for singing the psalm verses.

Hymns

The hymn section of the new hymnal has a familiar look. Over 400 hymns have been retained from *The Lutheran Hymnal*, though many have undergone a slight updating of language. The hymns are arranged according to the Christian year and topical headings. The hymn section also has a new look and sound. The last three decades have seen a strong resurgence of creativity and interest in the writing of hymns. Therefore, congregations will enjoy a greater variety of hymns than before.

In addition to Lutheran chorales and traditional English hymnody, a wide selection of plainsong hymns; spirituals; folk hymns from Appalachia, Wales, Ireland, and elsewhere; gospel hymns; and contemporary hymns in different styles are included. In addition to new texts and new melodies, a somewhat freer and fresher type of harmonization has been furnished for some of the hymns; descants and guitar chords are supplied for a few others.

A Christ-centered book

The hymnal is a unique tool for worship. It is a treasury of theology, poetry, music, history, liturgy, and praise. Because it is truly "the people's book," a good deal of care was taken to solicit opinion and reaction from the field. In addition to the *Sampler* of liturgy, hymnody, psalmody, and prayer distributed to all congregations early in the project, field-testing among groups of congregations was carried on throughout the project. Thanks is due to the many critical reviewers, proofreaders, and writers of several thousand letters of advice and reaction.

The overall intent of those who prepared *Christian Worship: A Lutheran Hymnal* is to produce a Lutheran hymnal that is at once forward-looking and also enriched by the faith and worship experience of the whole Christian church of the past. Specifically, the goal is to deliver to the church a strongly Christ-centered book, bringing together liturgies and a large number of hymns celebrating the life and atoning work of Jesus. May the new book proclaim the power of the Word of God and the foundation doctrine of forgiveness by God's grace through faith in Christ. May its use among us foster and strengthen appreciation of liturgical worship, and enrich and enliven our relationship with God and each other.

From the *Wisconsin Lutheran Quarterly*

Eggert was always examining and analyzing the use of music in the worship life of the church. As a teacher, director, and pastor, he tried to expose his students, choirs, congregations, and synod to music that he felt would fulfill this high calling. In the following article, published shortly after his death, he evaluates "gospel hymns" and how they might be integrated into the worship life of a liturgical church.

Gospel Hymns and Lutheran Worship
Wisconsin Lutheran Quarterly, Fall 1993 (Vol. 90, No. 4, pp. 262-267)

What is a "gospel hymn"? One might think that it is any Christian hymn that contains the gospel. Not so. Gospel hymns (or "gospel songs" or simply "gospels") are a specific kind of Christian song with well-defined characteristics. These characteristics are precisely those which have brought certain mainline and liturgical churches (particularly Lutheran and Episcopalian) to ignore this genre of hymnody, especially when it is hymnal-making time.

What are these characteristics?

1. The texts, though scriptural and atonement-centered, are generally shallow and theologically thin. The themes tend to be repetitious and consist of a rather small group of subjects.
2. Gospel hymns are personal and highly emotional, both in text and music. There is much repetition of phrases or single words which do not appeal to the mind but rather involve feelings by means of simple repetition.
3. The gospel hymn is concerned with the individual singer and not with the church as such. The vertical relationship with God is stressed, not the relationship to or participation in the body of Christ.
4. Musically, the gospel hymn is in form a solo song with a group refrain. The interest and attractiveness of these songs lie in their melodies, which are very easy, catchy, and sentimental. Some of their rhythmic patterns invite physical movement from gentle swaying to toe-tapping or hand-clapping. Harmonically, the gospel song is very simple, consisting mostly of three chords, inviting part-singing at the refrain. The bass line usually changes only at the bar lines and not within the bar.

Most of the above characteristics will be best observed by singing and playing about 15 or 20 gospel hymns, one after the other. One may sense that they call for no musical knowledge to understand them and no skill to sing them. One may also find that they are fun to sing.

The gospel hymn originated in the intense atmosphere of evangelistic mass meetings of preacher Dwight L. Moody and singer Ira D. Sankey. They brought the "Second Evangelical Awakening"(1859) to a culmination in 1872 and the following years. Moody met Sankey at a YMCA convention in 1870 where he watched Sankey rouse a slumbering audience into enthusiastic singing. Moody was unmusical and could not tell one tune from another, but he was immensely interested in music's power to move and sway an audience. He persuaded Sankey to follow him to England and Scotland. There they enjoyed enormous success, singing and preaching to audiences totaling 2,500,000. Biographer Gamaliel Bradford says of Moody's ability to judge a hymn's mass effect:

> He could form no judgment . . . by hearing it played or sung in private. He must see it tried in a crowd and could discover in an instant its adaptation to awaken the feelings which he needed to have in action. If it had the right ring, he used it for all it was worth. "Let the people sing!" he would shout. "Let all the people sing. Sing that verse again. There's an old man over there who is not singing at all; let him sing." No matter how long it took, he would keep the people at work until they were fused and melted.[2]

Ira Sankey was as unique a talent in his way as Moody. He accompanied himself at a small Estey reed organ, playing his own melodies and arrangements, which were sometimes improvised during the meeting itself.

Sankey was a powerful baritone but untrained. He sang, it is said, with the conviction that souls were receiving Jesus between one note and the next. A typical revival service included a musical program to stimulate the sensibilities of the people and prepare them for the rousing address which followed.

The extraordinary success of these meetings not only brought fame to Moody and Sankey but produced a great demand for the songs, both in the United States and in other countries. Expanding collections of Sankey's songs and those of some of his associates were published and widely used by evangelistic groups such as the Salvation Army and the YMCA. The gospel song became the standard type of music for mission use and the growing Sunday school movement. In 1903 Sankey published *Sacred Songs and Solos,* a compact volume of 1,200 songs. Unfortunately, Sankey's collections also spawned hundreds of imitative publications, increasingly marked by monotonous repetition and commercial excess. The most famous writer of gospel hymn texts was Fannie Crosby Alstyne (1820–1915), who authored more than 8,000 hymns, in addition to Sankey's associate, Philip Bliss, and Robert Lowry, William Doane, and George Stebbins.

The demise of the gospel hymn has over the years been prophesied or announced with some regularity. After more than a century, however, the gospel hymns are alive and well and still being written. They rest, mostly unchanged, in the hymnals of the Southern Baptist Convention and in songbooks of many evangelistic organizations.

---

[2]Quoted by Robert M. Stevenson in *Patterns of Protestant Church Music* (Durham, NC: Duke University Press, 1952), p.161.

So the beat goes on. Various movements to elevate the literary and musical tone of public worship are met with complete indifference by a large group of people whose taste is simply for emotional verse and light music. So it has been, and so it will likely continue.

Erik Routley calls the gospel hymns "nursery rhymes of Christian hymnody and designedly slight in musical content."[3] In his view these hymns are sometimes impressive but indigestible in large doses because of low theological protein content. Waldo Pratt, writing around the turn of the century, also expresses a negative opinion. He says:

> The defenders of this popular hymnody . . . very often gravely underestimate the capacity of the popular mind to rise above vulgar embodiments of truth and to shake itself free from perverted sentimentality, and they constantly mistake the zest of animal enjoyment in a rub-a-dub rhythm or the shout of childish pleasure in a "catchy" refrain for real religious enthusiasm.[4]

In the consideration of this genre of hymnody, or at least of specific examples, the WELS Hymn Committee, after considerable discussion, voted to reject most of the suggested gospel hymns. Originally the committee had placed gospel hymns in a special category and did not rate them because it was felt that they would not survive the theological, literary, and musical guidelines of the committee. They wished to leave open the possibility, however, that some might be included for other reasons.

Are there "other reasons" for their inclusion in our hymnal? Let us permit Louis Benson to set the stage for the defense by citing another quotation from his book *The English Hymn*. He writes as follows:

> They [the gospel hymns] were first sung in unison with a great throng of deeply moved people. Something of the spiritual impression they made was reflected from the simple and sincere personalities of the evangelists. They were plain men, employing the arguments and illustrations, the music and the verse, that appealed to themselves in the conviction that such preaching and song was best adapted to appeal to the hearers.

---

[3] Erik Routley, *The Music of Christian Hymns* (Chicago: GIA Publications, 1981), p. 137.
[4] Quoted in Louis Benson, *The English Hymn* (New York and Philadelphia, 1916), p. 489.

Why, then (so the argument runs), since the great majority of people who came under revival influences, whether of Moody or his successors, are likewise plain and uncultivated, is not the gospel hymn best adapted to the ends of evangelistic work? And if happily these people are brought into the worshiping congregation, why should they be asked to forgo the sentimental verse and popular melody that appeal to them in favor of a more literary hymnody and more artistic music? That there is some force in the argument is beyond doubting. Many hearts have been quickened through these hymns that seem to the critical to be crude in sentiment and unrefined in expression. And the editor of one of the choicest of modern musical hymnals has admitted that through the compositions of the gospel hymns school, "music" has become the expression of spiritual life for thousands who before were without a voice in public worship, and, as suppressed feeling easy does, were often without any share in public worship.[5]

Here Benson touches upon what I believe is the real issue: Are the gospel songs a good and useful thing for the Lutheran worship service today? Erik Routley makes the following point which provides a partial answer: The gospel songs "were very much used by the Salvation Army (in England) whose mission was to penetrate to all those places where religion had been squeezed out of life by artificial ugliness and poverty. But in America . . . the communities that have espoused them [the gospel hymns] are not necessarily underprivileged communities whose religion needs rescuing from infantilism (which is the disorder of wanting to remain a child when one should be growing up)."[6]

True enough. But we must be concerned if we are to pursue our synod's outreach. We have to be concerned about worship materials for outreach among the black community, who have adopted the gospel songs, usually via the Baptist Church. Also, what about the mission prospects, the catechumens, the new Christians, and those who enter our church from other church backgrounds where the gospel song is the norm? Will a scattering of gospel songs in our hymnal help them to have some comfortable part in the worship and help make the transi-

---
[5] Benson, p. 489.
[6] Routley, p. 137.

tion to Lutheran liturgical worship? We make a good deal from time to time of the doctrine of the universal priesthood of all believers. Can the gospel songs be a kind of temporary worship music, a stepping stone to the chorale and standard hymnody?

Perhaps the gospel hymn can be looked at also, however, as a kind of *Gebrauchsmusik* for certain times or occasions or for certain groups within our church. In one of the Anglican hymnals, a small section of gospel hymns is included which is headed "Not for Ordinary Use." Though this sounds patronizing and probably is, there is intended something like the above. And "regular" Lutherans also need something more than formal church hymns or chorales to hum or whistle around the house, or to sing at social gatherings, church dinners, youth organizations, and similar occasions.

Our new hymnal is strongly oriented to serious worship and to hymns which carry the gospel and "proclaim the wonders God hath done" (TLH 387:1). The dimensions that art adds to our Lutheran worship are also precious, but a discussion of that would take us too far afield.

Gospel hymns do not fit very well in the liturgical service which we have. They are oblivious to the church year and tend to be a kind of interruption in the flow of the service (as much of our choral music also is). On the other hand, the chorales for the most part do not whistle very well, and "Wake, Awake" does not fit the bill around the campfire. A judicious selection of gospel hymns can perhaps serve these needs without embarrassment and without the risk of tempting today's passive listeners and those who are looking for some sort of entertainment from the music in the service to feel they have found it in the gospel hymn.

Texts, Tunes, and Compositions by Kurt Eggert

Compiled by William H. Braun

Adam   CM (86 86)

Eggert wrote the tune ADAM to give Martin Franzmann's text "In Adam We Have All Been One" a new setting in *Christian Worship*. (Eggert felt the folk tune setting THE SAINTS' DELIGHT used in the *Lutheran Book of Worship* and *Lutheran Worship* was not appropriate for the text.) Franzmann was one of Eggert's favorite teachers at Northwestern Preparatory School and Northwestern College. Eggert admired the "highly poetic" nature and "panoramic sweep" of Franzmann's text. This tune was one of three he wrote for the text. The other two were written—one in a major tonality, the other in a minor tonality—to be used alternately, indicating the major (uplifting and inspiring) and minor (melancholy and confessional) characters of the various stanzas. The tune in *Christian Worship* was apparently a compromise between the composer and the Hymn Committee. The setting in *Christian Worship* (No. 396) was done by Eggert.

The Blessing

The SATB setting of the text below, by John Newton, was originally written for the 25th anniversary ordination service of the Reverend James P. Schaefer, Eggert's brother-in-law. It was used again in 1973 for Eggert's own 25th anniversary ordination service. The text is also used by the Lutheran Chorale of Milwaukee as the closing prayer for each rehearsal, a custom started by Eggert when he was the director.

> May the grace of Christ our Savior
> And the Father's boundless love
> And the Holy Spirit's favor
> Rest upon us from above. Amen.

God of Love and God of Marriage   87 87 89 87

Eggert wrote the tune and text of this composition for the marriage of his son John to Joanne Groll in August 1973. The original setting was for two guitars and included the following refrain, which was sung by the groom's brothers, sisters, and cousins:

> God of light and love and marriage,
> Bless, we pray, these your children,
> Bride and bridegroom, every day.
> Keep them faithful; keep them loving.
> Light their way.

This wedding song was adapted for use with organ accompaniment. The setting in *Christian Worship* (No. 602), written by Kermit Moldenhauer, does not use the refrain of the original.

God Was There on Calvary 77 75

Eggert wrote the tune and text for this choral piece in 1975. He composed the piece to complement a Lenten sermon series with the same theme preached by the pastors at Atonement Lutheran Church, Milwaukee, where Eggert served as one of the pastors. Kermit Moldenhauer wrote the setting in *Christian Worship* (No. 140).

How Lovely Shines the Morning Star!

This original poem, based on the Old Testament prophecy "there shall come a Star out of Jacob" (Numbers 24:17 KJV) and the New Testament fulfillment "I [Jesus] am . . . the bright and morning star" (Revelation 22:16 KJV), is not attached to any particular musical setting and does not follow any regular metrical scheme. It is given below in Eggert's original format.

> Men reach for stars,
>   for dreams that are too high,
>   too far away
> To capture and enjoy:
> A recipe for peace,
> A law to banish hate and greed,
> An antidote for death.
> —Such are the dreams men dream;
> —Such are the stars for which men strain.
>
> But grandest yet most hopeless dream,
> And brightest but yet farthest star
> Is this: salvation, heaven, eternal joy.
> This dream of men outshines all dreams
> As far as does the morning star
> At dawn, when all around
>   the other stars grow dim.

This is the dream beyond all dreams
Which man by his own efforts
Never can attain.
This is the Star above all stars
Which is the star above all stars
Which man must strive and reach for
All in vain.

So God sent down to this poor earth,
Through virgin birth,
His own dear Son
    to bear in his own self

All of our guilt and sin.
And thus to bring
Salvation down to men,
Himself became earth's Morning Star.

(How fitting that at his blest birth
God sent a star to point the place
Where in the hay
This Day-Star lay.)

Born thus a man, but yet true God,
Christ led for us a sinless life;
And by a shameful, painful death
Paid all our debts and thereby did
What we ourselves could never do:
Made our salvation's dream come true.

He died for all and rose again,
And reascended to the skies.
Do you ask why?
Because man's disobedience
    to God's command

Drove all perfection
    from the world
He made;
Sin separated man from God,
    and his in every age
Inclined his heart to pride,

> To selfishness
> And death.
>
> But God in love beheld lost man,
> Knew there was nothing man could do
> To pay for sin and thus to draw
> Down from afar
> Salvation's star.
>
> He rules as Lord of lords and kings.
>
> And through his Word shines day by day,
> As Morning Star, Light of the world
> To light the way
> To heaven's open door.
>
> Reach then and grasp this radiant Star
> —You can, by faith—
> Take Jesus Christ into your heart
> In humble trust.
> Thus you may live, safe in his grace,
> Until you step before his throne
> To see, with angels all around,
> The glory of his face.

If the Women Had Known

Eggert wrote the following poetic text, which was not attached to any special hymn tune or music, for an Easter celebration. It was published in *Focus on Worship,* Trinity 1976.

> If the women had known that Easter morn
> The mighty thing that God had done,
> How their hearts would have flown
> As they moved toward his tomb in the early dawn.
>   But they didn't know . . .
> So their steps were heavy and their heart a stone
> As they walked together in the silent dawn.
>
> If the women had known what awaited them there—
> The sight of an angel, shining fair,
> The tomb wide open, empty, bare,
> The grave clothes neatly folded there—

What tingling excitement would have urged them on
In trembling haste toward the beckoning tomb.
    But they didn't know . . .
So their steps were heavy and their heart a stone
As they walked along through the misty dawn.

If the women had known they would see the Lord,
Risen, living, standing, strong,
What shouts of joy would have muffled their sighs,
Given wings to their feet and made them fly.
    But they didn't know . . .
So their steps were heavy and their heart a stone,
Their eyes full of tears, their faith near-gone,
And only love still lingered on
As they walked in sorrow, despairing, forlorn—
A funeral procession on Easter dawn!

Introit for Reformation

This SATB choral setting of Psalm 46:1,2,11 was first used in a Reformation service at the Milwaukee Performing Arts Center in a Wisconsin Lutheran Choral Festival concert. After being copied and used for many years as a handwritten piece by Eggert, it was recently published by Northwestern Publishing House (order number OL28N6002).

Liturgical Music

Eggert had a special interest in the Psalms, in chanting, and in the liturgy of the church, as can be seen in his many essays, such as "Canticles for the Congregation" (*Church Music,* 75.2, pp. 10-13). As stated in the introduction to *Christian Worship,* an effort was made to preserve the Lutheran heritage of liturgy and at the same time improve and expand it. To that end, Eggert provided melodies for the *Kyrie,* "O Lord, Our Lord," and Preface in the Service of Word and Sacrament, with settings by Kermit Moldenhauer. Likewise, in the liturgy for the new Vespers called Evening Prayer, Eggert provided melodies for the opening versicles, responses, "Song of Mary" *(Magnificat),* and "Song of Simeon" *(Nunc Dimittis),* again with settings by Kermit Moldenhauer.

Not unto Us 12 10 13 10

Eggert wrote the text and tune for the hymn "Not unto Us" in 1975 for the 125th anniversary of the Wisconsin Evangelical Lutheran Synod. The hymn was first performed at a special service at St. John's Lutheran Church on Vliet Street in Milwaukee and has since been used for many district festivals and other occasions in the church. The opening line originally was "Not unto us, not unto us give glory, O Lord," and the first line of the concluding stanza was "Not unto us but to thy name all glory be giv'n." James Engel provided the setting in *Christian Worship* (No. 392).

The original hymn alternated between two sets of text and melody; however, *Christian Worship* uses only the first set. Eggert's concertato arrangement of this hymn employs both texts and melodies, with the congregation singing the first melody (as used in *Christian Worship*) and the choir responding with the second melody. The concertato setting is for congregation, SATB choir, and organ, with optional vocal and trumpet descants. It is published by Northwestern Publishing House (order number OL28N6003).

Oh, Come, My Soul 88 44 8

The tune, text, and setting of this hymn as published in *Christian Worship* (No. 99) were written in March 1976 by Eggert as a choral piece for a Good Friday Tenebrae service at Atonement Lutheran Church, Milwaukee. Peter Sordahl's concertato arrangement of this hymn for congregation, three-part choir, flute, clarinet, and organ is published by Northwestern Publishing House (order number OL28N6000).

Psalm 23

Eggert made a setting of the King James Version of this beloved psalm for flute and soprano. The melody is simple and graceful, with little repetition or elaboration. There was most likely an accompaniment part; however, as of this writing only the vocal part is known to be extant.

Ride On, Ride On in Majesty

In 1973 Eggert wrote a new tune and setting to Henry H. Milman's text "Ride On, Ride On in Majesty" (*Christian Worship* 132,133). The Palm Sunday piece was set for the junior and senior choirs and instrumentalists at Atonement Lutheran Church, Milwaukee. In 1991 this piece was used by the Lutheran Chorale of Milwaukee in a joint concert with the Treble Choir from Dr. Martin Luther College and the Wisconsin Lutheran Seminary Chorus. An estimated one thousand people were turned away from this concert at the seminary gymnasium for lack of room. Eggert played the piano section himself and thus did not write out that portion of the arrangement. His sister Hildegarde Fischer later made an arrangement with a new introduction and expanded brass part for the Lutheran Chorale's 40th anniversary concert in 1998.

Wedding Glory 87 87 887 887

The tune WEDDING GLORY and its setting (*Christian Worship* 219) were written for the sixth stanza of Paul Gerhardt's hymn "A Lamb Goes Uncomplaining Forth." This stanza was familiar to Eggert because his brother-in-law James Schaefer often quoted it in his sermons. The Hymn Committee was going to drop stanza 6 because of length, so Eggert composed a new melody for the single stanza. Dr. Carl Schalk was commissioned to write a setting of this tune and text for the Wisconsin Lutheran Seminary Chorus. This arrangement was premiered under the direction of Professor James Tiefel in May 1993 at the last seminary commencement concert that Eggert was able to attend before his death in June 1993.

Appendix: Bibliography of Articles

A complete listing (chronologically by date of publication) of the essays and articles written by Kurt Eggert on worship and music follows:

> Guide to the Church Year Series—Easter to Pentecost
> *Viva Vox*, 1955 (Vol. I, No. 1, pp. 15-17)
>
> Guide to the Church Year Series—Trinity III and IV,
> Advent, Christmas
> *Viva Vox*, 1955 (Vol. I, No. 2, pp. 13-18)
>
> Guide to the Church Year Series—Trinity I and II
> *Viva Vox*, 1956 (Vol. II, No. 1, pp. 19-25)
>
> Making the Propers of the Service Meaningful
> *Viva Vox*, 1956 (Vol. II, No. 2, pp. 3-6)
>
> A Narrative Service
> *Viva Vox*, 1956 (Vol. II, No. 2, pp. 11-15)
>
> Guide to the Church Year Series—Epiphany, Pre-Lent, Lent
> *Viva Vox*, 1956 (Vol. II, No. 2, pp. 21-24)

The Heart of Worship
Northwestern Lutheran, February 17, 1957 (Vol. 44, No. 4, pp. 59,60)

Living the Church Year with Our Children
Viva Vox, 1957 (Vol. III, No. 1, pp. 2-4)

Questions for Roundtable Discussion on Music in the Service
Viva Vox, 1957 (Vol. III, No. 1, pp. 3-6)

Hymns in the Service—The Easter Season
Viva Vox, 1957 (Vol. III, No. 1, pp. 9-20)

Hymn Festival
Northwestern Lutheran, April 15, 1957 (Vol. 44, No. 8, p. 123)

Hymns in the Service—The End-Time Season
Viva Vox, 1957 (Vol. III, No. 2, pp. 11-19)

Dear Fred (Imaginary Letters to a New Choir Director)
Viva Vox, 1958 (Vol. IV, No. 1, pp. 7-9)

Hymns in the Service—The Pre-Lent and Lent Season
Viva Vox, 1958 (Vol. IV, No. 1, pp. 13-24)

Hymns in the Service—Advent and Christmas
Viva Vox, 1958 (Vol. IV, No. 2, pp. 15-32)

Hymns in the Service—Trinity I and II
Viva Vox, 1959 (Vol. V, No. 1, pp. 3-14)

Integrating Organ and Choir with the Hymn of the Week
Viva Vox, 1959 (Vol. V, No. 2, pp. 3-5)

Hymns in the Service—Trinity III
Viva Vox, 1959 (Vol. V, No. 2, pp. 15-26)

Luther and the Singing Congregation
Northwestern Lutheran, October 1, 1967 (Vol. 54, No. 20, pp. 327-329)

The Case for the Propers in Liturgical Worship
Church Music, 69.1, pp. 19-26

An Open Letter on Singing Luther's Hymns
Northwestern Lutheran, October 25, 1970 (Vol. 57, No. 22, p. 360)

Meeting Contemporary Needs in Christian Worship
Presented at the Christian Worship Seminar, Dr. Martin Luther College, New Ulm, Minnesota, April 1971

Part One: Accent on Contemporary
Part Five: Accent on Balance

"Grace Notes": Michaelmas, Use These Tools, Your Own Worship Workshop
Focus on Worship, Trinity 1972 (No. 2)

A New Series of Introits for the Church Year
Focus on Worship, Advent 1972 (No. 3)

Focus on the Advent Wreath
Focus on Worship, Advent 1972 (No. 3)

"Grace Notes": Thinking the Liturgy, SPECMCWELS, What Child Is This?, Church Music
Focus on Worship, Advent 1972 (No. 3)

"Grace Notes": Our Policy, Choosing Hymns, Celebrate Ascension Day
Focus on Worship, Easter–Pentecost 1973 (No. 1)

"Grace Notes": Inchin' Along, Varying the Service, The Kyrie
Focus on Worship, Trinity 1973 (No. 2)

Worship Training—A Practical Method
Focus on Worship, Trinity 1973 (No. 2)

"Grace Notes": Baptismal Rite, New Calendar and Lectionary, Hymns for Christmas Morning
Focus on Worship, Advent 1973 (No. 3)

The Year of the Lord
Focus on Worship, Advent 1973 (No. 3)

The Lectionary—Where Do We Go from Here?
Focus on Worship, Pentecost 1974 (No. 1)

The New Lectionary—A General Introduction
Focus on Worship, Pentecost 1974 (No. 1)

Choirloft and Console: A Quiz for Church Organists
Focus on Worship, Trinity 1974 (No. 2)

"Grace Notes": Learning Takes Teaching, Try Unison Music
Focus on Worship, Trinity 1974 (No. 2)

Introducing the *Te Deum* to the Congregation
Focus on Worship, Trinity 1974 (No. 2)

Focus on the Communion Distribution
Focus on Worship, Epiphany 1974 (No. 3)

Choirloft and Console: Ye Good Olde Summertime, Practice Makes . . . , Keys to Choir Success
Focus on Worship, Trinity 1975 (No. 1)

"Grace Notes": Ah, Sweet Mystery of Love; Neglected to Death
Focus on Worship, Trinity 1975 (No. 1)

Canticles for the Congregation
Church Music, 75.2, pp. 10-13

"Grace Notes": Looking over the Overlooked, What about the Propers?, The Rhythm of the Liturgy
Focus on Worship, Christmas 1975 (No. 2)

Focus on the Wedding
Focus on Worship, Trinity 1976 (No. 1)

Here Comes the Bride
Focus on Worship, Trinity 1976 (No. 1)

Focus on the Wedding Music—The Solo
Focus on Worship, Epiphany 1977 (No. 1)

"Grace Notes": The Sung Processional, Alternate Prayers . . . Use 'Em, There's Got to Be a *First* Time!
Focus on Worship, Epiphany 1977 (No. 1)

The Wedding Solo
Northwestern Lutheran, May 1, 1977 (Vol. 64, No. 9, pp. 136,137)

"Grace Notes": Hallowed Be Thy Name, Gloria in Excelsis Deo
Focus on Worship, Trinity 1977 (No. 2)

"Grace Notes": Farewell and Godspeed, Familiar Variety, Attention: Piano Teachers, Quo Vadis?
Focus on Worship, Trinity 1978 (No. 1)

Choirloft and Console: Make Some Sound Improvements in Your Choir
Focus on Worship, Trinity 1981 (No. 1)

"Grace Notes": Hello Again; Alphabet Soup; Introit, Collects, Gradual; What Do We Bring to the Service?; NPH Music

Catalog, Worth Ordering
Focus on Worship, Trinity 1981 (No. 1)

Yes, We Need a New Hymnal
Focus on Worship, Trinity 1981 (No. 1)

WELS and Lutheran Worship
Presented at the Metropolitan-North Pastoral Conference, Milwaukee, Wisconsin, May 10, 1982

A New Hymnal for WELS?
Northwestern Lutheran, July 1, 1982 (Vol. 69, No. 13, pp. 200-203)

"Grace Notes": Forming an Opinion on LW, The Price of Change, A Balanced Book
Focus on Worship, Easter 1983 (No. 1)

God's Music Man
Prepared for the quincentenary of Luther's birth, Wisconsin Lutheran Seminary, Mequon, Wisconsin, November 1, 1983

The New Hymnal: A Blue Book
Northwestern Lutheran, February 15, 1985 (Vol. 72, No. 4, pp. 56,57)

Progress Report on the New Hymnal
Presented at the Metropolitan-North Pastoral Conference, Milwaukee, Wisconsin, March 18, 1985

The New Hymnal: A Gold and Silver Book
Northwestern Lutheran, January 15, 1986 (Vol. 73, No. 2, pp. 30-32)

Enriching Our Worship Heritage
Prepared for the convention of the Northern Wisconsin District of the Wisconsin Evangelical Lutheran Synod, June 23-25, 1986

Introducing the *Sampler*
Northwestern Lutheran, November 15, 1986 (Vol. 73, No. 20, pp. 386,387)

"Grace Notes": What Shall We Do with the Sampler?; Excuse, Please; Alternatum Hymn Singing; Why Do We Sing Hymns?
Focus on Worship, Pentecost 1987 (No. 1)

Our Changing Worship Language
Focus on Worship, Pentecost 1987 (No. 1)

Our Changing Worship Language
Northwestern Lutheran, October 15, 1987 (Vol. 74, No. 18, pp. 130,131)

A Quick Quiz for Church Organists
Focus on Worship, Winter 1988

"Grace Notes": The Focus Widens; Oh, No! Not the Creeds; Looking down the Road; What's Old? What's New?
Focus on Worship, Winter 1988

The New Hymnal: Master Hymn List
Northwestern Lutheran, January 15, 1989 (Vol. 76, No. 2, pp. 32-34)

Perspective on the New Hymnal
Focus on Worship, Spring 1990

Music for Communion Distribution
Focus on Worship, Summer 1990

The Shape of the New Hymnal
Northwestern Lutheran, April 1, 1991 (Vol. 78, No. 7, pp. 130,131)

Preserve, Improve, Enlarge
Northwestern Lutheran, March 1992 (Vol. 79, No. 5, pp. 88,89)

The Use of Silence
Focus on Worship, Summer 1992

Pressing On to the Future and Holding On to Our Past
Northwestern Lutheran, August 1993 (Vol. 80, No. 8, pp. 262,263)

Gospel Hymns and Lutheran Worship
Wisconsin Lutheran Quarterly, Fall 1993 (Vol. 90, No. 4, pp. 262-267)

The Life of Kurt John Eggert

Ruth Eggert

On a cold and blustery day, May 8, 1923, a son was born to the Reverend William and Paula (Kirchner) Eggert in Wausau, Wisconsin. The boy's father, pastor of four area churches, baptized him on May 26 and gave him the name Kurt John Eggert. Kurt was just four when his older sister, Margaret, was fatally injured by a car while crossing the street. But shortly afterwards, Kurt became a big brother when the Lord blessed his parents with three other daughters: Ruth, Gertrude, and Hildegarde. One of his mother's favorite stories was how at the age of three her son suddenly appeared on the chancel steps of the church during a Sunday service while his father was in the pulpit and she was playing the organ. Perhaps this was the first sign he wanted to become a pastor!

The family moved to Watertown, Wisconsin, in 1929 when William Eggert accepted a call as an associate pastor of St. Mark's Lutheran Church. Kurt was already reading, so he skipped kindergarten and entered the first grade at St. Mark's Lutheran School. His was a musical family: his father played violin and clarinet at Northwestern College in Watertown, and his mother played piano and organ. So it was natural for Mother Eggert to begin giving her son piano lessons at an early age. He continued lessons under Mr. Reichart and advanced rapidly under Josephine Sproesser, a well-known teacher in the area. Kurt excelled in school and was put to the test during his confirmation examination. After being quarantined to his room with scarlet fever, he was eventually examined alone in front of the church council, where he had to provide answers in both German and English.

After the eighth grade, Kurt began high school at Northwestern Preparatory School in Watertown. He continued playing the piano and was soon performing Rachmaninoff's Prelude in C-sharp Minor, Mendelssohn's "Rondo Capriccio," Mozart's Sonata in A Major, Bach's Little Fugue in G Minor, Chopin's "Fantaisie Impromptu," Liszt's Hungarian Rhapsody No. 6, Moskowski's "Il Caprice Espangol," and various Chopin etudes and nocturnes to the delight of his family and friends. Money was tight in those days, so delivering newspapers and making and selling lawn ornaments gave him spending money to buy phonograph records, sheet music, and tickets to concerts and plays. Eventually he was able to buy his own piano from his piano teacher. She sold him her Knabe grand piano for the sum of $200. Now there were two pianos in the parsonage, and Kurt was often joined by his mother or sister Hildegarde on the second piano. During his junior year of high school, he began directing choirs and often played organ for some of the local churches.

Kurt continued his studies at Northwestern College after graduating from prep school. One of his favorite professors, Martin Franzmann, instilled in him a love for theology in poetry, which enabled him to actually enjoy reading Homer's *Odyssey*. He began writing poetry, some of which was printed in the college publication, *The Black and Red*. He also enjoyed getting together with Rollin Reim, Jeb Schaefer, Winnie Schaller, Len Bernthal, and other friends in his family's basement club room. Father and Mother Eggert enjoyed having college students come to the parsonage, and whenever possible they encouraged them through discussions and literature to broaden their study of philosophy, theology, and music. The Eggerts often urged the students to use their talents in the ministry of the church.

During the summer, when Kurt and his sisters weren't working at the local ice cream parlor or pea canning factory, they spent much of their time at Lake Esador in Medford and at the family's trailer cabin in Lake Mills. Kurt and his close friend Rollin Reim were very interested in nature, so they spent many hours studying birds, moths, and trees on a small nature preserve in Watertown called Tivoli Island. Getting around got a lot easier when Dad Eggert bought Kurt an old police motorcycle—with a sidecar! The sporty wheels took him to campus for classes and many school activities. The vehicle also came in handy when he was selling religious materials or giving rides to two or even three passengers when necessary.

Kurt's musical talents started blooming at a young age. At age 16 he was giving professional-quality concerts and often was asked to perform for the local Euterpe Club and the Lion's Club. He had to buy his first tuxedo when he won the chance to be a finalist in a piano competition in Wausau through a radio contest. If you were looking for Eggert at the college, you could usually find him at the grand piano in the gymnasium. He also sang in the Northwestern College choir and directed the Male Octet as well as a special group of sixteen men who called themselves the Gleemen. At various school concerts he played accompaniment and soloed on the piano. His interest in choral music grew, and one of his favorite groups was the Robert Shaw Chorale. Perhaps that's why he later named his choir The Lutheran Chorale of Milwaukee.

Kurt Eggert graduated from Northwestern College in 1944. His plan was to gain a master's degree in music either before he entered the seminary or right after graduation. War and Uncle Sam dictated what would come first: the seminary. That summer he attended Christiansen Choral School in Lake Forest, Illinois. His studies at Wisconsin Lutheran Seminary in Thiensville, Wisconsin, were interrupted when he was asked to teach English and speech at Bethany Lutheran College in Mankato, Minnesota (1945–1946). Kurt took his turn playing organ for chapel and enjoyed tickling the ivories of two concert grand pianos with another gifted friend and teacher Bing Weller. Teaching piano, accompanying various groups, and monitoring the boys' dorm were also part of his duties at Bethany. This was probably the only time in Kurt's adult life that he didn't direct a choir, but other activities kept him busy.

While teaching at Bethany, Professor Eggert met a student in his class by the name of Ruth Westcott. She was a Southerner, born and raised in Alabama, who also lived in Watertown, where her dad was superintendent of Bethesda Lutheran Home. Professor and student worked together on various committees and were part of a trio (along with Clarice Huso) that traveled with Doc Ylivisaker, president of Bethany, to various congregations of the Evangelical Lutheran Synod. They spoke and performed musically to help promote Bethany College. Their friendship grew as they worked together and rode the "400" train between college and home.

The next summer Kurt returned to Wisconsin Lutheran Seminary for accelerated course work so he could catch up with his class and continue his theological education in the fall of 1946. His senior year he directed the St. Jacobi church choir, played organ for services at St. Peter's Lutheran Church on the south side of Milwaukee, and joined the Milwaukee Arion Chorus. While at the seminary, he sang in and helped direct the seminary chorus under Professor Hilton Oswald. He managed to travel to all his musical engagements with the help of an old model car called a Whippet. It was dependable transportation—until the universal fell off one day on the way back to the seminary. Besides his interest in music, Kurt and his buddy Rollin Reim found time to study astronomy and continue arguing the finer points of theology.

In 1947 Kurt Eggert graduated from Wisconsin Lutheran Seminary. He was assigned to be a tutor at Michigan Lutheran Seminary in

Saginaw. Besides teaching speech and typewriting, he directed the Girls' Chorus and the Male Chorus. He became more and more interested in choral music and even took a few voice lessons. At that time, portable audio recorders used wire instead of tape. He got his hands on one and was thrilled that he could record his Christmas concert and have his family hear it!

Meanwhile, his fiancée, Ruth, was teaching first and second grade at Atonement Lutheran School in Milwaukee, where William and James Schaefer were pastors. During vacations, Kurt and Ruth spent many hours listening to classical music on the family phonograph, which had to be wound up each time they played a record. Summer weekends were spent traveling to Milwaukee for Washington Park outdoor concerts, enjoying art displays, playing tennis under the lights, or canoeing on Lake Ripley. On June 27, 1948, Kurt John Eggert and Ruth Magdalene Westcott were united in marriage at St. John's Lutheran Church in Watertown, where Ruth's brother Ed, Jr., was the assistant pastor.

After a year at Michigan Lutheran Seminary, Tutor Eggert was assigned to St. Paul's Lutheran Church, a mission congregation in Valley City, North Dakota. Packing up some secondhand furniture, the family's revolving bookcase, his ebony grand piano, and their wedding gifts, the couple drove a 1936 Plymouth to their new home and church out West. They got there several days before the furniture truck, so the new pastor and his wife were taken in by some church members who were kind and generous. The ordination of Pastor Eggert proved nearly as interesting as the move. Pastor Jerry Ehlert was the officiant, but when the organist failed to show up, Eggert found himself alternating between his chancel chair and the pump organ in the front of the church.

Valley City was a beautiful town, with the distinction of having the highest railroad trestle in the United States and some very, very cold winters. The mission congregation was made up of a mixture of blue-collar workers and farmers. Pastor Eggert immediately immersed himself in all the necessary pastoral duties, including directing the choir. However, he found time to take some music courses at the State Teachers' College, studying harmony, counterpoint, and instrumental music (his clarinet playing later fell by the way). The area pastors and their wives traveled many miles to socialize and study. A Magnavox stereo was purchased at Christmas, and once again the budget found room for new records. His favorites were works by Chopin, Bach, Brahms, and Mendelssohn, but he enjoyed all classical music. On the lighter side, he and his wife enjoyed Gilbert and Sullivan's operettas, Burl Ives' folk songs, musical show tunes, and off-the-wall comedic artists like Alan Sherman and Spike Jones.

Ruth gave birth to their first child on July 14, 1949, while the new pastor was supervising the youth group at church. They named their son John Rollin, after Kurt's friend. In Valley City Pastor Eggert contributed regularly to the local newspaper by writing sermonettes for the religious page. One of these, called "How Lovely Shines the Morning Star," later appeared in the *Northwestern Lutheran*. He also helped promote the first Reformation rally for area churches in North and South Dakota.

Kurt received several calls and in 1950 accepted one to Immanuel Lutheran Church in Farmington, Wisconsin, a large rural congregation. He was installed by his father on March 12. At the time the congregation was still holding two services—one in German and one in English. His father, who lived just a few miles away in Watertown, faithfully helped his son prepare for the German service every week. It also was a time for the family and relatives to enjoy attending concerts together at Northwestern College. After a sudden heart attack took his father in 1953, Kurt's German preaching was limited to an occasional service. The members at Immanuel were very friendly and cooperative, and many changes took place in the congregation. Immanuel became an active member of the Wisconsin Synod and began to support the synod's mission programs. The constitution, which was still in German script, was rewritten in English. The Sunday school, Saturday school, and vacation Bible school were expanded and became important tools to teach hymns and God's Word. Pastor Eggert also helped foster the idea of a Lutheran high school in Lake Mills. He enjoyed working with both the junior and senior choirs and urged the members to join several churches in the Oconomowoc and Ixonia areas in presenting the cantata "Olivet to Calvary" during Lent. Church bulletins reflected his interest in having members better understand Scripture readings and the use of liturgy in Sunday services. The Ladies Aid programs were supplemented with slides and trips to see the new Northwestern Publishing House and the Northwestern College and Wisconsin Lutheran Seminary campuses. The promotion of missions was foremost in his ministry. Mission festivals were big events for the congregation and often featured music from various lands.

About 1954 Pastor Eggert began a number of projects to promote the use of edifying, quality music in our synod. Besides organizing joint concerts by area congregations and several church music seminars, he started publishing a quarterly circular for pastors and church musicians called *Viva Vox* (the Living Voice). The purpose of this paper was to chronicle the essays and discussions from the church music seminars. But with the help of Professor Ralph Gehrke from Northwestern College, it expanded to include liturgical and meaningful worship ideas like the Hymn of the Week. Writing and producing *Viva Vox* was a major undertaking because there were no computers, and the copier was an old-fashioned mimeograph. The artwork was tediously done by Kurt's wife, who used a stylus and stencils, and the pages were assembled around the dining room table.

Besides his pastoral duties at Farmington, Kurt found time to travel to Milwaukee for more piano lessons with the renowned Miss Adelaide Banazynski and harmony and composition classes at the Wisconsin College Conservatory of Music. Whenever possible he attended seminars, clinics, and classes to further his conducting skills and musical knowledge. Soon the family increased by three: Margaret, William, and Mark. The older children enjoyed playing in the large yard, which included the church's cemetery. They liked to toll the church bell and climb the apple trees. They also became very close to Grandma Eggert, since she often came over to babysit the children. She happily sang songs to them and helped Ruth can apples, cherries, raspberries, and pickles.

In 1955 Kurt accepted a call to be pastor at Gethsemane Lutheran Church on the south side of Milwaukee, where he led the congregation for 11 years. He enjoyed directing the larger senior and junior choirs. Sunday school and vacation Bible school were also places to nurture the learning of hymns and Christian songs. He often joined counselors Steve and Irene Kuklinski on weekend youth group trips, where the campers enjoyed singing around the campfire. On April 26, 1955, Easter Sunday, the family was blessed with a new daughter, Christine Paula. Three years later, there was another little surprise bundle, a beautiful daughter who was named Linda Rachel by the other children.

Kurt founded the Lutheran Chorale of Milwaukee in 1957 to present selected Lutheran church music in an appropriate manner at church music seminars. The choir grew to 70 members, and its scope quickly expanded to include regular concerts and participation in local and district anniversaries and functions. Chorale rehearsals went from once a month to every Sunday night. Soon the Chorale was sponsoring and presenting hymn festivals, church music workshops, and clinics in the Milwaukee area. This was all rather new to Milwaukee and the Wisconsin Evangelical Lutheran Synod (WELS) in general. But Kurt didn't stop there. He was instrumental in forming a WELS Federation of Churches in Milwaukee, which helped publicize Chorale events. The Lutheran Chorale's motto was "Sermons in Song." Between the musical pieces Pastor Eggert would explain the music and/or words to make the concert a more meaningful spiritual experience. The gospel content was his top priority when choosing music. The titles of some programs were "The Christian Life," "Our Liturgy," "Amazing Grace," "God's Time," "Tableaus of History," "Worthy Is Christ," and the traditional "Prelude to Christmas."

Kurt continued to publish *Viva Vox* with the help of Ralph Gehrke, a bachelor friend who had a great time with the Eggert kids while working four or five days at a time on the next issue. Ruth continued to produce the artwork and help assemble the booklet. Kurt also wrote a three-act play during his ministry at Gethsemane Lutheran Church. It was titled "Luther, Man of God" and was put on by the church youth group under the direction of Gil Shine. Years later, the play was reworked and produced by the Lutheran Chorale. "Lutherama" took place at the Wisconsin Lutheran High School auditorium with full staging and costumes. The middle act featured Luther at home celebrating Christmas and included Kurt's musical settings of 14 stanzas of Luther's hymn "From Heaven Above to Earth I Come."

Pastor Eggert's love of music rubbed off on Gethsemane, and the congregation purchased a new 21-rank Schantz organ under the consultation of Paul Bunjes. The congregation also purchased and remodeled a school building to open its own Lutheran elementary school. Franklin Zabell was called as principal and organist.

Mass choir festivals were being held in churches on both the south and north sides of Milwaukee, and Pastor Eggert promoted them throughout the city with the help of the Lutheran Chorale. He used the Chorale to introduce church banners, Chrismons (Christian symbols for decorating Christmas trees), and the arts in general by setting up vocal, instrumental, organ, and piano recitals at Wisconsin Lutheran High School and other places. From 1960 to 1962, Pastor Eggert taught liturgics and hymnody at Wisconsin Lutheran Seminary in Thiensville, Wisconsin, and directed the seminary chorus until Professor Martin Albrecht was called to fill the position.

During these years Kurt found time to give piano and recorder lessons to all the children and encouraged them to be involved in anything musical. Margaret, Christine, Linda, and later Jennifer played in many piano recitals, and all took honors in competitions. John, Bill, and Mark played in the band but were more interested in sports. The whole family enjoyed music appreciation records and early Leonard Bernstein television performances.

By this time Pastor Eggert was involved in yet another project. He was writing and producing a Milwaukee television program called *Lutheran Guideposts,* which aired on WITI-TV, Channel 6. For many years each program lasted a half hour. Later the programs were shortened to 15 minutes and included a sermonette and choir music or a panel of children discussing a Christian's faith and life. He used the programs to introduce the Luther Seal, the use of Christian symbols, the Christmas trees of sin and grace, and the Advent wreath. The Chorale also took its turn putting on special Christmas, Good Friday, and Easter programs on WTMJ-TV, Channel 4. One major undertaking was televising a Luther play in full costume. *Lutheran Guideposts,* one of the longest-running televised religious programs in Wisconsin, was written and produced by Pastor Eggert for over 30 years.

In 1959 Pastor Eggert and Professor Martin Albrecht were appointed as WELS representatives to the Synodical Conference Hymnal Committee to revise *The Lutheran Hymnal.* Kurt also was an original member of the Commission on Liturgy, Hymnody, and Worship (now known as the Commission on Worship), which the synod authorized in 1963. In addition, he was a member of the Association of Lutheran Church Musicians. Whenever possible, he met with other committees involved in producing new hymnals or worship materials. His summer vacations were often spent studying at St. Olaf College, Northfield, Minnesota; Concordia College, River Forest, Illinois; or the University of Wisconsin in Madison. Whenever possible, he would attend Christiansen Choral School, his favorite.

In 1966 Pastor Eggert accepted a call to head the music department at the newly established Milwaukee Lutheran Teachers' College (MLTC) and direct the choir. Until the synod's Board of Trustees found a house for the Eggert family, they were asked to store all their belongings and move into three adjoining motel rooms. At the time John was going to Northwestern Preparatory School; Margaret was attending Wisconsin Lutheran High School; Bill, Mark, and Chris were enrolled in

Atonement Lutheran School. Linda was too young for kindergarten, so she remained at home with her mother. Finally, the week before Christmas, the family retrieved all their belongings from storage and moved into a home on Grant Boulevard, where they once again settled down. The next year Ruth accepted a call to teach kindergarten at Atonement (how could she resist when Pastor Koeplin gave her one of his wife's freshly baked loaves of bread). By the end of the school year, she was expecting another family addition, so she gave up teaching. The last of the Eggert children was born on December 9, 1968, and was named Jennifer Ruth.

Meanwhile Kurt continued to carry out his calling at MLTC. The choir was small, but he enjoyed the perfection he could achieve when practice was held every day with eager young students. The choir made many tours, produced several records, and joined the Lutheran Chorale at Milwaukee's Performing Arts Center for a Wisconsin Lutheran Choral Festival concert. It was at this time that "Introit for Reformation" was written and performed.

When the synod closed the college in 1970, Professor Eggert declined a call to the music department of Dr. Martin Luther College in New Ulm, Minnesota. Instead, he accepted a call to be associate pastor at Atonement Lutheran Church in Milwaukee, a congregation of some 1,400 communicants. Besides his pastoral duties, he again took up the baton to lead the church's senior choir. In 1973 he wrote a new tune and setting for "Ride On, Ride On in Majesty." The Palm Sunday piece was set for the junior and senior choirs and instrumentalists. In 1974 he encouraged Mary Prange to accept a call to Atonement Lutheran School. He enjoyed working with her, organist Cris Sturm, and Pastor Kurt Koeplin in producing spiritually uplifting worship. During this time Pastor Eggert composed "God Was There on Calvary" (*Christian Worship* 140) and "Oh, Come, My Soul" (*Christian Worship* 99) to complement Lenten sermons with the same themes. The use of instrumental music was encouraged to enhance worship, and he spent many hours rehearsing with various soloists. Often "hymn sings" were used before the services to teach the congregation unfamiliar or new hymns. His choir practices were interwoven with spiritual truths, and the choir's emphasis was always on producing high-quality artistic pieces to the glory of God. Pastor Eggert had a special interest in the Psalms, chanting, and meaningful prayers. To increase the congregation's growth in evangelism and Bible study, he was instrumental in a year-long program called "By Grace Grow." All meetings and Bible classes opened with a hymn.

From 1971 to 1987 Pastor Eggert edited *Focus on Worship*, a publication printed by the Commission on Worship. During this time he also served as a member of the Board for Parish Education and the Coordinating Council. From 1971 to 1983 he was chairman of the synod's Commission on Higher Education, working closely with his friend the Reverend Robert Voss, who was executive secretary. It was at this time that the Campion campus in Prairie du Chien, Wisconsin, was purchased and became Martin Luther Preparatory School (MLPS). The family's youngest daughter, Jennifer, attended the school. She was quite advanced in piano and studied there under Professor Kermit Moldenhauer. Her father and mother were pleased to hear her senior piano recital and her many performances in MLPS musicals.

Pastor Eggert composed "Not unto Us" (*Christian Worship* 392) for the 125th anniversary of the Wisconsin Evangelical Lutheran Synod. It was first performed at a special service at St. John's Lutheran Church on Vliet Street in Milwaukee. He wrote "God of Love and God of Marriage" (*Christian Worship* 602) for the marriage of his son John to JoAnn Groll in August 1973. He arranged a special "Service of Light" for use with the wedding candle and this original song. The song was written for guitar accompaniment but was soon being used with organ at many weddings. The hymn in *Christian Worship* does not use the original refrain, which was sung at the wedding.

Pastor Eggert wrote the tune ADAM to give Martin Franzmann's text "In Adam We Have All Been One" a new setting in *Christian Worship* (No. 396). He felt the folk tune used in *Lutheran Worship* was not appropriate for the text. He composed two additional tunes for the text—one in a major key and the other in a minor key. They correspond to the major and minor characters of the various stanzas: three stanzas of the text are melancholy and confessional in tone and three are uplifting and inspire praise. The tune WEDDING GLORY (*Christian Worship* 219) was written for the sixth stanza of the hymn "A Lamb Goes Uncomplaining Forth." This stanza was familiar to him because his brother-in-law James Schaefer often quoted it in his sermons.

In 1991 "Ride On, Ride On in Majesty" was used by the Lutheran Chorale in a joint concert with the Treble Choir from Dr. Martin Luther College and the Wisconsin Lutheran Seminary Chorus. The concert was held in the seminary gymnasium, and an estimated one thousand people were turned away for lack of room. Kurt played the piano section himself, and to this day the music cannot be found because he never wrote it down. An arrangement by his sister Hildegarde Fischer, with a new introduction and expanded brass part, was written for the Lutheran Chorale's 40th anniversary concert in 1998. It was directed by Mary Prange and accompanied by Lynn Kozlowski.

Kurt loved music and theology, his pastoral duties, and Chorale rehearsals, but he never forgot to take time with his family. Many of their vacations were spent camping with the Hi-Lite trailer, checking out historical sites and national parks, and relaxing at the Mount Morris family cottage. In the later years, he enjoyed the north woods at the Alan Halter cottage in Rhinelander. He never left home without his trusty bicycle, pipe, typewriter, and briefcase of reading material and new music. These were his days to plan new and exciting things to do in upcoming concerts that would reignite Chorale members for another season of dedication and work.

Much effort and planning went into a jubilee year (50th) celebration for Atonement Lutheran Church and School in 1980. Each month had its own theme, with related artwork, music, and sermons. New paraments, tapestries, and picture displays were used. An addition was built onto the school, and handbells were purchased. On the 60th anniversary of the church, Pastor Eggert was part of the committee that selected a new Austin memorial organ as a thank offering to God for the Lord's many blessings to Atonement. An anniversary dinner and entertainment were held at Wisconsin Lutheran High School for all Atonement members and friends. Pastor Eggert is remembered as the white-gloved, blindfolded "mystery guest" who played "Rustle of Spring" with a sheet placed over the piano keys.

In 1983 the Wisconsin Synod resolved to begin work on a new/revised hymnal, and the Conference of Presidents called Kurt to be the full-time director of this hymnal project. After a farewell to the ministry at Atonement in June of 1984, he began his duties in an office at Northwestern Publishing House. His first act was to pick qualified men to serve on the committees. The appointees worked faithfully for the next eight years under his leadership and the Commission on Worship chairman, the Reverend Victor Prange. After the death of committee member Professor James Engel, Eggert's staff was expanded to include a full-time coworker, Professor Kermit Moldenhauer. His secretary, Joanne Gruber, ably fulfilled her position as copyright editor.

An important step in the hymnal project was to produce a sampling of new hymns and changes in the liturgy for possible use in the new/revised hymnal. The *Sampler* was introduced to many WELS congregations as a supplement to the regular liturgy and hymns in *The Lutheran Hymnal*. New uses of the psalms and prayers were included in this booklet. Kurt felt the hymnal was truly "the people's book," so he took great care to solicit opinion and reaction from congregations. Hundreds of letters and reactions were received. Some of them were more than just critical, and he often joked that when the book came out, he was "leaving the country." The *Sampler* was used by many congregations until the new hymnal was completed in 1993. A majority of congregations immediately began using the new hymnal in their services. Kurt composed the "Song of Mary" *(Magnificat)* and the "Song of Simeon" *(Nunc Dimittis)* specifically for the new vesper service called Evening Prayer. For the new Service of Word and Sacrament, he wrote "O Lord, Our Lord," a song of praise for use after the absolution. In the introduction to *Christian Worship,* he explains that the overall goal of those who prepared the book was "to produce a Lutheran hymnal that was at once forward-looking and also enriched by the faith and worship experience of the whole Christian church of the past. Specifically the goal was to deliver to the church a strongly Christ-centered book, bringing together liturgies and a large number of hymns celebrating the life and atoning work of Jesus."

In the fall of 1986, when he was rehearsing with the Lutheran Chorale at Wisconsin Lutheran College, Kurt suffered a heart attack. He had bypass surgery in December. Mary Prange, who had assisted with the Chorale, took over direction of the "Prelude to Christmas" concert. After Kurt recovered from his surgery, he continued to work with the various committees preparing the hymnal and with the Commission on Worship.

In 1993, after several medical setbacks, Kurt started experiencing congestive heart failure. He managed to rise from his sickbed to direct his favorite and final choral piece, "Song of Praise," by Felix Mendelssohn, at a joint concert with the Vesper Singers, Wisconsin Lutheran Concert Choir, and the Wisconsin Lutheran Seminary Chorus on April 25, 1993. Shortly afterwards, at the Chorale banquet, he turned over his baton of 36 years to his capable assistant, Mary Joy Prange. In May Kurt was able to attend the seminary commencement concert, where he was surprised and honored to hear a setting of his WEDDING GLORY commissioned by the male chorus and its director, Professor James Tiefel. The setting had been done by his friend Dr. Carl F. Schalk, an eminent Lutheran composer who was also in attendance.

Shortly after this concert, Kurt was hospitalized, with little hope of recovery. When his wife, Ruth, heard that the printing of the hymnals was finished and they were ready to be bound, she asked if it was possible to get a copy from Northwestern Publishing House to present to her husband. Five days before the Lord took him home, WELS president and Kurt's classmate Carl Mischke presented Kurt with the first bound copy of *Christian Worship: A Lutheran Hymnal,* with his family and close friends beside his bed. He had hoped to present one to the president himself in August at the synod convention in Saginaw, Michigan. The Lord, however, had better plans. On June 22, 1993, Kurt John Eggert fell asleep in Jesus to join the hosts of believers in heaven worshiping and praising God in eternal glory.

The Lutheran Chorale of Milwaukee and Kurt Eggert's Music Leadership

Mary Prange and Peggy Henning

A brief history of the Chorale by Mary Prange, current director

The Lutheran Chorale of Milwaukee had its beginnings in 1957 when Mr. Fred Bartel, then a teacher at Garden Homes Lutheran School, gathered a group to sing for the installation of the Reverend Werner Franzmann as editor of the *Northwestern Lutheran*. The participants, mostly teachers, found the experience so rewarding that they decided to continue meeting on a regular basis. Pastor Kurt Eggert from Gethsemane Lutheran Church was asked to serve as the director. The choir was asked to participate in a dedication service and several other functions during 1958 and began preparation for its first full-length program, titled "The Christian Life," which was presented in the spring of 1959. The accompanist for the choir at that concert was Hildegarde (Eggert) Fischer, and the narrator was Professor Gerhard Franzmann.

The Chorale's first officers were Arthur Griebling, business manager, and Marion Franzmann, librarian. In 1961 the officers were Gerhard Franzmann, chairman; Jerome Braun, first vice chairman; Paul Koehler, second vice chairman; and Arthur Griebling, business manager.

Over its 42-year history, the Chorale has been active in sponsoring hymn festivals, music clinics, and church music seminars. Many thematic programs, such as "The Year of Our Lord," "The Lutheran Liturgy," "The Lord's Prayer," "The Music of Bach and Mendelssohn," and "Amazing Grace" have been presented.

Over the years the Chorale has performed over 90 concerts and a Luther drama (written by Eggert) in many churches throughout Wisconsin, Illinois, and Minnesota. It has also taken part in various synod festivals, church anniversaries, and installations. For many years members of the Chorale appeared regularly on *Lutheran Guideposts,* a program that Eggert coordinated and that aired regularly on a Milwaukee television station.

In a typical season the Chorale draws its membership from about 40 Wisconsin Synod congregations in and around the Milwaukee area. Rehearsals were first held at Grace Lutheran Church in downtown

Milwaukee, followed by Parkside Lutheran Church (formerly located on Sherman and North), and Wisconsin Lutheran College, the current location. The Chorale has been served for most of its history by two fine accompanists, Hildegarde Fischer and Lynn Kozlowski.

Over 600 individuals can be counted as alumni of the choir, contributing nearly 3,000 years of devotion and loyalty to the group. Eighty-five members have sung in the Chorale for ten or more years, and 23 have given 25 or more years. Many who have sung with the group have been instrumental in organizing other "Lutheran Chorales" as they moved to various areas throughout the synod.

The motto of the Lutheran Chorale is "Sermons in Song." Choir members are grateful for the privilege of singing God's praise for so many years and dedicate all the music performed to the glory of our Lord.

Kurt Eggert was the driving force behind the choir from its beginning in 1957 through the spring of 1993. At the end of the 1993 season, Eggert felt that it was necessary to resign his position as director of the Lutheran Chorale due to poor health. After a meeting of the Chorale officers, Mary Prange was appointed to succeed her pastor, mentor, and friend as the director. Eggert's musical insights and dedication to ministry encouraged Chorale members and listeners alike to learn and appreciate the music of the church and to experience its power in carrying the gospel message.

Personal reflections on Kurt Eggert's music leadership by Mary Prange

I first became acquainted with Kurt when I was a freshman at Milwaukee Lutheran Teachers' College in 1966, the same year that he became a professor of music at that school. I had always been interested in music, so I was delighted to sing in his choir and have the opportunity to learn from him. Little did I know at that time what an influence he would become on my life.

I graduated from Dr. Martin Luther College, New Ulm, and was in my third year of teaching in Flint, Michigan, when I received a call to teach at Atonement Lutheran School in Milwaukee, where Kurt was the pastor and worship planner. He convinced me that Atonement was where I needed to be in order to develop the musical gifts that the Lord had given me, and so I moved to Milwaukee in 1974 to begin a long association with him as well as his entire family. What follows are some of my impressions of Kurt as a parish pastor, musician, and personal friend.

I think that Kurt's gifts as a parish pastor were sometimes overlooked because they appeared to be overshadowed by his musical involvement. He was a wonderful parish pastor, a gospel man in every sense of the word. You can tell from the texts of his hymns that he had a deep understanding of the grace of God in our lives, and he had a way of putting that into words. He also lived this understanding: he was a kind and gentle man who always appeared to have all the time in the world to listen to someone with a problem or wait with a family at the bedside of someone who was ill. He was innovative in worship, but the Word was always most important. He liked banners and artwork and had service folders and programs put together in very artistic ways—with symbols and pictures—and this was before the advent of computers and even copy machines!

Musically I would describe him as a romantic. Though we often sang Bach in his choirs, I feel that he liked the choral works of Mendelssohn better. And though he certainly used the Lutheran chorale often in worship, he also led me to appreciate the texts of hymns like "Rock of Ages" and "Amazing Grace." As a choral director, attention to dynamics and text always preceded attention to the notes. We could spend much time on two or three measures to get the musical sensitivity just right (and yet it never was quite right) in order to bring out the text of a piece. Yet in other parts of a piece, we wouldn't know the notes very well for lack of time. I learned musical sensitivity from him. He was a master at that—a talent lacking in many of our musicians today, I feel. But in order to learn, one has to have the opportunity to work with a really good teacher, a privilege that all who ever sang in one of Kurt's choirs had.

All who knew Kurt well relish what a wonderful sense of humor he had. This was not always evident to those who knew him only from Sunday worship, where he was always dignified and serious. But behind the scenes—and that includes his choir rehearsals—he had a marvelous wit. Even when he was angry with us in Lutheran Chorale rehearsals, the last line of his little rage often contained just enough humor to leave us asking, "Was that funny?" And it would be followed by laughter, which accomplished way more than the rage itself! When he was called upon at the annual Chorale banquet to make a speech, it was always cleverly done (I wish that the speeches had all been recorded or written down). Chorale members looked forward to his annual letters at the beginning of every season not only because of the information they contained but also because of the clever way they were written.

For as long as I can remember, the Lutheran Chorale of Milwaukee has rehearsed on Sunday evenings from September to May, from 7:30 to 9:30 P.M. The motto for all these years has been "Sermons in Song," as Kurt's purpose was not just to present a concert of beautiful music but to put a program together that might have a spiritual impact on the listeners. He often attended summer workshops where he found music that was on the cutting edge—20th-century church music written by composers such as Knut Nystedt and Egil Hovland. He loved the anthems of F. Melius Christiansen. He was a personal friend of both Carl Schalk and Richard Hillert, and we often sang compositions by those two very fine 20th-century musicians. Kurt had a wonderful gift for programming. I feel that he was instrumental in keeping the interest in quality church music alive in the Wisconsin Synod for many years. You can say that he was always looking for a "new song" to sing, as we are encouraged to do in the psalms. He accomplished much of this through the Chorale, whose members then took new things back to their home congregations. In that way he had a tremendous influence on the whole Milwaukee area and ultimately on the synod.

Personal reflections by Peggy Henning, a Chorale member

I first came to know Kurt when I joined the Lutheran Chorale in 1972. I had not sung for such a master musician before and was quite intimidated at first. But Kurt made it easy to relax, and I could tell his love of music by the intensity with which he attacked every piece. It didn't take long for me to become a "Bachophile" and truly learn to appreciate the finer points of good choral music. Over the years we learned the notes, but we also learned so much more about what was "behind the scenes" of the music and how the composer put a work together. I had had choral experiences in high school and church choirs, but no one had ever explained all the details the way Kurt did. He instilled a true appreciation of all things musical.

For Kurt there was so much more to singing than the technical aspects. He was truly a master director, composer, and pianist, but it was the soul of the music that drove him. His dedication to serving the Lord always preceded anything he did, and the music was used to share God's glory with many people. Whether a piece was an old favorite or something new and daring, the message was the key, and Kurt always focused on presenting that message in the best way possible so that it would touch the people who were singing or listening. His base was as a pastor, and the "Sermons in Song" were another means to inspire and help us grow in our faith. As people moved to different areas, they took that dedication with them and were inspired to do just a little more, work harder, try a new piece of music, and do everything to the glory of God. These are musical legacies of Kurt and his dedication, which he shared so willingly.

Kurt was a "people" person. He always seemed to have a mountain of things to do, yet he found time whenever someone needed guidance or help with a project. He inspired many of us, so we never questioned him when he asked us to serve extra duty, such as give a weeknight performance for a *Lutheran Guideposts* television broadcast or put together a play about the life of Luther for the Chorale's 25th anniversary. A big part of belonging to this choir, as encouraged by Kurt, was the social interaction of the people who practiced every Sunday night. We were drawn together by a common thread, and we made many new friends. Some took it beyond friendship: at least 15 couples met in Chorale and were married. One of the favorite warm-up exercises was a round that goes like this: "Make new friends, but keep the old. One is silver; the other, gold." There was often a reason to have a gathering and enjoy each other's company (especially if dessert was included). I'm sure Kurt's wife, Ruth, wondered how we could sing all day at concerts and then sing some more at the parties afterward!

Kurt was an intense person and always driven by the love of his Lord to do what he could for the education and welfare of the people around him. He was passionate about the music because he knew it could touch people in a way that nothing else can. The Lord gave him abundant talents, and he used them to inspire many others to give praise and honor where it is due. He has taught us many valuable life lessons, and we are truly blessed for having known him.

Many hearts and minds have been touched by Kurt Eggert. The Holy Spirit abundantly blessed this man with talent and the ability to share it with everyone around him. Singing under his leadership in the Chorale was considered a high privilege, but it was much more than his musical abilities that drew so many people and kept them coming for so long. There was a sense of fulfillment like no other this side of heaven when the concerts were performed. Kurt's enthusiasm was contagious! Following is a quote from a letter he wrote in October 1958: "May I say that I am delighted at the spirit and enthusiasm in our choir, and I count it a distinct privilege to direct the group. As we now number over 60 voices, the artistic results should be limited only by the efforts we are willing to expend. I feel that in continuing we will not only grow musically ourselves, but that our activities can be a God-pleasing inspiration and joy to our church choirs and congregations." How prophetic! We have to wonder if Kurt had any idea just how much effort would be expended over the next 35 years. He jumped in gladly with both feet and did not stop until health problems prevented him from leading us further.

A program from 1961 titled "The Chorale" was meant to demonstrate how this form of congregational hymn began and developed from the early church. From Kurt's narration at this concert, we also see the motivation behind the Lutheran Chorale as a choir: "The *heart* of the Chorale is its gospel message. . . . They proclaim Christ and bid us to rejoice." Rehearsals were often as much Bible lessons and church history classes as they were practices. Kurt would often stop to explain the references contained within the text and how the composers "saw" these in a musical context. I think that was one of the reasons people came back year after year every Sunday night. It was not the motivation to learn the notes; it was the study of the text within the music that took us to a deeper understanding of our messages. Even at concerts, Kurt often interspersed narration with the songs in order to explain the inspiration behind the particular pieces we would perform. I am sure many of the listeners over the years came to appreciate that feature as much as the singers did.

Kurt lived what he taught and was a fine example for many to follow. This was expressed by a member in a note when Kurt announced his retirement as director:

> Whether you realize it or not, you are a rare individual. The combination of a strong faith and deep love of music has created a powerful force on which we have learned to build our lives. This goes way beyond Sunday night rehearsals and a couple of concerts every year. I found that out many years ago, and it changed the direction of my life more than you will ever know. I'm sure there are many people who have had a similar experience, and we all thank God for your shining example!

In another note from a member who was a church choir director, we see how Kurt's example went beyond the Chorale:

> I was a little depressed as we started church choir rehearsal last night—about half the people were missing, we were still making the same mistakes on pieces we practiced for weeks, and nobody seemed to care. But we kept plugging along, and I realized how many times you must have had the same exasperating experience and how you taught us to be persistent, especially when we don't feel like it, and to try a little harder. You've given many of us a great musical education over the years—technique, history, styles (how many of us could pronounce "Knut Nystedt" much less find our way through his works?), and always how to make it better than last time. Then you encouraged us to expand our musical horizons; whether we sing in a choir, direct, or just put a little extra zip into the hymns during services. By the time we ended rehearsal with the Doxology, we could truly thank God for the blessings he gives us, particularly the precious gift of music. I just thought you should know that we appreciate the good example you set for us. Thanks!

That about sums up Chorale members' feelings toward Kurt: thankful. We are thankful to God for giving us this warm, funny, brilliant example of how we can make the most of our time on this earth by living our lives dedicated to the glory of our Lord. We are thankful to Kurt's family for sharing his precious time. We are thankful for Kurt's friendship and encouragement. How can we be anything but excited to be reunited with him in heaven and sing the never-ending praise of our most gracious Lord?

The Kurt J. Eggert Hymnological and Liturgical Memorial Collection

Arnold O. Lehmann

In November 1993 a proposal was presented to and adopted by the WELS Commission on Worship that a "Kurt Eggert hymnal collection be established at the Wisconsin Lutheran Seminary library." The initial funding for such a collection was to come from gifts given in memory of Pastor Eggert. Appointed to the committee to develop this collection were Rev. James Schaefer, chairman; Mrs. Ruth Eggert, secretary; and Dr. Arnold Lehmann, who had been a member of the Joint Hymnal Committee. Professor Martin Westerhaus, the seminary librarian, was an *ex officio* member of the committee.

The committee met for the first time in February 1994 and decided on the name: "The Kurt J. Eggert Hymnological and Liturgical Memorial Collection." At this meeting Dr. Lehmann spoke of other libraries that had established such a memorial library, for example, Concordia, River Forest, Illinois. He suggested gathering all hymn books, liturgical books, and other related resource materials in one place at the seminary library. It was also proposed that a designated archives section house all hymnal project surveys, correspondence, and articles relating to the hymnal project.

The committee continued to meet quite frequently over the next several years. The greatest concerns were how to collect this material, where to house it in the building, and how to make use of the monetary donations in a proper manner. When Rev. Schaefer was called to his eternal home, Dr. Lehmann was asked to serve as the chairman, and Professor Richard Balge was appointed to fill the vacancy. After Rev. John Hartwig accepted the call as seminary librarian, he also served as an *ex officio* member of the committee.

When the Eggert collection was ready to be placed into a section of the seminary library, Professor Hartwig suggested that the books, pamphlets, and other materials be placed in their proper location according to their topic and contents. This was approved with the addition that all the books in the Eggert collection be identified with some sort of sticker or symbol on the spine of each book. The committee also requested that a photograph of Pastor Eggert be placed in an appropriate place in the library, with brief details about the collection. This has also been done.

At this juncture the committee began to discuss its further importance and usefulness. The plans for organizing, collecting, and placing the items in the library were completed. The committee voted to ask the seminary librarian to continue the process of book and publication acquisitions for the Eggert library, a task that the present librarian, Professor Hartwig, accepted. Then the committee voted to disband and to inform the Commission on Worship that it felt its task was completed.

The hymnological and liturgical library is now available for use by the seminary students and others who have access to the library. It is a fitting tribute to a man who gave much for the advancement of Lutheran hymnody and liturgy.

Recollections of *Viva Vox*, 1955–1961

Ralph D. Gehrke

"Unique" is the only way I can describe the years of my collaboration with Kurt Eggert in a number of church music enterprises. "Why?" you ask. I respond, "Because our heavenly Father enabled us to participate in a very exciting and important mission." Such is the conclusion of this octogenarian after rereading and reflecting upon the 13 issues of our semiannual publication *Viva Vox*. In fact, despite some 40 intervening years, I am now as interested in and excited about the many and various church music ventures in which we collaborated as I was when Kurt and I first embarked on them. I am, therefore, most pleased to be asked to share my recollections of the beginnings of *Viva Vox* with readers of the Kurt Eggert Festschrift.

Easter 1955: a glimpse of the new child *Viva Vox*

Viva Vox was the name Kurt and I chose for our new brainchild, born shortly before Easter 1955. What we envisioned at first was a series of newsletters that would coordinate what Kurt had recently inaugurated in the Watertown area at Kurt's church, Immanuel in Farmington township: Sunday-afternoon hymn festivals and the first church music seminar. Such events continued and soon included an annual church music workshop, which would begin on a Friday evening and run through Saturday afternoon. It was often held outside the immediate Watertown area and involved church music leaders from a much wider area. Actually, it was part of a much broader movement of church music renewal, one in which we were enthusiastic learners.

Although *Viva Vox* itself spanned only the years 1955–1961, what it fostered continued to thrive in subsequent years. By God's wonderful grace it resulted in two landmark publications that brought to a closure the work in which each of us had played a major role: *Planning the Service: A Workbook for Pastors, Organists, and Choirmasters*, published by Concordia Publishing House in 1961, and *Christian Worship: A Lutheran Hymnal* (CW), published by Northwestern Publishing House in 1993.

The title page of the first and each subsequent mimeographed issue of *Viva Vox* (13 to 32 pages) focused readers' attentions on a tripartite symbolic masthead. At the center was (1) an open book, significantly labeled "The Gospel of Christ." That symbol was flanked on each side by (2) a five-line music staff on which church musicians could readily recognize the first eight notes of Martin Luther's "Dear Christians, One and All, Rejoice." That ballad narrates Luther's basic law-gospel experience. The publication's title *Viva Vox* was printed in (3) huge, eye-catching headline letters. The first four issues included a translation of the Latin: "The Living Voice" (that is, of the gospel). Thereby we wished to affirm that Scripture's life-giving gospel was central to the music making we wished to foster.

We knew, of course, that Luther's own church-music program was not confined to such popular, Reformation-age ballads, though he was good at that sort of thing. Luther proceeded to much more serious Reformation-age hymn tasks, such as Christianizing the Old Testament psalms (for example, Psalm 46:1 in "A Mighty Fortress Is Our God"), putting the basic songs of our liturgy into the vernacular (for example, the Creed in "We All Believe in One True God"), versifying the chief parts of the Small Catechism (for example, for Baptism, "To Jordan Came the Christ, Our Lord"), and providing congregations with versified versions of traditional medieval Easter and Pentecost chants (for example, "Christ Jesus Lay in Death's Strong Bands"). We also knew that orthodox and confessional Lutherans are not the only makers of great church music, glorious though the Lutheran heritage has been. We welcomed, therefore, the church-music contributions that had come to us from other Christian traditions.

**The scene on which *Viva Vox* appeared:
a goodly heritage now endangered**

Viva Vox's contributions to church-music renewal cannot be understood apart from its editors' backgrounds. What were the experiences with church music that Kurt and I had had at home in our youth and during our years at college and the seminary? The recollections I am able to give here of my personal experiences will not be mere personal reminiscences. They will explain, I trust, why Kurt and I undertook the task of reclaiming a godly heritage that was in great danger.

Kurt's church-music background was not as different from mine as people might at first imagine, even though Kurt came from a home that was enriched by both his pastor-father's and his music-teacher-mother's superior musical backgrounds. Nevertheless, his parents and mine worshiped within the same wholesome worship structures of their German Lutheran forebears, especially the hymnological heritage.

For instance, our common Christmas Eve "entrance hymn" was most likely Paul Gerhardt's "Once Again My Heart Rejoices" (CW 37). Thereby the gospel of our justification by grace through faith was put at the center of our celebration of the incarnation!

At the beginning of the distribution of Holy Communion, both our families most likely often sang Samuel Kinner's "Lord Jesus Christ, You Have Prepared" (CW 312), affirming the real presence of Christ's exalted humanity, his true body and true blood in the Sacrament. Similarly, the early Lutheran chorales (like "A Mighty Fortress Is Our God") were sung by both the young Kurt Eggert and Ralph Gehrke and their congregations according to their original rhythmic melodies (CW 200) rather than the isometric melody introduced by the logical Age of Enlightenment to give each syllable of the text one musical note in keeping with a precise overall metrical pattern (CW 201).

Of course, such singing of our great Lutheran hymnological heritage would not have occurred if our families had not emigrated from Lutheran lands to places where the hymnological heritage of our church continued to be fostered by well-trained, conscientious teacher-musicians and pastors. As it was, a good share of the Lutheran hymnological heritage was still alive in the congregations in which Kurt and I had grown up, even though, as we would soon learn, it was in increasingly grave danger.

Surprisingly enough, church music as such was not particularly prominent in Kurt's and my beloved alma mater, Northwestern College, then almost 70 years old. The school was located in the very German, southern Wisconsin city of Watertown. This unique eight-year, pretheological "boarding school" had more in common with a German preuniversity "prep school" like St. Michael's in Lüneburg, which the young J. S. Bach attended, than with an American private college like the Methodists' Lawrence College in Appleton, Wisconsin. Northwestern retained many characteristics of its European prototypes, including a four-year preparatory department, one that continued to use the traditional Latin names for its classes, grades nine through twelve, called sexta, quinta, quarta, tertia.

This prep school-college prepared future seminarians and pastors of the Wisconsin Evangelical Lutheran Synod with a liberal arts education that included major emphasis on biblical and theological languages. Hebrew was studied for two years alongside the classics, which were studied in their original Latin and Greek, for six and four years respectively. There were also excellent eight-year programs in German and English literature as well as in history. Classes were held five days a week, 8:00 A.M. to 2:20 P.M., plus on Saturdays, when classes ended at noon. Study-room radios and automobiles were forbidden; the dormitory observed absolutely quiet morning and evening study periods. A bell marked the times of the students' day, including those of morning and evening worship, "chapel."

"Hands-on music," as opposed to "canned music," was customary and very much alive. A full music program had not yet been integrated into Northwestern's academic program. That would soon come with the advent of Professor Hilton Oswald. Like sports and the two college literary societies, which met on Saturday evenings, music was mostly an extracurricular activity, carrying no academic credit and demanding no share of the college's slim budget. Professors served as volunteer directors of the various musical organizations. Of one's own volition, a student joined the orchestra or the band or one of the two vocal choruses, male and mixed. Those choruses never sang at the 15-minute morning (English language) or evening (German language) chapel services. At the concerts of the musical organizations, held in Northwestern's gymnasium, students, interested parents, and townsfolk heard both sacred and secular music on the same program. Sacred music received no applause at such concerts.

Chapel worship acquainted students like Kurt and myself with the Scriptures, which were read by presiding professors, chapter by chapter, with little or no exposition. We were also acquainted with the standard German and American hymn repertoire of our church. What we were unwittingly missing were the existing and promising contributions that could have come from the post-World War I German and English hymnological and liturgical renaissances. That began to come a bit later with the appearance of *The Lutheran Hymnal*. Holy Communion was not celebrated at the college, but in the local congregations; on Saturday evenings after chapel, students announced their intentions to commune to the dormitory tutor or dean, who relayed their announcements to the respective local pastor.

It was during my seminary years (1941–1944) that my interest in hymns grew exponentially. Such growth was fostered, of course, by our daily hymn singing. Now, however, I began to relate hymns (1) to their origins in various periods of church history, (2) to their expression of Christian theology, and (3) to the worship of the people I would soon be serving as parish pastor. As I now step back in these recollections to survey my experience with hymns in those seminary days, five experiences emerge as particularly significant:

1. In the autumn of 1941, my initial seminary year, *The Lutheran Hymnal* appeared. New hymns revitalized the already robust singing at daily worship. The new hymnal's various orders of worship provided us seminarians with many new forms of worship, especially Matins and Vespers. The Psalms were now available for use at worship. The Common Service put worship with Word and sacrament as the norm. It would take time, we realized, for us to assimilate all of this.

2. One pleasant summer morning my home pastor appeared, rather unexpectedly, in my father's hardware store, where I was working. He brought me a valuable gift. It was a cardboard box filled with his old *Theological Quarterlies (Quartalschriften)*. He said he had no more use for them but felt I could and would use them. He was right! Particularly interesting and helpful for me at that point were the articles by Professor J. P. Koehler on our Lutheran church-music heritage. They focused my attention on essentials: the gospel as it is expressed in the outstanding texts and superb melodies that give each of our Lutheran chorales its own distinctive personality.

3. For my final seminary year, I was appointed "seminary kapellmeister," the person in charge of the musical portions of our daily worship. I had served as college organist during my last years at Northwestern College. The depression had left our seminary chapel unpainted and without an organ. I therefore accompanied the hymn singing on a piano and supervised the a cappella hymn singing with the entire seminary student body forming one large male chorus. The unique "hymnal" we used for such a cappella hymn singing had been compiled some six or seven years previously by then seminarians Martin Albrecht and Martin Franzmann. This a cappella hymnal included a number of the hymn treasures Martin Franzmann had discovered shortly before in Cleveland, where he had taught in the school of the Missouri Synod's premier hymnological scholar, Pastor Arthur Katt. Because of the need to provide our synodical hymnal committee members with many important research sources as they worked on *The Lutheran Hymnal*, our seminary library was rather well stocked with some excellent hymnological books, including such significant hymn collections as *The English Hymnal* and Percy Dearmer's (and Ralph Vaughan Williams') *Songs of Praise* as well as a number of German-

language hymnological books. These helped interested seminarians like myself appreciate the full depth and breadth of our German-Lutheran and English-language musical heritage.

4. On Sundays during our final year at the seminary, several of us regularly took the earliest available interurban electric train into Milwaukee to visit (after attending the early service at one of our own churches) the services of various other denominations. In our symbolics course we were studying about them; such visits would, we felt, bring us into direct contact with them. For the first time in my life, I attended a pre-Vatican II Latin mass at the Jesuits' Marquette University's Gesu Church and also at a south-side Polish basilica where monks walked about on bare feet in winter! We visited Anglo-Catholics at the Episcopalian cathedral; the Greek Orthodox on Easter Eve; Presbyterian Calvinists, whose preachers came from Scotland; Haugian pietistic Norwegian Lutherans; and the Missouri Synod's English District "innovators" (not to forget a Sabbath eve service at an Orthodox Jewish synagogue). Each of these groups helped us understand, by comparison, our own unique heritage much, much better.

5. As I prepared for my kapellmeister duties, I often had occasion to consult the seminary library's hymnological section. There I discovered, quite by accident, a book that would become very important for my understanding and use of hymns. It was Wilhelm Nelle's *Die Festmelodien des Kirchenjahres*. For the first time, an expert made two things clear to me: *(a)* I must learn to appreciate the musical distinctiveness of each of the melodies that for centuries now had enabled us to celebrate with distinctive chorales each of the various seasons and festivals of the church year; and *(b)* somehow our great hymns were responses to the lectionary, especially the Gospel for the Day.

If our great hymnological heritage was to retain its vitality, the great hymns must in some way be "church year oriented." The melodies should characterize the season. For example, "Christ Jesus Lay in Death's Strong Bands" (CW 161) should not be used at other seasons, nor should it be confined to merely the first couple of Sundays of Eastertide. Rather, it and its companion sentence "Christ Is Arisen" (CW 144) should reecho many times, in variant settings, throughout the great 50 days of Easter.

Nelle carefully pointed out each hymn's unique melodic motif(s). In *Christian Worship* hymn 161, for example, a motif is expressed in phrase 3 at the words "But now at God's right hand he stands" that is already known or easily learned from its companion Easter classic "Christ Is Arisen" (CW 144). "Harmony," Nelle urged, "is best done away with when singing 'Christ Is Arisen.'" This melody should be played and sung with only in-unison (octave) organ support, but calling on all the registers from the organ's 2' treble to its 16' bass. Handel does this so dramatically in the "Hallelujah Chorus" at "and he shall reign for ever and ever." With such appropriate support even newcomers can begin to join in what would otherwise easily become a four-part "German dirge."

Thus I began to gradually realize that, as a future worship planner and hymn selector, I should abandon the almost unquestioned custom of choosing hymns, especially the hymns before and after the sermon, to amplify the particular theme of my sermon. Instead, Nelle urged, the Hymn of the Day, historic Lutheranism's de-tempore hymn, should be related to the church year season and the Gospel of the Day.

My parish ministry

The first test of my new approaches came in the 1943 and 1944 summer vacation Bible school teaching I did at St. John's in Wrightstown, Wisconsin. I discovered that children loved the "new songs" we sang in school. So did their parents, when their children helped them try some of the "new songs" in church on Sundays.

But the real test of my new approaches came during my four years on the prairies of South Dakota, where I served people of predominantly German-Russian origin, people whose forebears 150 years earlier at the time of Catherine the Great had emigrated largely from overcrowded southwest Germany to various German settlements in Russia. There they had lived until shortly before World War I, when the Pan-Slavic Movement threatened the very centers of their communities by attempting to curtail their German Lutheran schools and churches. They then emigrated, for a second time, to various new homelands, including the prairie states of the Dakotas. In Russia their well-trained pastors and teachers had been able to preserve a great deal of their Lutheran heritage, including Lutheranism's great hymns. My people knew a chorale like "Wake, Awake, for Night Is Flying" (CW 206) almost by heart and sang it with gusto not only in German but also in English!

In the second of the two congregations I served, in a village called Tolstoy, the Lutheran German-Russians were, however, a small minority, without the support of their own parochial school, which my first and much larger congregation had. In that village 90 percent of the people belonged to Zion Lutheran Church. Despite faithful church attendance, this Tolstoy congregation was, as a group, dispirited and, as I soon discovered, poverty-stricken in its hymnological repertoire. In spite of such handicaps, I also soon discovered that a new, vital hymn-singing tradition could be established, to the joy and edification of both older and younger members. Though the majority of the members were bilingual, 15 percent were not and hence were unable to worship (and usually didn't attend) on the alternating "German" or "English" Sundays. In its German-language worship, the congregation had all too often been reduced to singing the same rather limited number of well-known hymn melodies, season in and season out. These melodies were included in their German hymnals alongside Lutheranism's great hymns, which these people couldn't sing—hymns with easy isometric melodies such as MEINEN JESUM LASS ICH NICHT (CW 304). This tune could carry various alternative texts for each of the church year seasons: Advent, Christmas, Epiphany, Lent, Easter, Pentecost, and much more! Somehow the people recognized their hymnological poverty because the singing had become as monotonous and dull as the inferior texts they were to sing. What was to be done?

My response was to form (in anticipation of the upcoming Christmas celebration) a choir, a proposal that was initially greeted with universal, shocked disbelief: "We don't have enough male voices/tenors/basses, etc., etc." What I had in mind, however, and what soon became welcome reality was a small but competent group that sang in unison. This group could lead the congregational singing, first at the new-hymn practices and then in the actual service, sometimes singing antiphonally with the congregation. The new choir had its regular practice each Sunday while the children were at Sunday school, a time formerly spent waiting until Sunday school was over, visiting with one another. On Christmas the congregation was genuinely proud to be able to celebrate by singing several new hymns that were genuinely and exclusively for the Christmas season. Self-confidence grew, and so did the small congregation.

At my first and larger congregation, the parochial school children and a well-established church choir enabled that congregation to master even those hymns that were entirely new to them. For instance, "Christ Is Arisen" (CW 144) was sung as a Gradual response throughout all the Sundays of the Easter season. By the third year the congregation was ready to begin the retrieval of Luther's great "Christ Jesus Lay in Death's Strong Bands" (CW 161).

The Watertown-Farmington church-music connection

So much for my recollections of personal pre–*Viva Vox* experiences. The corresponding experiences of Kurt Eggert cannot, of course, be described by me. In fact, when we were together, we spent very little time discussing such matters. Kurt and I did discover that we had both been brought (1) to very similar assessments of the church-music situation of our churches and (2) to very similar desires to undertake appropriate action.

It was, however, Kurt—and Kurt alone—who initiated and led all the various church-music activities related to *Viva Vox:* the hymn sings, the church-music seminars, the church-music workshops. Later, Kurt and his wife, Ruth, performed all the various tasks of publishing and distributing *Viva Vox,* including the supervision of volunteers from Kurt's congregations who did yeomen's service at the final stages. I shall, therefore, conclude my recollections of the background of *Viva Vox* with a description of how we two first got into the working relationship that resulted in *Viva Vox*.

I had come to Northwestern College as professor of Greek and ancient history in 1948, some six and a half years before the appearance of *Viva Vox*. During those years I had sung in St. Mark's church choir; I had also served on St. Mark's centennial committee. One of my pastors at St. Mark's had been Kurt's father. In a way it was he who prompted me to pursue my church music and hymnological interests with his son. In fact, I can remember most vividly a dear father's playful description of his dear son's numerous enterprises in one inimitable "German" sentence, "*Mein filius* [son] *hat sehr viele* [irons] *im Feuer.*" One of Kurt's enterprises was church-music renewal.

I also recall rather vividly a visit to the Immanuel, Farmington, parsonage. The conversation made it obvious that we agreed on the need for renewal action, lest our precious heritage be lost. Also obvious was the fact that Kurt was well on his way toward instituting activities in our neighborhood that would spark concrete results. Also in this respect, Kurt was far ahead of me. He and his Immanuel, Farmington, church choir had, in fact, already joined with various choirs in the region in Sunday afternoon hymn sings; they had planned the region's first church-music seminar. Also, I learned that, along with Professor Hilton Oswald of Northwestern, Kurt had been attending some of the annual Valparaiso University church-music seminars. There a program of church-music renewal was in full swing under the capable leadership of people like Walter Buszin (Professor Oswald's brother-in-law) and Professor Hoelty-Nickel, with the full support of Concordia Publishing House's music department and its director, Edward Klammer. One of the recent results of this church-music movement was the four-volume *Parish Organist* (published by Concordia), to which Kurt introduced me. In fact, he surprised me by playing from it, on his grand piano, a very contemporary hymn prelude, Camil van Huelse's "Take My Life and Let It Be."

At the same time, there came from quite a different and unexpected quarter a valuable discussion of the theological renewal of our historic Lutheran liturgy of Word and sacrament by the German-Australian theologian Hermann Sasse. We had long since learned to value Sasse's two major books published by Augsburg: *Here We Stand: Nature and Character of the Lutheran Faith* and *This Is My Body: Luther's Contention for the Real Presence in the Sacrament of the Altar*. Now a number of his periodic "Letters to Lutheran Pastors," since edited by N. Nagel and published by Concordia Publishing House, gave us wholesome orientation on this related issue.

Four of *Viva Vox*'s significant features

The initial glimpse at *Viva Vox* in the first part of this essay led this writer to reminisce at some length on the various promising but largely unrecognized treasures this new child had inherited from its forebears. This final section will highlight some of *Viva Vox*'s unique and significant features. I will describe what I found, in my recent review, to be four significant features of the first issue, which appeared at Eastertide 1955. (Copies of each issue were sent to the libraries of the synod's various schools, where they may still be available. Some received bound copies of the issues from the first five years.)

1. **The response of the readers:** The response to the appearance of the new publication was remarkable! Many people not only read *Viva Vox* thoughtfully; they also responded in activities of various sorts. Several kinds of church-music events (hymn sings, seminars, workshops) that we sponsored were not restricted to one location. Even in Watertown they were hosted by the three different congregations and Northwestern College; they often took place in other locales like rural Farmington, Jefferson, Fort Atkinson, Janesville, Columbus, Sun Prairie, Mequon, and various parts of Milwaukee. The presenters and participants at the gatherings were not limited to a few "big name" experts.

Involved were many different pastors, teachers, organists, choir directors, professors, and students from our colleges and seminary. Interested people unable to attend could read perceptive, firsthand reports written by participants. The response of one such person, a pastor, was typical: "I am sure I never would have dared to have the congregation sing some of these hymns without your suggestion of hymn practice at the beginning or end of worship. Puzzled at first, the people now really like that." Our mailing list soon exceeded 200 addresses. Monetary contributions were unusually generous and almost always covered our modest expenses.

2. **Practice suggestions:** Each issue of *Viva Vox* provided practical suggestions for dealing with our immigrant church's basic church-music problem: "How can we sing the Lord's song in a foreign land?" Back in 1535, easily learned hymns like Ringwaldt's "The Day Is Surely Drawing Near" (CW 207) were a boon for village churches, where singing was not supported by the trained musicians and choristers of the large city or university churches. A great deal of our church-music heritage, however, was what we today would call "classical," presupposing a culture in which educated aristocratic people set the tone. Such was the setting, to take an example, of the young J. S. Bach as a chorister first in Eisenach and then at his "college," St. Michael's in Lüneburg. That part of our heritage could not be easily preserved by our struggling immigrant church. How would it fare in congregations without parochial schools, where even confirmation instruction was all too often minimal and with no emphasis on worship?

A typical *Viva Vox* response to the problem came, for example, in "Revitalizing Congregational Singing." That article pinpointed factors that were devitalizing current hymn singing: *(a)* tunes that were either boring or trivial, *(b)* inadequate texts, *(c)* absence of a church-year oriented celebration of God's great deeds of salvation, *(d)* lack of integration into the liturgy of Word and sacrament, and *(e)* failure to plan for improvements. The author urged the implementation of our church's historic "Hymn of the Day" program.

Similar articles were "Singing Hymns Antiphonally," giving steps toward reestablishing an earlier custom, one with great promises for the future; "Music and Worship: A Checklist of Questions," each with several possible matching answers; "For Discussion by Worship Planners"; and "A Narrative Service," the liturgy with brief explanatory comment. In spite of what might appear as a naive preoccupation on our part with hymn singing, Kurt and I were also aware of two dangers in hymn selection: that of "low church" advocates of "more hymns and less liturgy" and that of "high church" neglecters of the church's wholesome song heritage. On the one hand, we accepted C. S. Lewis' sharp warning against trying to replace the historic liturgy, the ordinary and the proper, with "folk songs." What we were suggesting was something quite different: the historic Lutheran practice of substituting for or adding to the historic Gradual a hymn reflecting the season and the Gospel for the Day, as, for example, "Wake, Awake, for Night Is Flying" on the last Sunday of the church year. On the other hand, we felt that Eric Routley was right when he noted that in practice "high church" advocates of "the liturgy! the liturgy!" were all too often careless in their choice of hymns. Many times "free church" worship planners, though functioning outside the lectionary, church year, and liturgy, chose preaching texts and corresponding hymns from Christendom's great heritage with much greater care and understanding than traditionalistic elitists.

3. **Series of articles:** Several series of articles offered valuable orientation for both beginner and veteran worship planners:

- "Guides to the Seasons, Sundays, and Festivals of the Church Year" listed, for example, for Easter Sunday: *(a)* a Scripture verse, Revelation 1:18; *(b)* the Gospel for the Day, Matthew 16:1-8, in capsule form (at the empty tomb the women hear heaven's announcement of Jesus' resurrection); *(c)* the Hymn of the Day, "Christ Jesus Lay in Death's Strong Bands."
- "Our Great Hymns, Their Seasons and Sundays" usually began by comparing, for example, the hymns of the great 50 days of the Easter season with those of the 12 days of Christmas (the former—vigorous, masculine, Dorian; the latter—gentle, feminine, Ionian) and then noting the contributions from the various periods of church history. Next, the significant characteristics of each great hymn were highlighted, especially key motifs like the rippling joy of "Awake, My Heart, with Gladness," especially as its last two lines ascend "like a soaring lark into the open heavens." Finally, brief practical suggestions were given regarding a hymn melody's dependence on extremely precise, clear-cut rhythm from the beginning and throughout.

- Organists and choir directors were the recipients of special attention in articles like "Music during the Distribution of Holy Communion," "Introducing Buxtehude," and "Basic Considerations in the Acquisition of the DMLC Memorial Organ." Newly published organ and choir music in packets left over from our workshops were often offered on a "first come, first served" basis.

4. **Kurt's vision:** A final significant feature of *Viva Vox* was Kurt's vision of the entire church-music renewal program, a vision that, under his leadership, became reality in each issue of *Viva Vox*. In the actual production of each issue, Kurt was ably assisted by his wife, Ruth, who was responsible for most, if not all, the stencil typing and the artwork that graced almost every page. Among Kurt's many down-to-earth contributions were articles of great merit also today, like "Improving Our Church Music," "Integrating Organ and Choir Music with the Hymn of the Week," editorial-like "Musings," and "Grace Notes." One such note recommended a new book, Erik Routley's *The Music of Christian Hymnody*, which was my introduction to that perceptive scholar's continuing, superb contributions to our hymn understandings.

One of Kurt's "Grace Notes" (Michaelmas 1959) reported that the synodical Committee on Hymnology and Liturgics was at work on a revision of the 1941 *The Lutheran Hymnal*. Kurt urged *Viva Vox* readers to respond carefully to a forthcoming questionnaire. Little did Kurt know that some years later he would become the project director for *Christian Worship: A Lutheran Hymnal*. When confronted with that daunting task, Kurt knew what the apostle Paul expresses so well, that the competencies we have for such gospel tasks come from God, who alone makes us able ministers of the new covenant (2 Corinthians 3:4-6). We also think of him when we repeat what the voice from heaven said to the seer John in the midst of trials and labors, "'Blessed are the dead who die in the Lord from now on.' 'Yes,' says the Spirit, 'they will rest from their labor, for their deeds will follow them'" (Revelation 14:13).

Hymnody and the Proclamation of the Gospel

Carl F. Schalk

It was the firm conviction of Kurt Eggert, whose life and work we honor with this volume, that the hymnody of the church truly must be the *viva vox evangelii,* the living voice of the gospel. The mission of the church is to proclaim the gospel. The role of hymnody—both text and music—in the life, worship, and mission of the church is to proclaim that same gospel with all the skill, craftsmanship, and art possible. It was precisely as proclaimer, as *viva vox evangelii,* as living voice of the gospel, that Luther could hold music as second in importance only to theology.

In the church, words and music are not devices for emotional manipulation, nor are they tools for inducing a variety of psychological states presumably conducive to worship. Luther was clear: "After all, the gift of language combined with the gift of song was only given to man to let him know that *he should praise God* with both words and music, namely, *by proclaiming [the Word of God]* through music and by providing sweet melodies with words."[1]

To proclaim the gospel was, for Luther, to speak and sing about what Christ has done. "I have no one to sing and chant about but Christ," Luther says, "in whom I have everything. Him alone I proclaim, in him alone I glory, for he has become my salvation, that is, my victory."[2]

For us, as for Luther, the song is the same: to sing and praise God for the victory won in the life, death, and resurrection of Jesus Christ. But it is especially in the gathering together of the Christian community that we sing that song: to each other as witness to the faith we hold, to God in praise and thanksgiving, and to the world as message and proclamation.

In the public assembly of Christians, to proclaim the gospel means to tell the story of salvation, or at least whatever significant part of that story the particular time, season, festival, or commemoration might suggest. To tell the story does not mean to "tell about the story," but to tell it, to tell the story of how God has accomplished our salvation. Just as in family gatherings where we tell and retell the stories that bind us

---

[1] Martin Luther, *Luther's Works,* edited by Jaroslav Pelikan and Helmut T. Lehmann, American Edition, Vol. 53 (St. Louis: Concordia Publishing House; Philadelphia: Fortress Press, 1955–1986), pp. 323,324; emphasis mine.

[2] *Luther's Works,* Vol. 16, p. 129.

together as families, so in the weekly gathering of the Christian community, we tell and tell again the story of what binds us together as Christians. We tell that story in liturgy and song. That story is the story of what God has done for us, the good news of Jesus Christ.

Luther wrote in his commentary on 1 Corinthians chapter 15: "And now St. Paul appropriately concludes with a song which he sings: 'Thanks and praise be to God, who gave us such a victory!' We can join in that song and in that way always celebrate Easter, praising and extolling God for a victory that was not won or achieved in battle by us . . . but was presented and given to us by the mercy of God. . . . But we must . . . sing of this victory in Christ."[3]

All this, of course, says a great deal about the texts of the songs Christians sing when they gather for worship. Texts that simply express vague religious sentiments will not do. When the texts of our songs sing of this Easter victory in Christ, they do what the tradition of Christian song and Luther enjoin us to do. When they consist in nebulous religious sentiment, they would best be set aside.

None of this should suggest that a mere mechanical repetition of the facts of the life, death, and resurrection of Jesus Christ is sufficient to gospel proclamation. The gospel is proclaimed not only with our lips, but with our lives as well, as we live out its implications in loving service to the world through our daily vocations. Nevertheless, as Richard R. Caemmerer suggests, "If the hymn is to fulfill its task, it must actually sing the gospel."[4] Obviously, this may not occur in every line or phrase. It is conceivable that in the celebration of the liturgy a hymn could possibly be a simple affirmation of reverence, thanks, or adoration, the totality of the liturgy providing a sufficient kerygmatic context in which pure adoration, thanksgiving, and reverence can appropriately occur. This possibility, of course, assumes that it is indeed the historic liturgy that is being celebrated, a celebration that provides just such a context.

It is particularly crucial that as the church gathers to celebrate the liturgy, she recognizes her duty and obligation to see that the gospel, whether spoken or sung, is indeed being properly proclaimed both in liturgy and hymns. The following gives several examples, among many that could be cited, of gospel proclamation in the history of the church's song.

---

[3]*Luther's Works,* Vol. 28, p. 213.

[4]"The Congregational Hymn as the Living Voice of the Gospel," *The Musical Heritage of the Church,* Vol. V, edited by Theodore Hoelty-Nickel, p. 170.

The Old Testament

How did the people of the Old Testament understand their songs of praise and thanksgiving? What was their content? The central event that shaped Israel's self-understanding was the Exodus, celebrated in two ancient songs of praise. The first was the song of Miriam, in which she sings: "Sing to the LORD, for he is highly exalted. The horse and its rider he has hurled into the sea" (Exodus 15:21). The Lord whom Miriam praises is not some lord or god in general, but the one who has thrown the horse and rider into the sea. The longer version of this song, the song of Moses (Exodus 15:1-18), tells the story at greater length and with more detail. In both cases, the story is of a great victory won as the Lord overcame the enemies of his people, as Pharaoh and his armies are cast into the sea.

A second example is the familiar Psalm 136, in which the second half of each verse repeats, "His loves endures forever." If the question is, "Who is this Lord to whom thanks is due?" the answer is found in the first half of each verse. Following a general exhortation to give thanks (verses 1-3), thanks is given to the creator of all (verses 4-9), to him who brought Israel out of Egypt (verses 10-15), and to him who "led his people through the desert" and gave the land promised to them as a heritage (verses 16-22). This is the God who "remembered us in our low estate," who rescued the Israelites from their foes, and "gives food to every creature" (verses 23-26). This psalm proclaims the story of God's rescue and deliverance of his people and of his victory over their enemies. In each of these examples the exhortation to sing, praise, and "give thanks to the God of heaven" was never simply a general one. To sing and praise God in the Old Testament was to "sing and praise the God who . . . ," the ellipsis being filled with the particular story of God's delivering his people.

The New Testament and early church

After the death and resurrection of Christ, the content of the gospel, as understood by the apostolic church, is Christ himself, supremely the message of the cross and the resurrection. Peter's Pentecost sermon, reflected in many other passages from the New Testament, set the model: "Jesus of Nazareth was a man accredited by God to you by miracles, wonders and signs. . . . You, with the help of wicked men, put him to death by nailing him to the cross. *But God raised him from the dead*" (Acts 2:22-24; emphasis mine). There was no substitute for this gospel, even if such a "different gospel" were preached by an angel from heaven (Galatians 1:6-9).

That the church took this gospel seriously in its song may be seen from such early outbursts of praise as the *Magnificat*, in which Mary proclaims the greatness of the Lord by rehearsing what God has done, culminating in that he has remembered his promise of mercy, the promise he made to our fathers, to Abraham and his children forever (Luke 1:46-55). Likewise, in the *Benedictus*, which exudes the joy in the fulfillment of God's promises (Luke 1:68-79). That the church has taken these "Lukan psalms" into its liturgy as a regular and recurring part of its worship reflects its concern that the story of God's salvation and victory continue to resound in the church's song of praise.

How this tradition of proclamation was carried into the early centuries of the church's existence may be seen in two representative examples. The first, "Christ Is the World's Redeemer" (*Lutheran Worship* 271), attributed to St. Columba (521–597), is a translation of "Christus redemptor gentium," the second part of a longer poem "In te Christi credentium miserearis omnium." The text, especially stanzas 2 and 3, tells the story of Christ's suffering, death, descent into hell, resurrection, ascension, and session, reflecting the statements of both the Apostolic and Nicene Creeds.

> Christ is the world's Redeemer, The lover of the pure,
> The font of heav'nly wisdom, Our trust and hope secure,
> The armor of his soldiers The Lord of earth and sky,
> Our health while we are living, Our life when we shall die.
>
> Christ has our host surrounded With clouds of martyrs bright,
> Who wave their palms in triumph And fire us for the fight.
> Then Christ the cross ascended To save a world undone
> And, suff'ring for the sinful, Our full redemption won.
>
> Down in the realm of darkness He lay, a captive bound,
> But at the hour appointed He rose, a victor crowned.
> And now, to heav'n ascended, He sits upon the throne
> Whence he had ne'er departed, His Father's and his own.
>
> Glory to God the Father, The unbegotten One,
> All honor be to Jesus, His sole-begotten Son;
> And to the Holy Spirit, The perfect Trinity,
> Let all the world give answer, Amen—so let it be.

The second example, "Pange, lingua, gloriosi," written by Venantius Fortunatus (530–609), is generally considered one of the finest of Latin hymns. This hymn, in the familiar translation by John Mason Neal, "Sing, My Tongue, the Glorious Battle" (*Christian Worship* [CW] 122), is particularly appropriate for use on Good Friday and is appointed for use by many Lutherans on that day. Its original ten stanzas sketch the life of Christ from birth to crucifixion, but its very first stanza heralds the victory of Christ over death. The stanza points us to "the ending of the fray" and reminds us that "Christ, the world's Redeemer, as a victim won the day."

> Sing, my tongue, the glorious battle;
> Sing the ending of the fray.
> Now above the cross, the trophy,
> Sound the loud triumphant lay.
> Tell how Christ, the world's Redeemer,
> As a victim won the day.

> Tell how, when at length the fullness
> Of th' appointed time was come,
> He, the Word, was born of woman,
> Left for us his Father's home,
> Blazed the path of true obedience,
> Shone as light amidst the gloom.

> Thus, with thirty years accomplished,
> He went forth from Nazareth,
> Destined, dedicated, willing,
> Did his work and met his death;
> Like a lamb he humbly yielded
> On the cross his dying breath.

> Faithful cross, true sign of triumph,
> Be for all the noblest tree;
> None in foliage, none in blossom,
> None in fruit your equal be,
> Symbol of the world's redemption,
> For your burden makes us free.

> Unto God be praise and glory;
> To the Father and the Son,
> To th' eternal Spirit honor
> Now and evermore be done—

Praise and glory in the highest
While the timeless ages run.

An eighth-century Greek hymn, "Come, You Faithful, Raise the Strain" (CW 142) by John of Damascus (c. 696–c. 754), also carries the theme of victory and combines it with the Exodus theme of freedom from bondage as reflected in Moses' song (Exodus 15).

This hymn, together with John of Damascus' "The Day of Resurrection" (CW 166), stands as a significant contribution to the church's treasury of song, praising God for the great victory won in the life, death, and resurrection of his son, Jesus Christ.

Come, you faithful, raise the strain
    Of triumphant gladness!
God has brought his Israel Into joy from sadness.
See the spring of souls today: Christ has burst his prison
And from three days' sleep in death As a sun has risen.

All the winter of our sins, Long and dark, is flying
From his light, to whom we give Laud and praise undying.
Neither could the gates of death
    Nor the tomb's dark portal
Nor the watchers nor the seal Hold him as a mortal.

But today among his own Christ appeared, bestowing
Blessed peace, which evermore Passes human knowing.
Come, you faithful, raise the strain
    Of triumphant gladness!
God has brought his Israel Into joy from sadness.

The Reformation

Luther's attitude toward the role of hymnody in Christian worship is most clearly reflected in the hymn that appeared as the first hymn in the very first collection of Reformation hymns, the *Etlich Cristlich lider* of 1524. The first stanza of this hymn, "Dear Christians, One and All, Rejoice" (CW 377), sets out the role of the hymn as proclaimer of the gospel:

Dear Christians, one and all, rejoice,
    With exultation springing,
And, with united heart and voice
    And holy rapture singing,

> *Proclaim the wonders God has done,*
>   *How his right arm the vict'ry won.*
> How dearly it has cost him! (emphasis mine)

    The exhortation is for Christians to sing with united heart and voice, proclaiming the wonders God has done. The subsequent stanzas of the hymn set out in great detail those "wonders": mankind is born into a lost condition; God plans for our salvation and sends his only Son; the Son obeys the Father's will, is born of a virgin, sheds his blood and wins the victory over death, ascends to heaven, and sends the Holy Spirit. No clearer proclamation of the gospel can be found than in this Ur-hymn of the Lutheran church.

    Equally important in this regard is another of Luther's hymns, the great Easter hymn "Christ Jesus Lay in Death's Strong Bands" (CW 161). As expressed in stanza 1, the joy of the Christian and the reason for thankful song is that "Christ Jesus lay [past tense] in death's strong bands" and the battle in which death and life contended has been won and Christ has conquered death! In the third stanza, Luther draws the parallel with the Exodus events: Christ is the slain Paschal Lamb whose blood marks our doors, and when faith points to the blood, the angel of death passes over. The fifth stanza (omitted in *Christian Worship*) takes note of the Eucharistic significance of the Easter event, that, like the Israelites in Egypt, we also feed on the Paschal Lamb in Holy Communion: "He is our meat and drink indeed; Faith lives upon no other. Hallelujah!" (*The Lutheran Hymnal* 195).

> Christ Jesus lay in death's strong bands
> For our offenses given;
> But now at God's right hand he stands
> And brings us life from heaven.
> Therefore let us joyful be
> And sing to God right thankfully
> Loud songs of hallelujah. Hallelujah!
>
> It was a strange and dreadful strife
> When life and death contended.
> The victory remained with life;
> The reign of death was ended.
> Holy Scripture plainly says
> That death is swallowed up by death,
> Its sting is lost forever. Hallelujah!

> Here the true Paschal Lamb we see,
> Whom God so freely gave us;
> He died on the accursed tree—
> So strong his love—to save us.
> See, his blood now marks our door;
> Faith points to it; death passes o'er,
> And Satan cannot harm us. Hallelujah!
>
> So let us keep the festival
> To which the Lord invites us;
> Christ is himself the joy of all,
> The sun that warms and lights us.
> Now his grace to us imparts
> Eternal sunshine to our hearts;
> The night of sin is ended. Hallelujah!

The present day

But such use of the hymn as proclaimer of the gospel in the sense described and illustrated thus far was not the case only in the church of the past. It continues as well into the present. Two examples will suffice. The first is the hymn recognized by the Hymn Society of the United States and Canada as the best new hymn in *Lutheran Book of Worship*: Ronald Klug's "Rise, Shine, You People." Since its appearance there in 1978, it has appeared in a number of other hymnals, including *Christian Worship* (No. 556).

> Rise, shine, you people! Christ the Lord has entered
> Our human story; God in him is centered.
> He comes to us, by death and sin surrounded,
> With grace unbounded.
>
> See how he sends the pow'rs of evil reeling;
> He brings us freedom, light and life and healing.
> All men and women, who by guilt are driven,
> Now are forgiven.
>
> Come, celebrate, your banners high unfurling,
> Your songs and prayers against the darkness hurling.
> To all the world go out and tell the story
> Of Jesus' glory.
>
> Tell how the Father sent his Son to save us.
> Tell of the Son, who life and freedom gave us.

> Tell how the Spirit calls from ev'ry nation
> His new creation.*

If telling the story is a criterion, Klug's text is an excellent example. It first tells that God in Christ the Lord has "entered our human story." It then tells of the victory over the powers of evil, bringing us freedom, life, light, and healing. We are then invited to celebrate our new existence by hurling our songs and prayers against the darkness, and then we're asked to go out and tell the story of Jesus' glory. The final stanza tells us what we are to tell: "Tell how the Father sent his Son to save us. Tell of the Son, who life and freedom gave us. Tell how the Spirit calls from every nation his new creation."

The second example is a recent text of Jaroslav J. Vajda written in 1999. "Around the World the Shout Resounds" tells the story of Jesus, the one who is risen from the dead. There is no "happier news" than this, the text proclaims: "Christ's life is ours, and we are his!" Stanza 2 speaks of the "cloud of witnesses who share the faith," while stanza 3 depicts the growing wonder and certainty "that sings convinced and unafraid: 'This is the day the Lord has made!'"

> Around the world the shout resounds:
> "Christ lives again, and life abounds!"
> The serpent's head is crushed, the grasp of death
> is broken;
> Atonement has been sealed, the empty grave its token.
> What happier news on earth than this:
> Christ's life is ours, and we are his!
>
> God bless the cloud of witnesses who share the faith that
> we confess:
> The women at the tomb, and Martha in her grieving,
> The thief upon the cross, and Stephen killed believing.
> With Job we know the life God gives:
> "We know that our Redeemer lives!"
>
> The wonder grows, remembering, considering
> and marveling,
> Not with fast-fading cheers, but with a steady knowing,
> A growing certainty, a peaceful, joyful glowing,

---

*Text: © 1974 Augsburg Publishing House. Used by permission of Augsburg Fortress.

That sings convinced and unafraid:
"This is the day the Lord has made!"*

The new millennium

All the preceding are examples reflecting the church's tradition of hymnody as a proclaimer of the gospel. The principle on which these examples are based is simply this: God is praised when the gospel is rightly proclaimed; and, conversely, the proclamation of the gospel is the way that God is rightly praised. There is no artificial division between songs that "proclaim" and others that "praise": unless "praise songs" proclaim the good news of the gospel, they are not, in any Christian sense, praise songs at all.

Some advocate that hymns in Christian worship "should be devotional rather than didactic or homiletical, and their direction Godward, not manward."[5] Such a view incorrectly implies that proclamatory hymns are merely teaching efforts, at best, or rhymed dogma, at worst. It forgets that the proclamation of the gospel is directed not only to the world as a message of hope and salvation, and to God as the community of faith pleads the good news of the gospel before the Father—just as the Son pleads for us before him—and praises him for it, but to the Christian community itself as it confesses and celebrates the faith.

There is, it must also be said, a great tradition of Christian devotional hymnody that must be accounted for. Much of it was written for private, personal devotional use and finds a valid use in just those circumstances. Some of this hymnody also finds especially appropriate use in corporate worship, particularly when used in the context of the historic liturgy with its inherent richness in proclamation. Where the historic liturgy of the church has been abandoned, replaced, or surrendered to a variety of passing fads, however, it is even more crucial that the proclamation of the gospel sound out clearly in the church's song.

Today, in too many congregations, liturgy has increasingly dissolved into what could honestly be described as a sea of fatuous wordiness, what Matthias Loy referred to as a "diarrhea of words and constipation of ideas,"[6] yet firmly believed by its advocates to be "creative." Likewise,

---

*Text: © 1997 Jaroslav J. Vajda. Used by permission.

[5] "Introduction to the Common Hymnal," *Service Book and Hymnal* (Minneapolis: Augsburg Publishing House, 1958), p. 286.

[6] *Lutheran Confessional Theology in America 1840–1880*, edited by Theodore G. Tappert (New York: Oxford University Press, 1972), p. 315.

while there are fine contemporary hymn texts, too many consist of pedestrian or narcissistic verbiage, centered on the individual and the self. In others the "I" and "me" no longer mean the individual worshiper, but presume to be the "voice of God," which worshipers sing to themselves in egoistic self-congratulation.

In view of all this, the church would do well to regain a greater sense of the proclamation of the gospel in its hymnody. As it enters a new millennium, the church could do so with no better song of praise on its lips, and no better model for its "new song" as "living voice of the gospel," than the ancient hymn, the *Te Deum* widely thought to be the work of Niceta of Remesiana (fifth century):

> We praise you, O God, we acclaim you as Lord;
> All creation worships you, Father everlasting.
> To you all angels, all the pow'rs of heav'n,
> Cherubim and seraphim, sing in endless praise:
> Holy, holy, holy Lord, God of heav'nly hosts,
> Heaven and earth are full of your glory.
> The glorious company of apostles praise you.
> The noble fellowship of prophets praise you.
> The white-robed army of martyrs praise you.
> Throughout the world the holy Church acclaims you:
> Father of majesty unbounded, your glorious, true, and
>   only Son,
> And the Holy Spirit, advocate and guide.
> You, Christ, are the King of glory, the eternal Son of
>   the Father.
> When you became man to set us free, you humbled your-
>   self to be born of a virgin.
> You overcame the sting of death
> And opened the kingdom of heaven to all believers.
> You sit at the right hand of God in the glory of the Father.
> We believe that you will come to be our judge.
> Come then, Lord, and help your people,
>   bought with the price of your own blood,
> And bring us with your saints to glory everlasting.[7]

---

[7] *Christian Worship: A Lutheran Hymnal* (Milwaukee: Northwestern Publishing House, 1993), pp. 48,49.

The Formation and Flow of Worship Attitudes in the Wisconsin Evangelical Lutheran Synod

James P. Tiefel

There is no official history of worship in the Wisconsin Evangelical Lutheran Synod (WELS). Several authors have traced the formation of the various hymnals published by and for the synod. Arnold O. Lehmann's article "Wisconsin Synod Hymnals and Agendas 1850–1950"[1] is the best of these studies, especially because it includes information from early Wisconsin Synod convention proceedings and official church periodicals. Lehmann makes no claims about going beyond the record of the official documents, however, and there is a great deal of history beyond those documents. The official histories of the church body (for example, John Philipp Koehler's *History of the Wisconsin Synod* and Edward C. Fredrich's *The Wisconsin Synod Lutherans*) include references to worship but offer nothing of more detail than the publication of a new hymnal or how worship was involved in a congregational controversy. There is no history of WELS worship similar to the official history of WELS world missions.

There will be no official history of worship in the Wisconsin Synod even with the publication of this essay, for it does not intend to be an in-depth study. This essay is narrative and anecdotal. It repeats stories that are retold, in the main, without documentation. The essay is more about sights, sounds, and sense than about facts and figures. If an official history of worship in the Wisconsin Synod can be written, it will have to wait for another day. The intent of what follows is nothing more than to give the reader of this commemorative volume a better understanding of the worship attitudes that formed and framed the work of Kurt J. Eggert.

After graduating from Wisconsin Lutheran Seminary, Eggert spent a year instructing high school students at Michigan Lutheran Seminary in Saginaw, Michigan, and then served a short pastorate in North Dakota. He spent the rest of his life in or next door to the two cities that hold center stage in the story of the Wisconsin Synod, Watertown and Milwaukee. He grew up in Watertown, where his father served the notable St. Mark's Lutheran Church. For eight years he attended

---

[1] *WELS Historical Institute Journal*, Vol. 16, No. 2 (October 1998), pp. 3-37.

Northwestern College and its preparatory department, located six blocks from the St. Mark's parsonage. His second pastorate (after the Dakota experience) was Immanuel Lutheran Church in Farmington, eight miles south of Watertown. In Milwaukee he served at Gethsemane Lutheran Church, at Milwaukee Lutheran Teachers' College, at Atonement Lutheran Church, and as a member of the synodical administration, headquartered in Milwaukee. If it can be said that the general attitude of the Wisconsin Synod, for at least the first one hundred years of its history and probably for longer than that, was most often molded and most consistently modeled in Watertown and Milwaukee, then it can also be said that Kurt Eggert grew up, attended school, and carried out his ministry in the two places where he would be most acutely influenced by the general worship attitudes of the Wisconsin Synod.

What are the attitudes of the Wisconsin Synod toward worship? Without a doubt, the attitudes have changed over 150 years. But it will be impossible to gain a genuine perspective of Wisconsin Synod thinking without a look that goes farther back than the formation of the synod in 1849 and 1850.

The worship mind-set of Martin Luther

Martin Luther inherited a worship tradition that was more than a thousand years old by the time he was born, that of the Roman Mass. The Roman Mass was virtually the only order of service used in the Christian church of western Europe after A.D. 1000.

As Luther began to understand the central theme of the Christian gospel and came to identify the errors of Roman Catholicism, he realized that parts of the mass would have to be changed. Most of the changes he made were in the liturgy of the Holy Communion, for it was there that the essence of the Roman false doctrine was found. Over a span of perhaps 500 years before A.D. 1000, the Roman Church had turned the Savior's gift of his body and blood for the forgiveness of sins and the strengthening of faith into a sacrifice by which the Savior's forgiveness could be earned. What Jesus intended as a means to impart grace had become a means to earn grace, and the Roman rite for Holy Communion was riddled with texts and ceremonies that accentuated that teaching.

Luther did not feel, however, that the historic Christian service had to be cast aside completely. Apart from the rite for Holy Communion, the Mass was nothing more than a set of psalms, prayers, and readings drawn directly from the Scriptures. He commended the continued use of pure and ancient practices, certainly those drawn directly from the Bible, as well as those that had authority in the long-standing practice of the church. He did not share the attitude of some of his contemporaries who insisted that everything inherited from Rome had to be abolished. He saw great value in retaining the ancient liturgical texts, prayers, music, and art. He often revised and rewrote, and he certainly suggested new elements and practices, but he retained the basic form of a five-hundred-year-old tradition. He wrote:

> It is not now nor ever has it been our intention to abolish the liturgical service of God completely, but rather to purify the one that is now in use from the wretched accretions which corrupt it and to point out an evangelical use.[2]
>
> Let all the old practices continue. Let the mass be celebrated with consecrated vestments, with chants and all the usual ceremonies, in Latin, recognizing the fact that these are mere external matters which do not endanger the consciences of men.[3]

The touchstone for Luther was the ability of the external worship form to communicate the gospel. Nothing was to be done in worship that encouraged or allowed worshipers to suppose they were earning forgiveness by means of their worship, for forgiveness comes only through the work of Jesus. He insisted that any practice that was used to gain merit before God had to be abolished—even if he himself had suggested the practice. He also insisted, however, that forms that served the gospel ought to be retained.

> What about the general precepts of the church, the fast and festival days? Answer: What has been established of old by the approval of the church and out of love for God and for just reasons must necessarily be observed, not because it is of itself necessary and unchangeable but because the obedience of love which we owe God and the church is necessary.[4]

---

[2]Martin Luther, *Luther's Works,* edited by Jaroslav Pelikan and Helmut T. Lehmann, American Edition, Vol. 53 (St. Louis: Concordia Publishing House; Philadelphia: Fortress Press, 1955–1986), p. 20.

[3]*Luther's Works,* Vol. 36, p. 254.

[4]*What Luther Says: An Anthology,* compiled by Ewald M. Plass, Vol. I (St. Louis: Concordia Publishing House, 1959), par. 903.

Luther prepared two orders of service, one in Latin, the other in German. Both retained the order and emphases of the historic liturgy. The Latin service, however, was more conservative; it retained the traditional participation of the choir for the singing of the ordinary and proper. It seems to have been Luther's intent that the German service would be used in congregations without a regular choir. In this second service German hymns replaced the Latin canticles and psalms. Over the years congregations tended to blend portions of the two services in ways that fit their situations.

Developments in Germany after Luther's death

Germany was not a united country in the years after Luther's death, but rather a set of kingdoms and provinces loosely knit together in what was called the Holy Roman Empire. What usually determined the worship style of a Lutheran congregation was the doctrinal position of the king or prince who ruled the province. If the prince was Lutheran but tended to be conservative in his thinking, many of the old traditions were retained. If the prince was influenced by Calvinism, worship in the congregations of his province tended to have less of the traditions. Only in lands where the prince was staunchly Lutheran could one expect to find worship attitudes that followed Luther's mind-set and principles.

Even in places where Lutheran doctrine was at its purest, however, the style of worship varied. City congregations had the resources to accentuate music and art. Especially if the prince was supportive, music and art flourished in worship. In country congregations or in lands where the prince was not supportive, worship could be artistically unimaginative. Lutherans in Leipzig, Lübeck, and Dresden, for example, experienced a rich liturgical life, but many other Lutherans experienced something far different.

The differing worship perspectives were minor, however, compared to the serious doctrinal controversies (eventually resulting in the writing of the Formula of Concord in 1577) that broke out between orthodox Lutherans and those who had been influenced by Reformed theology. The theological battles were heated and often waged in the pulpits and catechism classrooms. The people struggled to keep up, but many were left behind in the dust of debate and dialectic. Some sensed their pastors were more involved in solving controversies than in meeting the spiritual needs of the congregation.

The Lutheran churches were just beginning to recover from the doctrinal battles when the Roman popes and their Catholic allies began a determined effort to recapture the Lutheran lands lost during the Reformation. The Thirty Years' War raged in Germany between 1618 and 1648. Hundreds of Lutheran churches were destroyed, and their pastors and members were killed, scattered, or impoverished. Because the war left the church in disarray, many laypeople drifted away from regular attendance at worship and, without the attention of law and gospel, soon fell into a lifestyle that was decidedly unchristian. Those who remained faithful to God's Word found it difficult to understand why pastors continued waging doctrinal battles while church members were dying or drifting away in record numbers. Without doubt, an adjustment of some sort was essential. Tragically, the reaction became an overreaction, and the overreaction became known as Pietism.

The reaction of Pietism

As they observed the sad situation in German congregations, some Lutheran pastors and laypeople began to doubt the promises that God made about the power of the means of grace. When they went to worship, they heard the gospel proclaimed and saw children being baptized and many church members receiving Holy Communion, but these means of grace seemed to have little effect on the lives of their Lutheran neighbors. Little by little, Pietists began to talk more about deeds and emotions than about the promises of the gospel. They became less inclined to focus on God's working through the means of grace (since they couldn't see results) and more inclined to focus on how they lived and how they felt about God (responses they could see).

Despite this inclination, some Pietists retained their central focus on the Savior's cross. In other cases, however, the centrality of the cross was virtually lost. These Pietists lost interest in orthodox confessions and sermons. They saw little need to emphasize the sacraments of Baptism and Holy Communion. The Christian church year, with its readings, psalms, and prayers repeating the most important events in the life of Jesus, was abandoned for themes that concerned the Christian life and devotion. The Pietists' hymns sang of individual reaction to God rather than about the great things God had done in Christ. Invariably joined to these subjective hymn texts were tunes influenced by the emerging musical style of the opera, a style that was intended to arouse the emotions. Without an emphasis on the sacraments, the church year, or confessional hymns, the Pietists had little use for the Christian order of service, the liturgy. The worship of many Lutheran congregations came to include little more than a lengthy confession of sins, a sermon, and a series of sentimental hymns.

German Lutheranism at the dawn of the 19th century

Eventually the Pietists' strong focus on personal emotions began to seem shallow and empty to many Germans. Sadly, those who felt this way did not return to the doctrinal emphases of Luther and the Lutheran reformers. Instead, they turned their focus from their emotions to their intellect. Instead of gauging God's promises by how they felt about them, they looked at God's promises from the perspective of their human reason. The results were the same—the Word of God was despised and abandoned. This religious phenomenon was known as Rationalism; together with Pietism, it dominated the German Lutheran church at the dawn of the 19th century.

There were many Lutherans in Germany, however, who by God's grace retained their allegiance to confessional Lutheranism, and by the 1820s these "old" Lutherans were beginning to return to their Lutheran heritage. Often these confessional churches stood next door to pietistic or rationalistic congregations in the same city. Germany had few synods as we know them today, but different Lutheran congregations had very different confessions, and most people knew it.

The government knew it too and realized that efforts to unite Germany would be difficult as long as the churches held to so many different perspectives. The kings of Prussia, especially, were determined to bring the many German provinces together as a strong, unified nation, and they began concerted efforts to bring all Germany's Protestants—Calvinists as well as the various Lutherans—under the pale of one "evangelical" church body. Calvinists, Pietists, and Rationalists welcomed the move, but the confessional Lutherans deplored and opposed the Prussian union attempt. Prussia was a formidable enemy, however, and many confessional Lutherans began to emigrate to the United States so that they could practice their religion in freedom. One of these groups headed for Michigan and settled on the banks of the Cass River near Saginaw. Another arrived via New Orleans and settled in Perry County, Missouri, near St. Louis. Within ten years of their arrival in America, these confessional Lutheran congregations joined to form what we know today as the Lutheran Church—Missouri Synod (LCMS).

Confessional Lutherans were not the only Germans attracted to America. Pietistic and rationalistic Lutherans came too. They didn't come to gain religious freedom, however; in fact, many of them had been detached from active participation in church for years. They had little interest in church or its worship. They came seeking new opportunities in the new world. To their credit, many Pietists saw a need to serve these disattached Lutherans. Groups of Pietists joined with Calvinists to establish mission societies that gave basic training to men who were willing to go to America and gather Germans into congregations. One of these mission society pastors was a middle-aged baker by the name of Johannes Muehlhaeuser. Arriving in Milwaukee in 1848, he soon established Grace Lutheran Church. Together with two other mission society graduates, Muehlhaeuser formed a new church body known today as the Wisconsin Evangelical Lutheran Synod. At about the same time, Friedrich Schmid, another mission society man, was working to gather Lutherans in Michigan and trying to found a synod of sorts. In Minnesota, Pastor J. F. C. Heyer, a product of the pietistic General Synod, was gathering like-minded pastors into the Minnesota Synod. With similar roots, these three groups were drawn to one another and united as a joint synod in 1892.

Formation of worship attitudes in the Wisconsin Synod

Within 25 years of their founding, the "old" Lutherans of the Missouri Synod and the "new" Lutherans from Wisconsin had established a doctrinal unity that found expression in the Lutheran Synodical Conference of North America (1872). Primarily through the work of synod president Johannes Bading and seminary president Adolph Hoenecke, Wisconsin moved "to the right" of its pietistic doctrinal position and came to stand side by side with the confessional voices in Missouri.

Wisconsin's move away from Pietism was neither smooth nor swift, however, and its halting steps often can be observed in its worship practices. The constitution of Muehlhaeuser's Grace congregation in Milwaukee, for example, includes this paragraph:

> Be it resolved that our congregation, founded on the ground of the apostles and prophets, whereon Jesus is the cornerstone, makes confession of the Augsburg Confession and Luther's Small Catechism. However, never may or shall a preacher of the said congregation use the rite of the old Lutheran church, whether in Baptism or the Lord's Supper.

The pastors and people who were attracted to the Wisconsin Synod tended to have similar attitudes about worship forms. Now and then convention speakers in the 1850s and 60s asked the synod to adopt an order of service that was more Lutheran in its orientation and history, but no acceptable rite could be found or produced. Congregations continued to use the nonliturgical orders brought from their homeland. For many years after 1850, the most widely used hymnal in the Wisconsin Synod was the hymnal of the Pennsylvania Synod, recognized by more confessional Lutherans (and eventually also by Wisconsin) to include more than 100 hymns of dubious Lutheran integrity. So weak was the synod's early resolve in the matter of hymnody that its first official hymnal (1870) had to endure an immediate revision to cleanse it of nine hymns that should not have been included.

The pietistic worship practices in the Wisconsin Synod led to some serious skirmishes with Missouri Synod congregations located in the same vicinity. This was a battle that had begun in Germany, and the hard feelings and harsh words continued in America. The paragraph in the Grace constitution probably was aimed directly at Trinity Church, Missouri Synod's congregation across the Milwaukee River, where the old Lutheran rite was firmly in place.

The leading theologian of the Missouri Synod and the president of its seminary, C. F. W. Walther, was the undisputed American champion of a confessional worship rite and hymnody. The use of historic Lutheran worship practices was Walther's legacy from orthodox Lutheranism in Germany. To gain the freedom to use these forms without the interference of the German government was what led him to follow the immigration to St. Louis. Within ten years of their arrival in Perry County, the Missourians under Walther's leadership had published a hymnal, *Kirchengesangbuch,* which had as its chief consideration that its hymns be "pure in doctrine; that they have found almost universal acceptance within the Orthodox German Lutheran Church and have thus received the almost unanimous testimony; that they had come forth from the true spirit [of Lutheranism]."[5]

Walther's *Kirchen-Agenda,* containing the main Sunday order, arrived on the scene nine years later, in 1856. Visitors to the St. Louis congregations, where Walther served as senior pastor, would have

---

[5] Quoted in *Lutheran Worship: History and Practice* (St. Louis: Concordia Publishing House, 1993), p. 89.

experienced not only an elaborate liturgical rite based on Luther's Reformation revisions, but chasubles, chanting, candles, and crucifixes as well. They might also have experienced the thrill of hearing Walther at the organ; it is said that regular churchgoers did not have to glance to the balcony to know when Walther was taking his turn on the bench. Walther stood behind the efforts of his former students to establish his worship perspective and rite in every Missouri Synod congregation. So powerful was Walther's liturgical influence that even congregations in the synod that possessed their own confessional rites were led to abandon them for Walther's. (In his history of Frankenmuth, Michigan, *Teach My People the Truth,* Herman Zehnder bemoans the fact that St. Lorenz congregation was "forced" by Walther's contemporary Fuerbringer to give up its Wilhelm Loehe liturgy, thought by Zehnder to be far richer even than Walther's.)

The decided difference in worship practices in the Missouri and Wisconsin Synods is easily seen if one compares the following words of Walther with the paragraph Muehlhaeuser inserted into the Grace Church constitution:

> We refuse to be guided by those who are offended by our church customs. We adhere to them all the more firmly when someone wants to cause us to have a guilty conscience on account of them. . . . It is truly distressing that many of our fellow Christians find the differences between Lutheranism and papism in outward things. It is a pity and dreadful cowardice when one sacrifices the good and ancient customs to please the deluded American sects, lest they accuse us of being papistic.
>
> Indeed! Am I to be afraid of a Methodist, who perverts the saving Word, or be ashamed in the matter of my good cause, and not rather rejoice that the sects can tell by our ceremonies that I do not belong to them?
>
> We are not insisting that there be unity of perception or feelings or of taste among all believing Christians, neither dare anyone demand that all be minded as he. Nevertheless it remains true that the Lutheran liturgy distinguishes Lutheran worship from the worship of other churches to such an extent that the latter look like lecture halls in which the hearers are merely addressed or instructed, while our churches are in truth houses of

prayer in which the Christians serve God publicly before the world.[6]

Walther's words about Christian liberty might have been included in his defense of the Lutheran liturgy for the sake of his Wisconsin Synod brothers. Despite the heartening move toward Lutheran confessionalism, Wisconsin was not ready to abandon the nonliturgical practices of Pietism. This was certainly true of its members, but especially true of its pastors. The move toward confessionalism, guided, of course, by the Holy Spirit, was an intellectual move, born out of study of the Scriptures and the Lutheran confessions. But Missouri's brand of liturgical worship and its tastes in hymnody ran counter to what Wisconsin's founders and early leaders had experienced from their youth. Wisconsin was ready for a confessional adjustment, but the assimilation of liturgy, ceremony, and objective hymns didn't feel right to many pastors and people born and bred in Pietism.

It might be supposed that Walther's liturgical leadership would have been powerful enough to have changed the prevailing attitude in the Wisconsin Synod, but this was not the case. Lehmann's article reveals that although Walther's hymnal and service order were available for its use, Wisconsin never formally adopted them or even considered adopting them. An 1874 resolution calling for the adoption of Walther's *Agende* specifically rejected Walther's order of service. It is difficult to document this, but one senses that early Wisconsin Synod pastors (perhaps more often than their leaders) saw in Walther a certain "pushiness" that they resented. It makes good sense that the very qualities that made Walther the premier confessional spokesman in America occasionally would have seemed overbearing to little pietistic Wisconsin. It is likely that Wisconsin—smaller, poorer, and generally less sophisticated than Missouri—compensated for a subtle inferiority complex by dismissing Missouri's ways as somewhat grandiose and ostentatious. The less lovely sister often deals with the lovelier sister's beauty by considering her vain. Anecdotal history leads one to sense that such a compensation occurred in Wisconsin more often than the official histories admit. One gets the impression that Wisconsin tended to look at Missouri's liturgical emphases from what eventually became a rather skeptical perspective. Join this phenomenon to the worship experiences of their pietistic past and it

---

[6] C. F. W. Walther, *Essays for the Church*, Vol. 1 (St. Louis: Concordia Publishing House, 1992), p. 194.

becomes easy to understand why Wisconsin pastors did not take to Missouri's worship rite, to say nothing of the "chasubles, chanting, candles, and crucifixes" that had been among Walther's practices.

Wisconsin had no liturgical champion of its own. There is no doubt that Adolph Hoenecke had as much theological influence in the Wisconsin Synod as Walther had in the Missouri Synod, but Hoenecke did not carry the dual mantle of synod and seminary president as Walther did and thus could not influence his synod in the same way that Walther influenced his. Hoenecke's practical theology field was homiletics, not liturgics, and although he served on several hymnal review committees, he does not seem to have had as much interest in music and the arts as Walther did. Not until J. P. Koehler (Walther's student in St. Louis) arrived at the seminary in 1900 was there an emphasis on teaching confessional hymnology at the seminary, and not until after Hoenecke's death in 1908 was there a course on liturgics.

Roots in Pietism, few financial resources, resentment of Missouri's perceived overbearing leadership, and a resulting skepticism over practices considered show and ostentation—these combined to establish a generally negative attitude toward liturgical worship, ceremony, music, and art that lasted well into the second century of Wisconsin's history.

The history of two hymnals

One might have supposed that J. P. Koehler, seminary professor (1901–1930) and president (1920–1930) would have become a liturgical leader to match Walther, his teacher. Koehler had a deep interest in history (he authored the first synodical history), church music (he founded the seminary chorus), and ecclesiastical art (his paintings of biblical scenes hang in the seminary library and his influence led to the classic design of the present seminary campus). But Koehler's knowledge of history (and to a certain extent an observation of church life in his own era) led him to the conclusion that too often liturgy and ceremony were imposed on the church in a legalistic way and led not to a faith-wrought liturgical life but to one that was formalistic instead. This concern may have been so deep that he could not bring himself to become a champion for liturgical enrichment in his own synod. His writings on hymnody in the *Wisconsin Lutheran Quarterly* run to several hundred pages; his lone article on the liturgy includes nothing more than the outline of his seminary liturgics course.

Some have deeper reservations about Koehler's liturgical thinking. In an article in the first issue of the *WELS Historical Institute Journal,* Victor Prange (who married Koehler's granddaughter) observed:

> Koehler shows an appreciation for protestantism; one misses an equal appreciation for that which is catholic. Koehler speaks of how the life of the church so easily "becomes materialistic." One suspects that he might have been just a bit uncomfortable with some of Luther's writings on the Sacrament of the Altar. At times one gets the feeling that Koehler would have felt right at home in a Zwinglian church building cleansed of all distractions so that in that plain and bare setting the Word alone could impact the soul. Koehler appreciated hymnody; I find little evidence that he cared much for the liturgy. The liturgy is catholic; hymnody is protestant.[7]

It is interesting to note that the first scholarly article on the history and value of the Lutheran liturgical service did not appear in the *Wisconsin Lutheran Quarterly* until 1938, 34 years after the publication's first issue. Entitled "What Benefits May Be Derived from More Emphasis on the Study of Liturgics," the article was written not by a seminary professor, but by a parish pastor, Gervasius Fischer, who also served on the liturgics subcommittee for *The Lutheran Hymnal* (TLH).[8]

The lack of liturgical leadership became obvious in the publication of Wisconsin Synod's first English hymnal, the *Book of Hymns* (1917). Missouri had published a major English hymnal in 1912, the *Evangelical Lutheran Hymn-Book with Tunes.* Not surprisingly, that volume contained the 1888 Common Service, prepared by east-coast Lutherans and purportedly based on the best and most widely used liturgical orders of the Reformation Era. The Common Service was more than an order of service; it included translations of the Introits, Graduals, and collects for all the Sundays and festivals of the Christian year. The musical settings had been prepared by Luther Reed and Frederick Archer in 1901. The *Book of Hymns* borrowed a few of Reed's and Archer's settings from Missouri's hymnal, but very little else. In fact, a May 1918 article in the *Northwestern*

---

[7] Victor Prange, "Review of J. P. Koehler's *History of the Wisconsin Synod,*" *WELS Historical Institute Journal,* Vol. 1, No. 1 (Spring 1983), p. 40.

[8] *Wisconsin Lutheran Quarterly,* Vol. 35, No. 2 (April 1938), pp. 109-130, and Vol. 36, No.2 (April 1939), pp. 97-118.

Lutheran included a determined defense of the rejection of portions of the Common Service. Despite the fact that the *Agnus Dei* had been attached to the Holy Communion service since at least the second century and was positioned in the Communion liturgy by Luther in both of his orders, the author concluded, "There is very good reason for singing . . . 'O Christ, Thou Lamb of God' immediately after the Confession of Sin; hence we put it there, but omitted it later where it is often found." He followed with another incredulous observation: "We believe the average churchgoer will thank us for not putting in more than one Scripture lesson." With the *Agnus Dei* (or the *Kyrie* in the alternate service) following the Confession of Sins and with only one Scripture lesson, the *Book of Hymns* had no need for either Introits or Graduals. Perhaps this is part of what Martin Albrecht, longtime liturgics professor at Wisconsin Lutheran Seminary, noticed in his early ministry in the 1930s. Asked what he felt was the most significant change in WELS worship practices over his 60 years of service, he said, "When I first entered the ministry, our pastors had no sense of the Christian church year." The liturgical rites in the *Book of Hymns* substantiate his observation.

Almost from its initial publication date, the *Book of Hymns* met with disappointment. Subsequent issues had to include numerous corrections. And there were pastors who were chagrined by the book's liturgical and hymnological poverty. Already by 1925, WELS convention resolutions were looking for something better: an appendix to the *Book of Hymns* containing more and/or better hymns, or perhaps a completely new book, maybe even a joint effort with Missouri and the other synods of the Synodical Conference.

Work on the former suggestion began but was never completed. The latter suggestion eventually led to the joint effort that produced *The Lutheran Hymnal*. The primary work was done over a period of 12 years, from 1929 to 1941. The Wisconsin Synod sent representatives to the meetings—among them seminary professors John Meyer and August Zich and Pastors Otto Hagedorn, Gervasius Fischer, William Schaefer, and Arthur Voss—and these men contributed. Fischer was especially active in the work of the liturgics subcommittee. Several hymn tunes by Fritz Reuter, the renowned Dr. Martin Luther College musician, were included: REUTER (TLH 283) and NEW ULM (TLH 50). The book contained an original hymn text by WELS poet Anna Hoppe: "O'er Jerusalem Thou Weepest" (TLH 419). Several WELS members produced hymn translations. But in the main, *The Lutheran Hymnal* was Missouri's book. The Order of the Holy Communion was essentially the order from the 1912 *Evangelical Lutheran Hymn-Book*, and Wisconsin's men could not prevail upon the Missourians to include some of the WELS favorite hymns, for example, "Jesus, Shepherd of the Sheep" from the *Book of Hymns*. The leadership of the synod sensed a new hymnal was necessary, but old prejudices died hard. When synod president John W. Brenner appointed William Schaefer to the joint committee, Brenner specifically stated, "I want a person on that committee who has both feet in the congregation so that we don't get a monument to the musicians of the Missouri Synod."

Whether or not Brenner's concerns were realized with the publication of the new hymnal is difficult to know. What we do know is that Wisconsin Synod congregations purchased copies of *The Lutheran Hymnal* by the thousands. Northwestern Publishing House encouraged the purchase of the new book with an ingenious offer: During a 15-month window, WELS congregations could purchase the book for the special price of 81 cents on the mere declaration that an equivalent number of older books was being replaced. That was a mighty incentive for thrifty WELS members! Most congregations were willing to make the change for other reasons too. In articles throughout the 1930s, the *Northwestern Lutheran* had done a good job preparing the people for the new hymnal. There were many new hymns, and some of them quickly became popular, for example, "God's Word Is Our Great Heritage" and "For All the Saints." There was enough interaction between WELS and LCMS congregations in those days that many Wisconsin Synod members knew Missouri's Common Service (in fact, more than a few WELS congregations used Missouri's 1912 hymnal). Where the service was less familiar, worshipers remained after services and practiced. While there are no official records to substantiate this, it can be safely said that *The Lutheran Hymnal* was being used in almost every WELS congregation by the end of World War II.

A significant number of WELS congregations, however, usually pastored by synodical veterans, still felt uncomfortable and put off by the new order of service. Martin Albrecht recounted an incident that took place in the fall of 1941 in the sacristy at Calvary, Thiensville, Wisconsin, where he was serving as pastor. He was preparing for the opening service of the Milwaukee pastoral conference and had posted "page 15" (*The Lutheran Hymnal*'s The Order of the Holy Communion) on the hymn board. Just before the service, his district president and the chairman of the synod's Board of Trustees arrived at the sacristy door and suggested that Albrecht not use "that high-church liturgy." Albrecht was not deterred, but the Trustees chairman never did inaugurate the service in his congregation, First German in Manitowoc, Wisconsin. First German's old Mecklenburger rite (in translation, of course) was used until he retired in 1966. Grace Lutheran Church in Yakima, Washington, never did adopt the Holy Communion rite in *The Lutheran Hymnal*; it moved straight from the liturgy in *Book of Hymns* to that of *Christian Worship: A Lutheran Hymnal*! Fifteen years after the publication of *The Lutheran Hymnal*, another district president, Pastor E. Arnold Sitz, was still criticizing the Holy Communion rite in a lengthy essay presented to his Arizona-California District brothers in the mid-1950s. Commenting on the conclusion of *The Lutheran Hymnal*'s Vesper service, he wrote: "This long post-sermon drag merits a short German epithet '*Sopf*' (pigtail)! Not only good liturgical principle, but plain common sense dictates the shears for it."

Younger pastors took to the new hymnal with more enthusiasm, perhaps more out of pragmatism than on principle. *The Lutheran Hymnal* had arrived on the WELS worship scene with auspicious timing. The years after World War II were good years in the synod. The war economy had allowed the synodical debt, so crippling during the 1930s, to finally be retired. Discussions about mission expansion, on both the home and world fronts, highlighted conferences and conventions. English was replacing German at the main Sunday service in most congregations. Elementary schools were growing, and their success soon encouraged the birth of a dozen or more Lutheran high schools. Wherever the Wisconsin Synod went, *The Lutheran Hymnal* went along. Converts, children, and even old-line Germans learned its hymns and liturgy, and various tracts and booklets helped make the hymnal's contents understandable.

Encouraged by growth and a post-war economy, congregations and schools embarked on notable church and chapel projects. The formality of *The Lutheran Hymnal*'s liturgical rite seemed to fit well with the neo-Gothic style, the style of choice for church architects and building committees in the 1940s and 1950s. Dozens of WELS congregations erected churches with high ceilings; long, narrow naves; deep chancels; and notable pulpits, lecterns, and altars. An individual gift enabled Northwestern College, the synod's preseminary institution in Watertown, to erect a fine neo-Gothic chapel in 1955. Eventually that chapel housed a set of stained-glass windows given by Professor Ralph Gehrke in memory of his parents and a Schlicker pipe organ designed by Paul Bunjes, thought by many to be America's leading expert on the classic north-German organ. In the 1950s, through the influence of growing liturgical thought, both an organ and an altar were added to the chapel at the seminary, which for many years had neither.

Already in the 1920s, Professor Koehler had begun encouraging the use of the great hymns of Lutheranism's golden age. Until then these hymns were usually unknown by most WELS members. A weekly class period was devoted to singing and learning the Lutheran chorales (seminary students from the 1920s through the 1980s will recall this class being held in the fifth hour on Wednesday). Koehler encouraged the formation of a male chorus at the seminary and then created an opportunity for the seminary men to form a choir with young women from Lutheran High School in Milwaukee to take these hymns "on the road." (There is evidence that this mixed choir eventually became the Lutheran A Cappella Choir, still active in Milwaukee today.) A similar effort was taking place at Dr. Martin Luther College (DMLC) in New Ulm, Minnesota. Frederick Reuter (d. 1924) had laid the foundation for a solid music education program and had encouraged the teachers he trained to carry out his principles in their congregations by using his own organ and choral compositions. Emil D. Backer (d. 1958) carried on Reuter's work and helped create a musical atmosphere in which the great chorale-based music of classic Lutheranism could flourish. The music of Bach, Schuetz, and Scheidt, with its roots sunk deeply into the Lutheran liturgical rite, was a regular feature of DMLC concert programs and remains so to this day.

Difficult days

The musical scene in the synod's pastor-training track was not as bright, although this was no fault of the man at the center of it, Professor Hilton C. Oswald. Oswald had been called to Northwestern College in the 1930s to teach German and Latin. The fact that he later accepted the position as an editor of the American Edition of *Luther's Works* attests to the reality that the languages remained his first love and interest. Oswald also enjoyed music, however, and was persuaded (with some persistence) to accept the responsibility for Northwestern's band and choirs when Depression realities made it impossible to call a replacement for a departed music director. Oswald's task was formidable.

Northwestern was a predominantly male school; actually, it was two schools, a preparatory school and a college. Many of his "boys" arrived on campus either as ninth graders or college freshmen with little inclination toward music and less training in it. Add to this that during his tenure, first Northwestern's basketball teams and then its football teams gained national recognition. From 1945 until 1960, Oswald also served as director of music at the seminary. He dutifully traveled to Thiensville (Mequon) every Tuesday and rehearsed the choir (at 9:00 P.M.) and taught the courses in hymnology on Wednesdays. Then he returned to Watertown. It is not surprising that musical interest lagged in the pastor track during those years, although this problem dare not be placed at Oswald's feet. Under the best of circumstances, a man would have found it difficult to maintain enthusiasm with students who had no other music teacher for 12 years of school!

If the musical scene at Northwestern College and Wisconsin Lutheran Seminary failed to move pastoral interest forward, unhappy developments in the Lutheran Church—Missouri Synod moved enthusiasm backward.

At first glance, Missouri's worship activities in the 1930s and 1940s hardly seem unhappy. With more innate interest, more financial resources, and more opportunities for scholarship, the Missourians stood at the forefront of efforts to reclaim the rich worship heritage left by the Lutheran reformers. I mentioned previously the reputation of Paul Bunjes in the pipe organ world. Bunjes' doctoral dissertation on the Praetorius organ set the standard and supplied much of the impetus for the *Orgelbewegung*, a worldwide movement that sought to reestablish the dominance of the organ that had been designed to accompany the hymns and music of Lutheran worship. Often working with organ builder Herman Schlicker, Bunjes designed organs for many of Missouri's schools and sensitized a whole generation of students in the Concordia system to the glories of the classical Lutheran instrument. William Heyne, professor at Concordia Seminary, St. Louis, directed the Seminary Male Chorus at the same time he led the St. Louis Bach Choir. Both ensembles regularly supplied the music for the *Lutheran Hour* and its nationwide audience. Heyne's colleague at Concordia, Walter Buszin, earned a solid reputation among Lutherans and non-Lutherans for his scholarly commentaries on Lutheran liturgy and hymnody. Carl Halter at Concordia College, River Forest, Illinois, was the first in a long line of capable and well-loved musical leaders who exerted enormous influence on future LCMS church musicians. Arthur Carl Piepkorn, another St. Louis professor, produced a meticulously researched monograph on the history and use of the liturgical vestments, which was and is recognized as the standard work on the subject.

By any gauge, these men from the Missouri Synod were giants in Lutheran liturgical studies. Most of them carried on their activities within the context of the Lutheran liturgical movement, however, and this is where their work was often compromised and came to be suspect among WELS pastors. Begun in the 1930s, the liturgical movement attracted pastors, teachers, church musicians, and laypeople from various Lutheran synods who were interested in the liturgical, musical, and artistic legacy of orthodox Lutheranism. Unfortunately, many of these individuals were also interested in Lutheran ecumenicity and arrived at conferences and symposiums not only for the study of worship but also to discover how the confessional walls that existed between Lutherans might be broken down. Among those quietly pushing for Lutheran unity were theologians who had begun to accept the conclusions of the historical-critical method of Bible interpretation. One can hardly blame Wisconsin Synod pastors, cautious and conservative by nature (and generally wary of ostentation anyway), for their disapproval of and distaste for the emphases of the Lutheran liturgical movement. Attending the sessions of the Valparaiso Liturgical Institute or subscribing to the publications of the Liturgical Society of St. James could put an ugly brand on a man during the 1940s and 1950s. The essay by Pastor E. Arnold Sitz (cited previously) included this paragraph:

> It is our opinion that men like Dr. Luther Reed of the United Lutheran Church and Dr. Piepkorn of the Missouri Synod have done the Lutheran Church in America grave disservice in departing from the sober-minded and simple dress and ritual of the past century into the labyrinth of the high church movement. Fred Lindemann and many others are pressing so on this high church trend as to insist that the climax of the service can be nothing other than Holy Communion or, as they prefer to term it, the Eucharist, which in itself already gives a biased slant toward Roman Catholic terminology and toward Roman sacramentarianism, from which Luther set us free. Sad to say, they are losing sight of the position Luther rightly took that the Word

is central; also of the stand of Luther that of the two sacraments, Baptism outranks Communion.

There is a story that somehow leaked out of a Wisconsin Lutheran Seminary call meeting that suggests that a certain board member spoke against calling Kurt Eggert to the seminary because wearing the "high church" cassock and surplice (which Eggert wore) rendered him doctrinally "unsafe."

There were a few pastors and teachers in the synod who understood that there was much to learn from the Lutheran liturgical movement and that one need not buy into the ecumenical agenda to learn it. There were few opportunities, however, to share or put into practice what had been learned. The great debate with Missouri was waged during the 1950s, and that debate dominated the scene at conferences and conventions and in the synod's schools and congregations. Hardly anyone in the Wisconsin Synod was left untouched by the battle. Countless families were divided, not only those with Missouri Synod ties but also those who experienced the defection of family members to the Church of the Lutheran Confession. Three of its largest and most historic congregations (Immanuel in Mankato, Minnesota; St. Martin in Winona, Minnesota; and St. John in West Bend, Wisconsin) and dozens of smaller ones left the synod, most to the Church of the Lutheran Confession but some to the Missouri Synod. The president of the seminary resigned. The Synodical Conference disbanded after 91 years of glittering history.

By the time the battle ended—Wisconsin ended its long fellowship with Missouri in 1961—the anti-Missouri spirit was high, and whatever good would come out of Missouri in the area of worship in the years following the break was more or less disregarded by the majority of WELS members. Besides, the synod was ready to go its own way and do its own thing in missions, benevolences, and worship.

New attitudes

If pastors and teachers tend to exert more influence on worship practices than laypeople, then the role of the schools that train pastors and teachers is vital—and the four schools that prepared pastors and teachers in the 1960s witnessed the inauguration of new worship and music leaders. For the first time in its history, the seminary established a full-time liturgics chair in 1962 and called Dr. Martin Luther College's music division head, Professor Martin Albrecht, to fill it. Albrecht reorganized the school's liturgics and church-music curriculum, revitalized the

Seminary Chorus, and kept students up to date on worship activities in the wider Lutheran world. Professor Meilahn Zahn succeeded Albrecht at Dr. Martin Luther College and presided over the expanding music program that was needed to serve a growing student body. Zahn guided the school's choral activities to a new level of sophistication that enabled complete performances of Brahm's "Requiem" and Bach's "St. John Passion." It was during Zahn's tenure that the Memorial Organ was installed in the school's auditorium, a three-manual Casavant organ designed by Paul Bunjes, perhaps the finest instrument in the Wisconsin Synod at the time. Arnold Lehmann, a Northwestern College graduate with a Ph.D. in liturgical history, arrived at his alma mater in 1962. Lehmann grabbed Northwestern's musical reins with dogged determination, insisting on high standards for the school's musical groups, refusing to excuse students from music rehearsals for sports activities (a new experience for this school), and insisting (he stood against the school's most illustrious president on this issue) that a classically voiced pipe organ be placed in the chapel. The fourth of the synod's worker-training schools, Milwaukee Lutheran Teachers' College was born during this era. It began with the objective of supplying more teacher candidates for the synod's overcrowded and understaffed elementary school system. Everything about the school was new and somewhat disorganized, and its first music director often found himself working in less than ideal circumstances. But from his position at the new college, located in the center of the synod's constituency and in view of the synod's administration, Kurt J. Eggert was able not only to serve the greater Milwaukee area, as he had already begun to do (see Professor Ralph Gehrke's contribution to this commemorative volume), but also to influence the synod at large. These four men, and especially Albrecht and Eggert, were to have profound influence on the emerging worship attitudes in the Wisconsin Synod as they trained future pastors and teachers and as they carefully led the church body to new levels of liturgical appreciation.

    Despite its break with the Missouri Synod, the Wisconsin Synod was still dependent on Concordia Publishing House for its hymnal and service books. When Missouri began to consider a revision or replacement of *The Lutheran Hymnal,* therefore, Wisconsin was invited to join the discussions. The 1963 synod convention, reacting to a memorial from the Conference of Presidents and recognizing the need for broad-based involvement in these discussions, authorized the formation of a standing committee on worship. The Commission on Liturgy, Hymnody, and Worship was born with Martin Albrecht (chairman), Kurt Eggert (secretary), and Meilahn Zahn among its original members. At the same time Missouri was moving toward the 1969 publication of *Worship Supplement* (that is, supplemental to *The Lutheran Hymnal*), it also became involved with the Inter-Lutheran Commission on Worship (ILCW), an organization that had as its stated objective the dream of the original Lutheran liturgical movement—a common hymnal for all of North America's Lutherans. Although the Wisconsin Synod did not join the group officially, Albrecht and Eggert began attending the Chicago sessions of the ILCW in 1965.

After Martin Albrecht arrived at the seminary and as he began to chair the Commission on Worship, he and Kurt Eggert formed an interesting partnership. Their personal and social interests were not the same—Albrecht was Eggert's senior by 14 years—but their individual abilities were complementary. Albrecht was the technician; Eggert was the artist. Eggert wrote the music, and Albrecht scribed it with his meticulous hand. Eggert philosophized, and Albrecht summarized. Eggert stood on the front lines encouraging the synod to reclaim its worship and musical legacy and to strive for catholicity in form and excellence in performance. To this effort Albrecht supplied his substantial reputation and thereby allowed a discussion of worship issues to be considered legitimate and prudent. Each man, in his own way, influenced a slow change in the worship attitudes of the Wisconsin Synod. Professor Albrecht, by his 19-year tenure at Dr. Martin Luther College (1943–1962) and his long association with the seminary, had personal contact with thousands of pastors and teachers. He was, in fact, a graduate of both schools. Because he edited music for church choirs and produced the very popular "Our Favorite Hymns" series (some 3,000 cassette tapes were sold over 30 years), his name was well known to many who had never met him. Choir tours carried him to WELS congregations from Tacoma to Miami and from Tucson to Ottawa. Choir members sensed that someone knew him well at every church on the itinerary. Eggert's sphere of personal influence was narrower but perhaps conceptually deeper. Those who came under his influence tended to attach themselves to him and his priorities with intense loyalty. He set high standards for those who followed him, and never being quite convinced that the best had been achieved, he encouraged them to strive for what was better. This quality was especially obvious in his work with the Lutheran Chorale of Milwaukee, a choir of WELS members from various churches that he directed for 36 years.

The *Worship Supplement* was published in 1969, and the Commission on Worship analyzed the book's contents and shared its resources with the synod on the pages of its publication, *Focus on Worship*. The new supplement did not enjoy wide use. It was in the pews at the seminary and at the Wisconsin Lutheran Chapel in Madison and was used by the choirs at Dr. Martin Luther College, but it was not purchased by Northwestern College or by any congregation known to this author. It was not above suspicion, either; seminary students often referred to it as "the worthless supplement" (it was from Missouri, after all). Its influence was deep, however, deeper than anyone might have expected in 1969. It exposed future pastors and teachers to dozens of new hymns, among them the hymns of Martin and Werner Franzmann, and to many fine old hymns as well. The book's service orders notated the liturgical chants for both the congregation and the pastor, something WELS members had not seen before, and a few pastors gained permission to copy these services for experimentation at pastor and teacher conferences. The book included prayers arranged for leader and congregation, another concept that seemed innovative in 1969. The *Worship Supplement*'s contemporary setting of the Matins was regularly used in the seminary chapel.

The *Worship Supplement* was never intended as a replacement for *The Lutheran Hymnal*, and it became obvious to the Commission on Worship that the final product of the ILCW probably would not be acceptable to the Wisconsin Synod. (As it turned out, *Lutheran Book of Worship*, completed in 1978, was not acceptable to the Missouri Synod either.) The commission did analyze the ILCW's revision of the Christian calendar and its proposed three-year lectionary. A committee chaired by Pastor Victor Prange advised the 1974 synod convention that nothing stood in the way of using the new calendar and lectionary. The convention agreed, and soon thereafter Northwestern Publishing House began printing the lessons from the three-year cycle on the back of its bulletin covers. The Commission on Worship determined that its wisest course of action was to prepare materials to supplement *The Lutheran Hymnal*. Contemporary translations of the historic collects and Graduals were produced. The commission developed a new concept for the Introit (psalm sections were placed between hymn stanzas) and shared several sets of these with the synod. In 1971 the commission produced a booklet entitled *Service of the Word,* which contained a new rite for Holy Baptism and a set of responsive General Prayers besides a worship order for services at which Holy Communion was not offered. Plans for a booklet offering new hymns were begun but never brought to completion.

There was a certain urgency in the Commission on Worship's work in the late 1960s and early 1970s. Mission expansion was occurring at a breakneck pace in the southern, northeastern, and southwestern regions of the United States, and evangelism efforts were attracting many people who were not Lutheran from birth. The synod was on the verge of going from 9 districts to 12. "In every state by '78" was a quasi-official synodical motto. Old-line city congregations gave birth to daughter congregations in the suburbs as their members moved away from the central city. Congregations located in rural communities for their entire history became located in bedroom communities without changing their addresses. A hymnal that contained old English language, old English script, less than a dozen 20th-century hymns, and no liturgical canticles newer than 1750 began to seem somewhat out of sync with the space age. Pastors began looking for something more relevant. They looked for hymns in a variety of resources, many decidedly non-Lutheran. Homemade orders of service proliferated. It seemed occasionally that the synod was living in the liturgical period of the judges, "where everyone did what was right in his own eyes." The commission sensed that a new hymnal was vital if the synod was going to avoid a liturgical chaos it had experienced at the beginning of its history.

As the 1980s dawned, there was some hope that Missouri Synod's new hymnal, *Lutheran Worship,* could be adopted or at least adapted by the Wisconsin Synod. Pastoral conferences studied the new volume in earnest after its 1982 publication. But the book's thick liturgical section simply highlighted the long-standing differences between worship concepts and practices in the Wisconsin and Missouri Synods. Once again, Wisconsin might have been willing to accept Missouri's hymns but not its liturgies. Although the concern ran deep in many places that Wisconsin lacked the talent to produce its own hymnal and the necessary accompanying publications, the Commission on Worship recommended to the 1983 convention that the synod embark on the production of its own hymnal. As they say, the rest is history, and Victor Prange tells the story of *Christian Worship: A Lutheran Hymnal* elsewhere in this commemorative volume.

Conclusion

One wonders what Johannes Muehlhaeuser would think were he to visit his Grace Church 150 years after its founding. The worship rite used twice every month in the four weekend services with Holy Communion is *Christian Worship*'s Service of Word and Sacrament, which purports itself to be "a version of the historic liturgy of the Christian Church." Grace's two pastors are vested in alb and stole and regularly chant the liturgy. The Psalm and Verse of the Day are sung by a cantor, a children's choir, or one of several adult choirs. The Hymn of the Day is always sung in its historic liturgical position, connected to the Gospel and Sermon. Processions with crucifix and candles begin worship on festival days. By any gauge, "the rite of the old Lutheran church" is in place at the congregation Muehlhaeuser founded. Although he died apparently convinced that his synod's move toward a more confessional position was the right move, we're guessing he would react to worship at Grace with a frown.

One wonders what Kurt Eggert would think were he to have attended either the 1996 or 1999 version of the National Conference on Worship, Music, and the Arts, sponsored by the Commission on Worship he served for so many years. He would have witnessed many of the historic Christian and Lutheran rites he had endeavored to restore. He would have experienced rituals that, while new to his synod, he knew had edified countless Christians in many eras and many places. He would have listened to music that may finally have met the standards he had set in his mind but was not always able to achieve in his concerts. He would have noticed the chasubles, chanting, candles, and crucifixes! And he would have observed the joy that this worship elicited from several thousand Wisconsin Synod participants. By any standard, the attitude of the synod that Eggert served has changed over 150 years. How would he react? We're guessing he would react with an incredulous smile!

On the other hand, he might have expected the change. He might have supposed that an appreciation for a rich liturgical life would eventually flow from his synod's love of the Scriptures and its commitment to the doctrines of the Reformation and the Lutheran Confessions. He might have expected attitudes to change as the synod overcame the prejudices of its early history and began to do the work of worship on the basis of its own studies and perspectives. He might have sensed that *Christian Worship: A Lutheran Hymnal* would effect such changes. Such was the desire he had in the Introduction, which he wrote: "May [the hymnal's] use among us foster and strengthen appreciation of liturgical worship and enrich and enliven our relationship with God and each other." He might have longed to see the fruits of his labor, but the Lord took him to heaven, where the richest sort of worship is more than a dream; it's a reality.

The Shaping of
Christian Worship: A Lutheran Hymnal

Victor H. Prange

Early in the process leading to the publication of *Christian Worship: A Lutheran Hymnal*, project director Kurt Eggert presented an essay titled "The Shaping of the New Hymnal." This essay was read at the fall 1984 meeting of the Confessional Lutheran Forum. Eggert described the significance and the difficulty of the hymnal project in the opening paragraphs of that essay:

> Before us lies a task of considerable dimension and unusual importance. The hymnal is our major resource and guide for congregational worship. It is a book for all the people, handled by more of our members in the course of a week than the Bible.... The preparation of such a book poses considerable challenge, and we have no specific experience in producing a hymnal. However, we trust the Lord will provide sufficient talent and ability, willingness and dedication, to produce a hymnal for our Christians of today and tomorrow which will constitute a significant improvement over our present hymnal.[1]

Kurt Eggert did not live to see how the hymnal he did so much to shape was received by the members of the Wisconsin Evangelical Lutheran Synod (WELS). They received it in a way that would have thrilled and surprised him; it was a reception far beyond anything he had envisioned. The hymnal is shaping the worship life of many believers, young and old, and will continue to do so in the future. To honor the memory of this talented man of God who did so much to nurture and improve the worship life of our synod, this story of the shaping of *Christian Worship: A Lutheran Hymnal* is recounted.

A new hymnal needed

One can point to the year 1959 as the genesis of the hymnal project. That's when the Lutheran Church—Missouri Synod (LCMS) extended an invitation to the members of the Synodical Conference to

---

[1] Published in the *Wisconsin Lutheran Quarterly*, Vol. 82, No. 2 (Spring 1985), pp. 114-140.

share in a revision of *The Lutheran Hymnal* (TLH). Many of the new materials for this contemplated revision were published in the 1969 *Worship Supplement,* a book that substantially influenced future Lutheran hymnals.

The focus for the Missouri Synod changed in 1965 from a revision of *The Lutheran Hymnal* to the production of a totally new hymnal together with the other Lutheran church bodies in America. The Inter-Lutheran Commission on Worship (ILCW) was formed, and in 1978 the *Lutheran Book of Worship* (LBW) was published. The Wisconsin Synod was not a member of the ILCW but did observe the work being done to produce this new hymnal. Though the Missouri Synod was a member of the ILCW, it declined to endorse *Lutheran Book of Worship* and in 1982 published its own revised version called *Lutheran Worship* (LW).

In the words of Kurt Eggert, this "unpredictable series of events . . . led to some frustration on the part of the WELS Commission on Worship [CW]." With hope that *Lutheran Book of Worship* and later *Lutheran Worship* might be suitable for use in the synod, the commission waited and spent the time in working on a new non-Communion service (Service of the Word) and in revising some of the propers for trial use. When it became apparent that *Lutheran Book of Worship* would not serve our congregations, the synod resolved to publish its own supplement to the hymnal, *The Worship Companion*. This project was derailed when Missouri's decision to publish *Lutheran Worship* gave renewed hope for a hymnal suitable for our use.

The 1979 WELS Convention directed the synod's Commission on Worship "to continue a careful study and review of the proposed *Lutheran Worship*."[2] For the next several years this study became the focus of the commission's work. The results of this evaluation were reported in some detail to the 1981 convention.[3] Members of the commission recognized that *Lutheran Worship* has merit but also certain flaws that made it impossible for them to recommend the hymnal's use in WELS congregations. The commission was convinced "that a new hymnal is a vital worship need in our congregations." The convention agreed, resolving "that the synod at this time recognize that there is a growing need for a new hymnal within the next decade."[4]

---

[2] 1979 WELS *Proceedings*, p. 194.

[3] 1981 WELS Reports and Memorials for the Forty-Sixth Biennial Convention (BORAM), pp. 210-216.

[4] 1981 *Proceedings*, p. 157.

The Commission on Worship prepared a document for distribution at the 1982 district conventions titled "Guidelines: A Study Guide Looking toward Hymnal Revision for the WELS." This booklet first of all carefully reviewed the need for a new hymnal, citing specific hymn and liturgical concerns. There were also some paragraphs titled "The Language of Our Worship." Section II of the booklet was a study guide for *Lutheran Worship*. In this booklet one hears the voice of Kurt Eggert speaking: "Let us be bold enough and wise enough to set about providing a hymnal that will as fully as possible reflect our heritage, enfold the best of contemporary forms and worship materials, and invite us and our children to lift up our hearts and voices in praise to God and proclaim with joy the mighty works that he has done" (p. 6). The Commission on Worship concluded: "We need a new hymnal" (p. 27).

The 1983 synod convention authorizes a new/revised hymnal

The 1983 WELS Convention was held at Dr. Martin Luther College, New Ulm, Minnesota. Floor Committee No. 8 (publications), chaired by Forrest Bivens, had the responsibility of studying the report of the Commission on Worship. The committee recognized the immediate need to shape a new hymnal and submitted the following series of resolutions to the synod convention:

> That the synod now begin work on a new/revised hymnal of its own, one that under the blessings of God will be scripturally sound and edifying, welcomed and judged to be highly satisfactory for purposes of devotion and worship by a majority of our members, in harmony with the character and heritage of our church body, and will reflect the larger perspective and mainstream of the worship of the Christian church.
>
> That the Conference of Presidents, in this biennium, call a full-time project director for the new/revised hymnal.
>
> That the Conference of Presidents, in consultation with the project director and the Commission on Worship, appoint the committee members deemed necessary for the development of our new/revised hymnal.
>
> That the Coordinating Council and the Board of Trustees give this project high priority within the total work program of the synod.

> That each congregation, throughout the development of the new/revised hymnal, periodically receive samples of prepared materials—both liturgies and hymns—for their trial use, evaluation, and response.
>
> That we invite and seek to involve ELS representatives in the preparation of the new/revised hymnal in a manner agreeable to both parties.[5]

The delegates to the 1983 synod convention approved all of these resolutions. They agreed that a new hymnal was needed.

Shaping the organization for the hymnal project

In order to move the hymnal project along, Northwestern Publishing House (NPH) offered to fund the project director's salary and housing and provide office space and secretarial help. This allowed the Conference of Presidents to issue a divine call in January 1984. There was little question that Pastor Kurt Eggert would be the one chosen for this position. After some initial hesitancy because of his desire to remain as pastor of Atonement Lutheran Church, Milwaukee, Eggert accepted this call. He was installed as hymnal project director by synod president Carl Mischke on the Tuesday after Easter 1984, in a service at Atonement. Victor Prange, who replaced Eggert as a voting member of the Commission on Worship, preached the sermon based on the words of the *Gloria in Excelsis* (Luke 2:14) and titled "Celebrate a New Beginning."

Eggert's first task was to work with the Commission on Worship in shaping the organization that would produce the new hymnal. He consulted with several synodical leaders to discuss how best to accomplish this challenging task. His recommendations were included in a five-page report that he made to the commission on August 3–4, 1984. The commission approved the following resolutions that outlined the organization:

> That there be two committees of six members each: the Hymn Committee and the Liturgy Committee.
>
> That the Liturgy Committee divide its work into two subcommittees, one dealing with orders of worship and the other dealing with propers, rites, calendar, lectionary, and other liturgical materials.

---

[5] *1983 Proceedings,* pp. 90-92.

That the Hymn Committee be divided into a hymn-text committee and a hymn-music committee.

That the Commission on Worship (CW), in consultation with the project director, propose candidates from outside the CW membership to serve as chairmen of the Hymn and Liturgy Committees. These candidates are to be proposed to the Conference of Presidents for their approval and appointment.

That the responsibility of each subcommittee chairman shall be to direct the work of the subcommittee and report to the CW.

That the committee chairmen be given the privilege of the vote on hymnal decisions.

That each subcommittee include one member of the CW.[6]

A critical organizational question, which later provoked some heated debate, was this: Who has the final decision concerning what will be included in the new hymnal? At first the Commission on Worship granted this voting privilege only to its own members and the four subcommittee chairmen (see the second last resolution above). In so doing, the commission failed to follow the recommendation that Eggert had made at its April 1984 meeting: "That for purposes of approval and decision on materials produced or selected for the new hymnal, the *Commission on Worship* and the *full membership of the Hymnal Committee (WELS members)* constitute the decision-making body."[7] In August 1986 the commission reversed its initial resolution and gave "each of the members of the CW and the two committees equal voice and vote in approving of materials for inclusion in the hymnal."[8]

The original organization also failed to designate one person as chairman when the two committees met jointly. For a time the chairmen of the Hymn and Liturgy Committees rotated this assignment, but this did not work out well. Finally the chairman of the Commission on Worship served also as the chairman when the two committees met jointly. In the course of time this larger group, at first called the Hymnal Committee, was named the Joint Hymnal

---

[6]CW minutes, August 3–4, 1984.

[7]Eggert, "Development of the Hymnal Project," April 6, 1984, p. 2.

[8]CW minutes, August 29–30, 1986, p. 1; the vote on this motion was 4 to 2.

Committee (JHC), which made it easier to distinguish the group from the Hymn Committee.[9]

Appointment of the members of the Joint Hymnal Committee

The 1983 synod resolution stated "that the Conference of Presidents, in consultation with the project director and the Commission on Worship, appoint the committee members deemed necessary for the development of our new/revised hymnal." Finding the right people to produce the new hymnal was a critical task.

Eggert wrote to all the ordained clergy of the synod requesting the "names of pastors, teachers, and laypersons who have *exceptional* talent or knowledge in one of the following categories: *(a)* all-around knowledge and good judgment in the area of worship; *(b)* creativity in preparing or arranging services of worship; *(c)* facility in writing prayers for worship; *(d)* ability in writing new hymn texts; *(e)* ability in translating hymn texts from the German; *(f)* ability in composing hymn tunes; *(g)* ability in harmonization of hymn tunes; *(h)* exceptional ability as organist; *(i)* exceptional ability as choir director; *(j)* ability as a writer, sensitive in the use of language."[10] This search produced a long list of persons suggested as having the kind of talents needed for the project.

In October the Commission on Worship recommended to the Conference of Presidents the names of eight persons to serve on the Hymn and Liturgy Committees. The seven who accepted the appointments were Mark Jeske, Iver Johnson, Harlyn Kuschel, Arnold Lehmann, Kermit Moldenhauer, James Tiefel, and David Valleskey.[11] Three members of the commission also agreed to serve on one of the committees: Bruce Backer, Theodore Hartwig, and Victor Prange. The two vacancies were filled at the December meeting with the appointments of Richard Buss and James Fricke.[12] James Fricke was designated as chairman of the Hymn Committee; David Valleskey, as chairman of the Liturgy Committee. The remaining members of the Commission on Worship at that time, Martin Albrecht, Elfred Bloedel, and Gordon Pape, also attended the joint meetings of the two committees.

---

[9]In this essay the term *Joint Hymnal Committee* will be used whenever there is a reference to what at first was called the Hymnal Committee.

[10]Report to the Commission on Worship, August 3–4, 1984, p. 2.

[11]CW minutes, October 5, 1984, p. 1.

[12]CW minutes, December 7, 1984, p. 2.

In the course of time there were several changes in the Joint Hymnal Committee personnel. Early on, David Valleskey was forced to resign because of the press of other duties. His place was taken by Wayne Schulz, and Victor Prange became chairman of the Liturgy Committee. When James Fricke resigned from the JHC, he was replaced by Loren Schaller on the Hymn Committee, with Richard Buss designated as the chairman. In the summer of 1987, Martin Albrecht retired as chairman of the Commission on Worship, and James Tiefel was appointed as his replacement on the commission. Victor Prange was elected commission chairman and also began to chair the JHC meetings. Theodore Hartwig was appointed Liturgy Committee chairman. James Engel served a brief time as hymnal music editor before the Lord called him to his heavenly glory on April 17, 1989. When Kermit Moldenhauer accepted the call as full-time hymnal music editor, his place on the Hymn Committee was taken by Elfred Bloedel. Joining the Commission on Worship in later years and serving on the JHC were C. T. Aufdemberge, Carl Nolte, and David Prillwitz. Mark Jeske and Carl Nolte served as JHC secretaries.

The members of the four subcommittees were organized as follows (parentheses indicate members who resigned or were replaced):

1. Hymn-text committee 1: Richard Buss, (James Fricke), Mark Jeske, Loren Schaller
2. Hymn-tune committee 2: Bruce Backer, Elfred Bloedel, Harlyn Kuschel, (Kermit Moldenhauer)
3. Liturgy committee (major rites): Theodore Hartwig, Iver Johnson, chairman, James Tiefel
4. Liturgy committee (minor rites): Arnold Lehmann, Victor Prange, Wayne Schulz, (David Valleskey)

In the early stages of the project, the Hymn and Liturgy Committees met jointly; later they divided into the two subcommittees. The procedure set up for final adoption of materials to be included in the hymnal had these steps: (1) approval of item by subcommittee and distribution to Hymn or Liturgy Committee; (2) approval of item by Hymn/Liturgy Committee and distribution to the JHC; (3) initial approval of item by the JHC; (4) selected critical review with possible field-testing; (5) evaluation of critical review, field-testing, and suggestions for revision; (6) final approval by the JHC and final copy for the printer.[13] Often items

---

[13] JHC minutes, January 2, 1987, p. 1 (referring to Prange's letter of December 11, 1986, to the JHC).

presented to the JHC were referred back several times to the subcommittees for further study and revision. This procedure allowed for a careful evaluation of all items finally included in the hymnal. Some proposals that came to the JHC were accepted by common consent, but many matters had to be decided by majority vote. Decisions were seldom unanimous on either major or minor questions on which there was disagreement.

Members of the JHC not only spent many hours together in meetings, but they also came to know each other very well by conversing informally, especially over food and drink. This provided an opportunity to talk things over when difficult decisions had to be made. One downside of frequenting restaurants was the lament Prange sounded on more than one occasion in his diary: "ate too much." Despite a lot of hard work and some distressing situations, the experience of participating in shaping the hymnal was regarded by all members of the JHC as a wonderful privilege.

Meetings of the Joint Hymnal Committee

Orientation for members of the Joint Hymnal Committee took place at the Ramada Sands Motel, Milwaukee, on January 17–18, 1985. At the Thursday evening dinner meeting, synod president Carl Mischke welcomed the newly formed committee and reminded them of the important task that was before them. The keynote address was given by James Schaefer, editor of the *Northwestern Lutheran*. Kurt Eggert spoke on the topic "Surveying the Task Ahead." It is interesting to note that Mischke, Schaefer, and Eggert were classmates. Mischke and Schaefer were very supportive of the effort to shape a new hymnal. This dinner meeting gave all members of the JHC an opportunity to become acquainted with each other. One person's evaluation of the evening was, "Got to meet everyone, and I think it is a good crew."[14]

The Joint Hymnal Committee had a full agenda the next day, including three formal essays delivered by members of the Commission on Worship. Hartwig described the strengths and weaknesses of *The Lutheran Hymnal;* Backer outlined ways in which he felt the hymn section could be improved; Prange did the same for the liturgical section. Prange reminded the JHC that producing a new hymnal was only a first step in improving worship in the Wisconsin Synod, pointing out that

---

[14]Prange diary, January 17, 1985.

"when we have finished the task of producing a hymnal, then really the work has only begun. . . . We will not better our worship if only we have produced a better liturgical section and a better selection of hymns and tunes. The forms lie as dead music and words until they are put to good use. Our pastors and organists need to become more aware of how to lead worship in a better way."[15]

A significant item on the agenda was the series of questions posed by project director Eggert. These questions deserve to be quoted in full because they highlight in a very specific way the task that lay before the JHC and some of the pitfalls the members would likely encounter along the way.

1. For whom are we preparing the new hymnal?
2. How will contemporary needs be reflected in the new book?
3. What principles will guide the language change in the liturgies? in the hymns?
4. What kind of balance is desirable between the liturgical and hymn sections?
5. What kind of changes should be effected in the collects and prayers?
6. How large dare the hymnal be?
7. What set of principles will guide the selection of hymns?
8. Which factors will guide us in determining the number and nature of liturgies?
9. Will chants be provided for the pastor's part in any of the liturgies or portions of them?
10. If new music is produced for a liturgy, of what sort should it be?
11. How will we provide for congregations with small musical resources (no choir) and also for those well-endowed?
12. Should special consideration be given in the hymnal for mission churches or those with a large number of members from a non-Lutheran background?
13. On what basis will the hymn sections in the hymnal be balanced?

---

[15]Prange, "Improving the Liturgical Section for the New Hymnal," January 18, 1985, p. 4.

14. How much revision can or should be undertaken in the pages 5 and 15 liturgy?
15. Will psalms be used in the Sunday service?
16. If so, what musical provision will be made for their singing by the choir? by the congregation?
17. Shall pronouns for the Godhead be capitalized?
18. How much consideration should be given to the use of the hymnal for devotional or educational purposes?
19. What kinds of materials should be field-tested?
20. Which factors need to be considered in deciding on the basic type of hymn harmonizations?
21. What will the guidelines be for lowering the pitches in hymns or liturgies?
22. If the new three-year lectionary is basic for the new book, what provision will be made for the present one-year series?
23. For what reasons will the Catechism be included or omitted in the hymnal?
24. Which rites should be included in the hymnal: Baptism? Confirmation? Marriage? Burial?
25. What principles will guide decisions on revised wording for common texts such as the Creeds, Lord's Prayer, *Te Deum,* etc.?
26. Will more chorales be included? Fewer?
27. Will hymn types not now represented in TLH be included?
28. What guideline will determine the arrangement of hymns in the new book?
29. What factors should determine the length of hymns?
30. How much importance should be attached to keeping hymn texts or tunes from LW or LBW unchanged?
31. What will we do when congregations are strongly in favor of including certain hymns and we are strongly in favor of exclusion?
32. What will be the name for the new hymnal and the color of its cover?
33. How long will this list eventually be?[16]

---

[16]Eggert, "Guidelines for the New Hymnal," January 18, 1985, pp. 1,2.

At the next meeting of the Joint Hymnal Committee on February 21, 1985, Eggert's list had grown longer. In preparation for that meeting, he sent to the committee members a list of 47 questions for their consideration. One of Eggert's unique contributions throughout the hymnal project was his ability to raise searching questions. Sometimes committee members grew impatient at the slow pace that resulted because of the need to answer these questions, but in the end it proved highly beneficial.

A final agenda item at the January orientation meeting was the opportunity given to each of the appointed members of the JHC to briefly address this topic: "The Kind of Hymnal I Would Like." Several mentioned the need to offer more variety. One person scored the liturgy rather severely: "A new hymnal must improve over the old in the area of liturgy. Especially in sounding out younger people or newcomers to our Lutheran worship, I find that to them our present liturgy is often illogical, tedious, and boring . . . rather than joyful response to the means of grace." Prange noted this in his diary on January 18, 1985: "I was the defender of the liturgy much of the day." This suggests that there was much criticism of the liturgical section of *The Lutheran Hymnal*. Other suggestions for the new hymnal were to include a collection of practical prayers and responsive prayers, to make more use of the Psalms, to have good chant tunes, to avoid making the hymnal provincial, and to have the largest possible typeface.

Eggert would have supported the observation of one member of the JHC that "the pastor is still, in most cases, the key to a congregation's worship life. If he is interested in worship, he will offer a richer worship no matter what appears in our new hymnal. If he is not interested, he will not offer any enrichment even though there is richness in a hymnal."

The initial meeting of the JHC concluded with the Hymn and Liturgy Committees meeting to review their specific assignments. Eggert outlined for each of them a proposed schedule and suggested some basic procedures. This orientation meeting set in high gear the shaping of a new hymnal. It was most beneficial for all members of the Joint Hymnal Committee. After that initial meeting, the JHC had 17 more plenary sessions over the next eight years.

ELS representatives and their role in the hymnal project

The 1983 synod convention, which authorized the hymnal project, also resolved "that we invite and seek to involve ELS representatives in the preparation of the new/revised hymnal in a manner agreeable to both parties." The Evangelical Lutheran Synod (ELS) designated Walter Gullixson, Paul Madson, and Erling Teigen to be their representatives. These men were invited to attend the orientation meeting and future meetings of the JHC as advisory members.

At the February 28, 1985, meeting of the JHC, Teigen presented an essay, "The Worship Tradition of the *Lutheran Hymnary*." The minutes for that meeting note that "it was a thorough, detailed discussion of the historical background of the *Hymnary*, paying particular attention to the areas where the *Hymnary* differs from the TLH liturgy, for example, opening and closing prayers, confession and absolution, and the order of the liturgy for Holy Communion." In January 1986 Teigen presented ELS concerns and perspectives for the hymn section. He presented two lists compiled by the ELS Worship Committee: one listed 20 "most urgently desired" hymns from the *Hymnary* that do not appear in *The Lutheran Hymnal*, and another listed 25 "desirable" hymns.[17]

Over the years Teigen and especially Gullixson attended quite a few meetings of the JHC and took an active part in the discussions. However, it became increasingly evident that neither the hymn or liturgy sections of the new WELS hymnal would include items that the ELS desired. This ultimately led the Evangelical Lutheran Synod to publish their own hymnal in 1996, the *Evangelical Lutheran Hymnary*.

Regional meetings in the fall of 1985

Among Eggert's initial proposals was what he termed "focus meetings." He wrote: "After considerable pondering, I am convinced that small group meetings of pastors, teachers, and laypersons knowledgeable in the area of worship and church music would be valuable. Such meetings held in the various areas and districts of our synod would have the following objectives: (1) Satisfy the general expectation for input from the synodical membership. (2) Give us some in-depth opinion and reaction on the proposed hymnal from those with the most knowledge and background in worship and music. (3) Provide us with firsthand information about prospective members of the hymnal committees and a pool of prospects for other needs."[18]

---

[17]JHC minutes, January 3, 1986, p. 2.
[18]Report to the Commission on Worship, August 3, 1984, p. 4.

Five such focus meetings were held in various regions of the synod in fall 1985: Winona, Minnesota (September 27,28); Detroit, Michigan (October 21,22); Denver, Colorado (November 4,5); Milwaukee, Wisconsin (November 8,9); and Fond du Lac, Wisconsin (November 22,23). Those leading the sessions in addition to Eggert were JHC members Jeske, Kuschel, Moldenhauer, and Prange; Gordon Snyder also served as one of the leaders. An average of 30 persons attended each of the meetings.

Break-out groups responded to four requests: (1) list the strengths of *The Lutheran Hymnal*; (2) list the weaknesses of *The Lutheran Hymnal*; (3) list hymn-section improvements you would like to see; (4) list liturgy-section improvements you would like to see. An additional work session asked the participants to rank the most significant responses in each of these four categories. A long list of suggestions was compiled that was available to the Joint Hymnal Committee as it shaped the new hymnal.[19]

A concluding plenary session provided an opportunity to discuss several special questions and concerns: (1) What revisions should be made to the pages 5 and15 liturgy of *The Lutheran Hymnal*? (2) How can our congregational worship be improved? (3) What can be done to prepare congregations for the new hymnal? Finally, those present were encouraged to bring up any other question they wanted discussed. These regional meetings provided an excellent opportunity for worship leaders in our synod to share their ideas with the JHC about how to shape the new hymnal.

The Liturgy Committee

The Liturgy Committee met for the first time separate from the Hymn Committee on March 1, 1985. Eggert had prepared an agenda that outlined the work that lay before the committee. He listed as the ultimate goal "a significantly improved liturgical section." He went on to spell out some general objectives: (1) retain from *The Lutheran Hymnal* what appears to be eminently satisfactory for today and the next 25 or 30 years, revising where necessary; (2) drop or replace what appears to be unsatisfactory, providing alternate materials by borrowing from other hymnals or creating new; (3) provide entirely new liturgies or forms where it is deemed useful.

---

[19]Eggert compiled a 44-page report of these suggestions, listing them for each of the five regional meetings. This report is in the synod archives.

To accomplish these objectives, the following procedures were suggested: (1) review liturgical contents of *The Lutheran Hymnal*, noting problem areas and other concerns; (2) study *Lutheran Worship* and *Lutheran Book of Worship* carefully for possible alternatives or new materials; (3) review liturgical sections of other hymnals; (4) draw up a preliminary table of liturgical contents for the new hymnal.

In the first few meetings of the Liturgy Committee, these suggestions of Eggert were carried out. The entire liturgical section of *The Lutheran Hymnal* was reviewed and evaluated. In June 1985 the Liturgy Committee presented to the JHC a proposed list of items from *The Lutheran Hymnal* to retain (usually with revisions), to drop, and to hold for a future decision.[20] This report sparked considerable debate and served its purpose of starting the discussion as to what shape the new hymnal's liturgical section should take.

The Hymn Committee

Eggert had also outlined some objectives and procedures for the Hymn Committee, also meeting on March 1, 1985. He proposed that the committee (1) prepare a set of guidelines for the ideal hymn section for our new book; (2) retain from *The Lutheran Hymnal* the hymns that are eminently worthy, historically important, strongly in use, or adjudged to be necessary for a special reason, revising hymns where deemed necessary; (3) add new hymns of *good quality* as needed to accommodate the church year and topical balance; (4) drop hymns used very seldom and not fitting any of the categories mentioned in objective 2 above; drop hymns to make room for definitely superior hymns; (5) decide on church year and topical headings for the sections; (6) revise, on the basis of agreed guidelines, hymn texts where necessary; (7) determine, on the basis of agreed guidelines, which tunes or settings need revision or replacement and prepare new tunes and harmonizations; (8) refine the hymn list (review "expendable" hymns) on the basis of available space, balance in church year and various topical sections, and the desirability of increasing or decreasing the number of hymns of a certain character or from a certain era.

In order to determine which hymns to retain, add, or drop, Eggert suggested a rating system. First, all the hymns in *The Lutheran Hymnal* would be reviewed and rated by the committee. Then hymns from

---

[20]Progress report of the Liturgy Committee to the JHC, June 3–4, 1985.

Lutheran Worship and *Lutheran Book of Worship* would be reviewed in the same way. Attention would also be given in a less thorough way to non-Lutheran hymnals in order to find excellent hymns that may have been overlooked. Finally, hymn suggestions from the Evangelical Lutheran Synod and new hymns from WELS sources would be reviewed and rated.

The committee decided to use a rating system with *5* being the best and *1* the poorest. The long task of reviewing hymns from various hymnals was carried out in 1985 and 1986.[21] With six committee members voting, the best rating a hymn could receive was a *30*. Another important factor in developing the master hymn list was the 1984 survey of WELS congregations, asking pastors to report how many times each hymn in *The Lutheran Hymnal* had been used that year. After receiving the survey results, the Hymn Committee reviewed its original ratings, "giving special attention to those TLH hymns rated 16 or lower by the committee with a WELS-use rating of 200+ as well as those rated from 22 to 30 by the committee with a WELS-use rating of 400+."[22] This rating system and congregational hymn use survey proved to be highly useful to the Joint Hymnal Committee in shaping the master list for the hymn section.

Language changes

One of the most critical issues faced by both the Hymn and Liturgy Committees was updating language. Eggert provides an excellent summary of the issues: "It is necessary to view the hymnal against the backdrop of a changing worship language, from the KJV Bible to the NIV Bible, from the Elizabethan language of the Book of Common Prayer to the language spoken today in America. This is a widespread change in Christian churches, not a product of the Hymnal Committees. It is a change that has already taken place in most WELS churches. We are not *initiating* change, we are merely *recognizing* it. . . . It should not be a huge shock if the liturgies adopted today's English. What is also happening is that common prayers or texts such as the *Te Deum,* the Creeds, the Lord's Prayer, the *Venite,* the *Magnificat,* the *Gloria in Excelsis,* the *Nunc Dimittis,* etc., are struggling to find a common text. It may take another

---

[21]The report of the Hymn Committee to the JHC at the January 2–3, 1987, meeting lists all of the hymnals reviewed. A total of about 1,200 hymns were rated.

[22]Hymn Committee progress report to the JHC, August 13, 1987, p. 2.

generation to settle into the same kind of agreement as we have had in the past."[23]

In an editorial in the *Northwestern Lutheran,* Prange discussed "The Language of Worship." In response to the charge that our modern worship language is "too plain and lacks dignity," he observes that "in fact our English language today is less ornate compared with Shakespeare's day. The King James translation, made when Shakespeare was in his prime, is more literary than most contemporary Bible translations. There was opportunity for more variety in Elizabethan English. One example is the second person pronoun. The King James translation works with eight different forms of the second person pronoun: thou, thy, thee, thine, ye, you, your, yours. A modern translator is limited to three: you, your, yours. This results in language which is flatter, tending to monotony when often used as in the liturgy. It is a price which must be paid if we would speak the language of today."[24]

Prange concludes: "What is the proper language of worship? Our goal must be to use the best possible contemporary English. It must be language well-crafted and expressive, yet readily understandable; there needs to be rhythm and balance; worship requires language which is vibrant, not drab and dull. The words we sing and speak in worship glorify the Lord of heaven and earth; they proclaim his saving gospel to people he loves. The language of worship needs to be the very best we can bring forth."

Throughout the process of shaping a new hymnal, the members of the Joint Hymnal Committee struggled to find the right words to use in writing and revising hymns, liturgies, and prayers. Several times the JHC thoroughly discussed the subject of inclusive language. Not every JHC member agreed with each suggestion for wording changes, but there was no disagreement that some language updating was essential in the new hymnal.

The JHC realized early on that worshipers would resist language change especially when it came to the Lord's Prayer. In the orders for corporate worship, it was decided to print the Lord's Prayer side by side in a revised and traditional wording. The revised wording is exactly the same as in *Lutheran Worship,* the hymnal of the Lutheran Church—Missouri Synod. It differs slightly from *Lutheran Book*

---

[23]Eggert, "Gaining a Perspective on the New Hymnal," p. 8; essay presented to the JHC on August 11, 1987.

[24]*Northwestern Lutheran,* June 1, 1987, p. 204.

of Worship, which has the following text for the sixth and seventh petitions: "Save us from the time of trial and deliver us from evil." The JHC did follow *Lutheran Book of Worship* in printing the revised wording in the left column, thus showing a certain preference for using this revised version.[25]

Contrary to what some members of the synod perceived, updating language was not the main reason for the publication of a new hymnal. There were many other reasons why a new tool for worship was needed. With the passage of time, people became more comfortable with the revised language and began to appreciate *Christian Worship* for the many other worship resources that were provided.

The revision of *The Lutheran Hymnal* services on pages 5 and 15

Eggert suggested that the first major task of the Liturgy Committee should be a revision of the pages 5 and 15 liturgies of *The Lutheran Hymnal*. The reference is to The Order of Morning Service without Communion (pp. 5-14) and The Order of the Holy Communion (pp. 15-31), the two chief services in *The Lutheran Hymnal*. Both of these services were very familiar to synod members from long use. At the second meeting of the JHC in February 1985, there was a consensus that "there is a strongly conservative mood in the synod, which makes almost imperative our retention of the pages 5 and 15 liturgy."[26] The revision of these services proved to be a long and difficult assignment.

On one matter there was agreement: the two services should be combined. The major points of disagreement were the following: (1) How completely should the language and music of the services be revised? (2) How should the "Lord, have mercy" (*Kyrie*) be handled? (3) Where and how should the Psalm be used? Throughout the fall of 1985, the Liturgy Committee struggled with revising these services in the most appropriate way. Several members of the committee presented special studies on individual topics.

The Liturgy Committee presented its proposals at the January 3, 1986, meeting of the Joint Hymnal Committee. The minutes summarize two of the areas of disagreement: "Considerable debate ensued as to whether the *Kyrie* should be used as a cry for forgiveness in the

---

[25] JHC minutes, January 22, 1988, p. 4: "Resolved, that in all liturgies where the two Lord's Prayer versions are to be printed side by side, the contemporary one is to be printed at the left and the traditional one to the right."

[26] JHC minutes, February 28, 1985, p. 1.

Confession of Sins or as a more general cry for mercy."[27] The JHC went on record as favoring the placement of the *Kyrie* into the Confession of Sins by a vote of 9 to 3.

On the question of the use of a psalm in the service, the minutes report: "There was considerable discussion on the role of the Introit/psalmody/sentence. Some pleaded for its retention in the traditional place before the *Gloria;* some urged that provision be made for greater singing of the psalmody; some . . . pleaded for more encouragement for using full psalms." On this question the JHC favored by a vote of 8 to 4 the placement of the psalmody between the Collect (Prayer of the Day) and the Scripture readings.

But the dissatisfaction with the proposed revision was broader than just over the matter of the placement of the *Kyrie* and Psalm. That is evident from a letter addressed to the Liturgy Committee by a member of the Hymn Committee shortly after the January JHC meeting. He questioned many aspects of the proposed revision of pages 5 and 15 and pleaded for a reconsideration of what had been done. He wrote: "You are heading in the wrong direction. The revision which the members of our constituency are expecting, those whom this revision is to serve, is one that will have an absolute minimum of change." He went on: "We do not want a WELS that uses two hymnals, or three. LCMS is plagued with this now, as you know. . . . One step toward winning the highest percentage of our constituency is to present a page 5/15 combination at the beginning of the new hymnal that will attract the worshipers who were worried about change."

The Hymn Committee, by a unanimous vote of 6 to 0, asked the Liturgy Committee to reconsider its proposed revision. Even Eggert wondered if perhaps it would not be better to regard the proposed revision of pages 5 and 15 as a second service and include the *TLH* version in the new hymnal without change.[28]

The Liturgy Committee met February 21–22 and March 17–18, 1986, and once again agonized over the revision. The committee itself was divided as to the best course of action. One Liturgy Committee member reporting on those meetings wrote: "There were votes and revotes on items that had already been decided, disagreements on what constituted major or minor changes, and some hesitancy on whether we were always heading in the right direction, where it was suitable to

---

[27]JHC minutes, January 3, 1986, p. 2.
[28]Prange diary, March 9, 1986.

depart from the historical past and where not . . . whether the Elizabethan English should be retained in the liturgical songs and responses or whether they should be updated to correspond with the language of America in this age."[29] Another committee member summed up those meetings: "It is hard and slow work."[30] By a vote of 3 to 2, the committee resolved to stay with its proposals and also to eliminate all the Elizabethan English throughout the service (though offering the Lord's Prayer in two versions). The committee asked chairman Prange to communicate this decision by letter to the rest of the members of the JHC.

Prange's letter dated March 19, 1986, pointed out that the Introit from *The Lutheran Hymnal* had lost a great part of its original intent because of three things: (1) an opening (entrance, introit) hymn had been added to the old mass; (2) a confession of sins prior to the Introit had been introduced; (3) we generally do not have processions into the service (the original function of the Introit psalmody).

The *Kyrie*, likewise, had lost a great deal of its original intent. From its original place in the western rite, it had been moved around and shortened. The WELS *Book of Hymns* included it as part of the Confession of Sins. Other hymnals had created a kind of "minilitany" from the *Kyrie* and placed it prior to the Song of Praise.

Concerning the placement of the Psalm, Prange wrote: "We tried various solutions. The majority came to the conclusion that the most suitable place for the psalmody was prior to the readings." In later revisions of this service, the position of the Psalm was changed.

The charge was addressed that this was a radical revision. "We have heard many times that this revision in the structure of the service as found in TLH is radical. The majority of the members of the Liturgy Committee continue to believe that ours is a conservative revision improving the flow of the service, one which the person in the pew will accept. Our service breaks up the '*Gloria Patri–Kyrie–Gloria in Excelsis* progression' and makes these individual parts of the service more meaningful. . . . We believe that this kind of change in structure will prove more acceptable than changes in language and much more so than changes in the music. . . . We are suggesting only few, very minor, changes in the music."

---

[29]Wayne Schulz, "Goals and Implementation of the Liturgy Committee"; presented to the JHC on August 11, 1987.

[30]Prange diary, February 22, 1986.

To support the Liturgy Committee's revision, the results of the five regional focus meetings were cited. The responses showed that 39 persons wanted "a revision that changes as little as possible"; 65 opted for "a revision that changes rather freely, seeking to improve wherever possible"; and 29 wanted "printing two versions of the page 5/15 liturgy: *one*, a reprint of the present, and *two*, a version that makes improvements wherever they seem to be indicated."

The music for the revised service was prepared by James Engel of Dr. Martin Luther College. The Joint Hymnal Committee took a break during its May 31, 1986, meeting to travel to Apostles of Christ Lutheran Church to sing through the revised liturgy and a few hymns. Since this proposed revision of the pages 5 and 15 liturgies was intended for field-testing by synod congregations in the forthcoming *Sampler,* the Commission on Worship had to give final approval to "The Service" (as it was then called). There the debate continued, as will be reported in the next section. And once the revised service was published in the *Sampler,* it soon became the subject of much discussion throughout the synod. Later this service was reconsidered by the JHC, and the revision called The Common Service was included in the new hymnal.

Sampler: new hymns and liturgy—Advent 1986

At the June 4, 1985, meeting of the Commission on Worship, project director Eggert raised the question of "Field-Testing of Hymnal Materials." The 1983 synod resolutions had called for distribution of materials to all congregations. Eggert raised the question, "How much of this can realistically be done?" He went on to suggest that "if the revision of the pages 5 and 15 liturgy is completed in time, we might submit this to the district conventions in June of 1986" and that "this liturgy together with a number of new approved hymns be sent out in summer or fall of 1986 to all congregations."[31]

The commission resolved to follow these suggestions that the revised pages 5 and 15 liturgy and 20 hymns be offered to the 1986 district conventions. The motion continued: "This convention *Sampler* will be presented as tentative material to be included in the new hymnal. It should contain new translations, revisions, unchanged hymns, hymns from other books, as well as new hymns."[32] This set in motion

---

[31] Agenda notes from CW meeting, June 4, 1985, p. 2.
[32] CW minutes, June 4, 1985, pp. 1,2.

a significant phase in the shaping of the new hymnal: the publication of the *Sampler*.

In September 1985 Eggert could report that "both committees are working on this project." But he also expressed his personal opinion "that the contemplated 20 hymns and entire revision of pages 5 and 15 may be too ambitious a goal for completion by March or early April [1986]. Perhaps key sections of the revised liturgy and a somewhat smaller number of hymns should be planned."[33] At the next meeting of the Commission on Worship, the plan was separated into two parts: "a *convention report* containing preliminary examples of the work done by the Hymn and Liturgy Committees, and a *field-test sampler* to be available for our congregations by Advent 1986, to contain about 20 new hymns and the completed revision of the pages 5 and 15 liturgy proposed for inclusion in the new hymnal."[34]

Even though the revision of the pages 5 and 15 liturgy and the selection of hymns was the responsibility of the Liturgy and Hymn Committees respectively, the Commission on Worship passed a resolution "that the approval of the contents of the *Sampler* is the function of the Commission on Worship."[35] As a result of this motion, the debate over the pages 5 and 15 liturgies revision continued at the June 2, 1986, meeting of the commission. Hartwig, a supporter of the revision, was absent from this meeting but did send a letter urging approval. When the vote was taken to approve the revision, two were in the affirmative and two in the negative. One member's vote was not at first audible. After being questioned, he voted in the affirmative, which meant approval of the liturgy revision by a vote of 3 to 2.[36] The 21 hymn suggestions were approved with little debate. At the next meeting of the commission, the policy for approving items for the new hymnal was changed. From that time on, all members of the Joint Hymnal Committee had an equal voice in approving materials for inclusion in the hymnal.[37]

Final editing of the *Sampler* was done by an executive committee authorized by the Commission on Worship: Albrecht, Eggert, Jeske, Prange, and Tiefel. That summer Eggert presented an essay at the

---

[33] Agenda notes from CW meeting, September 20, 1985, p. 1.
[34] CW minutes, January 2, 1986.
[35] CW minutes, April 3–4, 1986, p. 2.
[36] CW minutes, June 2, 1986.
[37] CW minutes, August 29–30, 1986, p. 1.

Northern Wisconsin District Convention that reported on the hymnal progress and outlined the contents of the *Sampler*.[38] In October Prange reported: "We got the *Sampler* (100,000 copies are stacked in warehouse). Nice job."[39] Later that month Kurt Eggert suffered a heart attack during a practice with the Lutheran Chorale of Milwaukee.[40] The strenuous schedule and tensions of the preceding months had obviously taken their toll on our project director's body, and in the future he would lack some of the energy that had driven him in the past.

The *Sampler*, which many of the congregations of the WELS began to use during Advent 1986, had a foreword and an introduction to the revised service and the hymns. They gave the reasons for the changes being made and were meant to prepare the people to worship with this new service. Responsive prayers for "All Times and Occasions" and for the "Epiphany Season" were included. Twelve psalms from *Lutheran Worship* with tones and pointing for singing were included by permission.[41] The 21 hymns, none of which appeared in *The Lutheran Hymnal*, were (numbered 701 to 721):

> Lo, He Comes with Clouds Descending
> Once in Royal David's City
> Your Little Ones, Dear Lord
> The Only Son from Heaven
> Down from the Mount of Glory
> Sing, My Tongue
> This Joyful Eastertide
> Alleluia! Sing to Jesus
> Holy Spirit, Ever Dwelling
> We Praise You, Lord
> Thy Strong Word
> Here, O My Lord, I See You Face to Face
> Amazing Grace
> Love in Christ Is Strong and Living
> Lift High the Cross
> Forgive Us, Lord, for Shallow Thankfulness

---

[38] Eggert, "Enriching our Worship Heritage," June 1986.

[39] Prange diary, October 3, 1986.

[40] Eggert suffered the attack on October 26, 1986, and was taken to County Hospital. Immediate surgery was ruled out but later scheduled in December.

[41] Psalms 1, 2, 16, 23, 24, 98, 104, 105, 118, 130, 142, 146.

Son of God, Eternal Savior
In Christ There Is No East or West
Our Father, by Whose Name
Lord Jesus Christ, the Children's Friend
Let All Things Now Living

Each hymn was annotated, a feature that was much appreciated. The *Sampler* concluded with a listing of the propers for Advent to Pentecost, including a Verse of the Day but no Prayer of the Day.

Eggert was soon back to work after his heart attack and reported to the JHC on the reception of the *Sampler:* "The big surprise was that the number of participating congregations, and the total number of copies ordered, far exceeded our projection. It appears that well over a thousand WELS pastors ordered copies, and since some have two congregations, it would seem that most all the churches of the synod are going to use the *Samplers* in one way or another. Our first order was for 100,000 copies, and a second printing of 90,000 (!) is within 4,000 of being shipped out."[42]

The introduction assured the worshipers: "Your reaction to this service is very important to those working on the hymnal. At first you may not like this service as well as those in *The Lutheran Hymnal*. But give yourself (and the service) a chance. And remember that the new hymnal must serve all the people of our synod as well as the coming generation. You will be given opportunity to fill out a questionnaire at the end of this trial period. Your reactions as well as those of worshipers throughout the synod will be seriously considered in preparing the final version of this service for our new hymnal. Thanks for your help in seeking to improve our worship of the Lord." The promised questionnaire was prepared by the Commission on Worship and distributed to congregations for their use at the conclusion of the six-month field test of the *Sampler*.

Critical reaction to the *Sampler*

Long before the end of the six-month trial period, letters began to pour in that were critical of the *Sampler*. They came to project director Eggert;[43] they came to synod president Mischke; they came to *Northwestern Lutheran* editor Schaefer; they came to Prange, who had written

---
[42] Eggert's letter to the JHC, November 25, 1986.
[43] Eggert reported that 1,300 letters were received.

an editorial in the *Northwestern Lutheran* on the *Sampler* titled "A Tool for Worship."[44]

One letter that came to Prange read: "Re: your editorial in NW Lutheran. The cries against the 'Sampler' service are dyeing [sic] down simply because we *lay* people are getting tired of beating our heads against the clerical brick wall. If the *Sampler* is the best the panel can come up with I have fears for the future of WELS. I have talked to people from 20-25 congregations in the 5 western states and have yet to meet anyone who can say one word for the *Sampler*. The old saying still goes 'if something works, don't fix it.' The *Sampler* is the devil's work and nothing less. If you people in Milwaukee and Wisconsin would just listen, you might hear something."

Excerpts from other letters included statements like this: "I'm scared and upset. I've gone to church for 61 years. I've never thought God's word was drab or dull, and when pastors think so and try to change His Holy word, what are people coming to?" Another: "This new hymn book and *Sampler* are a big mistake. They should be buried before any more divisive mischief occurs. God should not be referred to irreverently as 'you.'" The criticism of referring to God as "you" was echoed by many other letters. One writer said that using *thee* and *thou* was a way to "set God aside as holy, shows respect and awe, and love."

Editor Schaefer published two pages of letters about the *Sampler*, a total of 21 letters.[45] In his column in the *Northwestern Lutheran*, "From This Corner," he also reflected on the issue: "Few things have stirred the synod as much as the appearance of the *Sampler*. . . . No other issue has brought more letters to the *Northwestern Lutheran*: there were about 75, 90 percent of them critical. . . . The most common complaint was the dropping of 'thee' and 'thou' in addressing God."[46]

Schaefer's father was a member of the Intersynodical Committee on Hymnology and Liturgics, which produced the 1941 *The Lutheran Hymnal*. Schaefer continues: "Recently I went through my father's correspondence from this stormy period. The letters, mostly from pastors, reflected emotions ranging from outrage to warm acceptance. They ran something like ten to one in favor of our old *Book of Hymns*. Most of the critical letters deplored the new 'high church' liturgy, the new transla-

---

[44]*Northwestern Lutheran*, January 15, 1987, p. 24.
[45]*Northwestern Lutheran*, August 1987, pp. 271,272.
[46]*Northwestern Lutheran*, July 1987, p. 259.

tions, and the unnecessary cost to congregations just emerging from the Great Depression."

Eggert and members of the JHC, as well as many WELS pastors, wrote and spoke in defense of the *Sampler*. Having the strong support of many pastors who had a good understanding especially of the language issue was of great benefit. The sharp criticism of the *Sampler* did have a sobering effect on those at work shaping the hymnal. It particularly troubled Eggert as is evident from this diary note: "Kurt looks good, but all the negative comments on the *Sampler* seem to have him down a bit."[47]

But in the end, based on the questionnaire responses, the silent majority of synod members spoke and gave their support to the *Sampler*.[48] There were a total of 57,135 responses, 30.9 percent of synod members (obviously the most active worshipers since the questionnaires were usually filled out at the conclusion of a Sunday service). On all eight of the questions, the majority of respondents judged the *Sampler* in a favorable light. The closest vote came on this statement: "Updating the language of the liturgy to make it conform more closely to today's English." It was judged to be "desirable" by 61 percent. Language revision was the most troubling aspect of the *Sampler* service. One pastor wrote: "By far the main objection to the *Sampler* liturgy in my congregation is the change in language. This feeling is overwhelming in *all age groups*." Pastors, however, favored the change in worship language by a margin of 712 to 29.[49] The most highly approved item (85 percent) by the people was the regular use of the Psalm in the service. Eighty-three percent did prefer having *Amen* printed at the close of hymns, an issue over which the JHC later agonized. Of the 21 *Sampler* hymns, the two favorites were "Amazing Grace" and "Lift High the Cross." At the bottom of the list were "The Only Son from Heaven" and "Forgive Us, Lord, for Shallow Thankfulness."

The results of the *Sampler* questionnaire obviously heartened Eggert and the members of the Joint Hymnal Committee. Eggert could even report to pastors in the fall of 1987 that "*Sampler*s are again in demand as many congregations continue to use them. If you will have no further use for your copies, why not ship them back to NPH, and we will redis-

---

[47] Prange diary, June 23, 1987.

[48] Grand totals (all ages) for the congregational survey on the *Sampler* were compiled in August 1987.

[49] Eggert's letter to WELS pastors, October 1987.

tribute them."⁵⁰ The results of the survey showed that there was considerable support for shaping a new hymnal. This field test of the *Sampler* had the effect of letting many people blow off steam, fire off their cannons as it were, and no doubt helped to prepare the way for a much more favorable reception of the new hymnal.

Project music editor and secretary

As work on the hymnal project accelerated, it became obvious that Kurt Eggert needed some additional help. Professor James Engel of Dr. Martin Luther College had been asked to prepare the musical setting for the *Sampler* but had no official capacity with the project.⁵¹ In August 1986 the Commission on Worship informed the Conference of Presidents of Eggert's need for full-time assistance.⁵² Northwestern Publishing House responded by providing a part-time secretary for four days per week in April 1987.⁵³ Later Joanne Gruber became the full-time project secretary, and her assistance was invaluable, especially in securing the necessary copyright permissions for the hymnal.

What the project also needed was a music editor. In September 1987 Eggert proposed that the Commission on Worship request the Conference of Presidents to appoint a music editor and musical consultant for the hymnal project. This person would have two basic functions: (1) to review music manuscripts of liturgies and hymns and be responsible for the final form of music manuscripts prior to publication and (2) to advise and assist the project director and committees regarding the production of liturgical music and hymns.⁵⁴ The Conference of Presidents responded positively to the commission's request and appointed Engel to the position of part-time music consultant.

During 1988 Engel served the project director and the JHC in this role. He was present at the August JHC meeting and met with the Liturgy Committee in West St. Paul in October. The Commission on Worship by resolution asked him to serve as editor for the *Organist's Accompaniment to the Liturgy*.⁵⁵ However, Prange reported that he was not present in

---

⁵⁰Eggert's letter to WELS pastors, October 1987.
⁵¹CW minutes, June 2, 1986.
⁵²CW minutes, August 29–30, 1986, p. 1.
⁵³CW minutes, March 20–21, 1987, p. 1.
⁵⁴CW minutes, September 25–26, 1987, p. 1.
⁵⁵CW minutes, September 23, 1988, p. 1.

December for a meeting of the Liturgy Committee: "Discussed settings for Morning Worship; Engel sick so this was somewhat hindered."[56] The JHC learned that he was terminally ill with cancer.[57] Our heavenly Father called James Engel to his eternal rest on April 17, 1989.

Fortunately the Lord provided the project with a gifted replacement who was one of the committee members, Professor Kermit Moldenhauer of Martin Luther Preparatory School. He served first on a part-time basis as music editor, but the next year he was called by the Conference of Presidents to serve full-time. Moldenhauer was installed in an evening service on August 8, 1990, during a Joint Hymnal Committee meeting.[58] At the same time, Professor Richard Hillert of Concordia University, River Forest, Illinois, agreed to serve as a part-time musical consultant for the project. Moldenhauer's services proved to be especially valuable when increasing health problems slowed down the activities of project director Eggert.

Critical review and field-testing

All congregations of the synod had the opportunity to field-test the *Sampler*. It was obvious, however, that not all items to be included in the new hymnal could receive such a thorough testing. What needed to be decided was how materials prepared by the Joint Hymnal Committee would be reviewed and tested. The Commission on Worship took responsibility for developing the guidelines for this aspect of the project.

At the commission's meeting in August 1987, the chairman was asked to "have a draft of guidelines prepared for our next meeting covering critical review and field-testing of worship materials."[59] The guidelines that Prange prepared were reviewed and amended at the next meeting.[60] These guidelines, given final approval in November 1989, are in three sections:

    1. *Critical Review*
        a. That the Hymn and Liturgy Committees seek critical review for those items which each has produced

---

[56]Prange diary, December 9, 1988.
[57]JHC minutes (February 10, 1989, p. 1) report that Engel was ill and excused from the meetings.
[58]JHC minutes, August 8, 1990, p. 7.
[59]CW minutes, August 10, 1987.
[60]CW minutes, September 25–26, 1987, p. 1.

and which have been given tentative approval by the JHC.
b. That the method and scope (extent) of this critical review be determined by the Hymn and Liturgy Committees.
c. That the District Worship Coordinators be among those selected for the purposes of critically reviewing materials produced.

2. *Field-Testing*
a. That the Commission on Worship determine the necessity and scope for field-testing items which are tentatively approved by the JHC.
b. That the commission carry out field-testing in one of several ways depending on the nature of the item being considered: synodwide, random, representative (type, size, location of congregation), and volunteer.
c. That the project director construct the reporting instrument for the field-testing in consultation with the Hymn and Liturgy Committees.
d. That the Commission on Worship approve the reporting instrument and implement its use.

3. *Informational Distribution of Materials*[61]
That all congregations of the synod periodically receive copies of major liturgical items and a sampling of hymns as determined by the commission.[62]

The commission asked Eggert to develop field-testing procedures, which he presented in some detail at the March 1990 commission meeting.[63] Eggert listed items that were ready for field-testing and some that were not. The four major new/revised services received the most extensive field test: Service of Word and Sacrament, Service of the Word, Morning Praise, and Evening Prayer. Other items were tested less thoroughly. The critical review and field-testing were valuable tools in helping the JHC determine how their work was being received. In some cases the results led to major changes in services. This process also helped to identify problem areas that needed correction.

---

[61] CW minutes, November 17–18, 1989, p. 2.
[62] Guidelines for Critical Review, Field-Testing, and Distribution of Hymnal Materials.
[63] CW minutes, March 23–24, 1990, p. 2.

The master hymn list

One of the major assignments of the Hymn Committee was to develop the master hymn list. The working assumption was that the new hymnal would contain about 600 hymns, 400 of them from *The Lutheran Hymnal* (which had a total of 660) and 200 from other sources. This list was ready for presentation to the JHC in August 1988.[64] At this meeting members of the JHC had the opportunity to offer motions to add to the list and delete proposed hymns. Some of the votes on either adding or deleting were very close. One hymn from TLH, "Lo, Judah's Lion Wins the Strife," was first restored to the master list by a vote of 7 to 6, but later it was deleted by that same 7-6 vote. At that meeting 16 hymns were added to the list. Motions were defeated to add 33 other hymns, 14 of these from TLH. Motions were approved to drop 26 hymns from the proposed list, 16 of these from TLH. Finally, motions were defeated that would have dropped an additional 27 hymns. When all the voting was finished that day, the master hymn list numbered 579, of which 409 came from TLH.

Already at the January 1988 meeting of the JHC, the question was raised how best to publicly release the names of hymns on the master list. There was considerable debate over the wisdom of doing this in the *Northwestern Lutheran*.[65] But ultimately this was the course followed. A total of nine articles appeared (authored by various members of the JHC), listing the hymns proposed and those from *The Lutheran Hymnal* that had been dropped.[66] Releasing the master hymn list gave members of the synod an opportunity for input as to the final selection of hymns.

The master hymn list continued to be altered by additions and deletions in the next few years. One major addition was to include the canticles in the hymn section. *The Lutheran Hymnal* had printed the texts of nine canticles, in addition to those found in worship orders; but these texts were without music.[67] At the August 1987 JHC meeting, the minutes report: "The role of the canticles came under much debate.

---

[64]JHC minutes, August 8, 1988, p. 1.

[65]Prange diary, January 22, 1988: "Much debate about the use of the NWL."

[66]*Northwestern Lutheran*, October 1, 1988, pp. 332,333; October 15, 1988, pp. 353,354; November 1, 1988, pp. 372,373; November 15, 1988, pp. 392,393; December 1988, pp.413,414; January 1, 1989, pp. 12-14; January 15, 1989, pp. 32-34; February 1, 1989, pp. 52,53; and February 15, 1989, pp. 70,71; additions to the master hymn list: October 1, 1990, p. 333, and March 1, 1991, p. 93.

[67]*The Lutheran Hymnal* (St. Louis: Concordia Publishing House, 1941), pp. 120-122.

How many? Which?"[68] Lehmann of the Liturgy Committee did considerable research into the texts and tunes for these songs, and it was decided to recommend a few of them for inclusion in the new book. The JHC decided to number the canticles along with the hymns and place them in the "Hymns of the Liturgy" section. The August 1989 minutes report that this brought "an anguished plea from the neighborhood of the Hymn Committee that these canticles should not be counted as part of the hymn total when determining the size of the hymn section."[69] Later two additional chants from the pages 5 and 15 services of *The Lutheran Hymnal* were added to the "Hymns of the Liturgy" section: "Glory Be to the Father" *(Gloria Patri)* and the first setting of "Create in Me a Clean Heart, O God" (Offertory).[70] At the second last JHC meeting, "Preserve Your Word, O Savior" (TLH 264) and "The Day You Gave Us, Lord, Is Ended" were added.[71] One of the last hymns that found its way into the hymnal was "Where Shepherds Lately Knelt," a text by Jaroslav Vajda that had appeared in Augsburg's 1987 *Christmas: The Annual of Christmas Literature and Art*.[72]

As the new hymnal was readied for publication, there was a concern that it might be necessary to delete a few hymns to keep within the planned 960 pages. And so the JHC decided that each member should compile a list of hymns for possible deletion if necessary. This came to be referred to as the "hit list."[73] Fortunately, it was not necessary to make use of this hit list. The final number of hymns in *Christian Worship* is 623. Included in this total are eight that have two tunes:

> A Mighty Fortress Is Our God
> Come, Holy Ghost, Creator Blest
> God Be with You till We Meet Again
> Lift Up Your Heads, You Mighty Gates
> O Little Town of Bethlehem
> O Lord, How Shall I Meet You

---

[68]JHC minutes, August 12, 1987, p. 1.

[69]JHC minutes, August 4, 1989, p. 6.

[70]JHC minutes, September 27, 1991, p. 3; *The Lutheran Hymnal,* pp. 6,12,13.

[71]Agenda notes from JHC meeting, January 4, 1992.

[72]C. T. Aufdemberge, *Christian Worship: Handbook* (Milwaukee: Northwestern Publishing House, 1997), p. 74.

[73]JHC minutes, January 6, 1992, p. 7.

On My Heart Imprint Your Image
Ride On, Ride On in Majesty

Gospel hymns

One category of hymns that elicited special discussion was the so-called "gospel hymns," the kind of songs that had not traditionally been included in Lutheran hymnals. Eggert pointed out the need to study "new types of hymnody such as folk hymns and 'gospel' hymns."[74] At the August 1987 JHC meeting, the minutes report that the Hymn Committee had discussed the "role of gospel or spiritual hymns in the new book."[75]

The *Sampler* questionnaire revealed that even some members of congregations were not happy with the idea of including gospel hymns in the new book. One person included this note on the survey: "Beware of including too many folk songs, for example, "Amazing Grace." This one, in particular, is overused by the sectarians. Do we have to join the crowd?" This person also raised the question as to whether "How Great Thou Art" was going to be included, commenting, "Songs of this genre are unsuitable for an orthodox Lutheran hymnal. . . . Are we watering down our Lutheran heritage in order to become a generic church like the one 'down the street'?"

The topic of gospel hymns got a full airing in August 1988. The minutes report that "at this point the floor was given to Eggert for a presentation on gospel music and spirituals ('The Case for and against Inclusion of Gospel Hymns in the New Hymnal'). At the close a letter was read from a parish pastor pleading for inclusion of a few hymns of this genre, and later a similar letter was read from Prof. David Valleskey of the Seminary."[76] The JHC also sang a number of gospel hymns at the meeting room in the Dillon Motel.[77]

The minutes go on to report that "vigorous debate followed." The meeting was resumed that evening at the Synod Administration Building, where the minutes report that "the matter of gospel hymns and spirituals was again vigorously debated. Although the chairman warned against putting off a decision too long, the vote on this genre of

---

[74]Eggert, "Hymnal Planning—Year III and Long Range," August 29, 1986.
[75]JHC minutes, August 13, 1987, p. 2.
[76]JHC minutes, August 9, 1988, p. 3.
[77]In fact, the singing became so lusty that the management asked the JHC to hold it down.

hymns was deferred" till the next morning.[78] Prange reports: "I was a bit testy because there was a plea for more time."[79]

The next morning by a vote of 9 to 5, the following resolution was approved: "to include no fewer than 6 and no more than 12 gospel hymns and spirituals on the master list; these are to be placed in the topical categories to which they belong."[80] The Hymn Committee suggested that four such hymns were already on the master list: "How Great Thou Art," "Come, Sing the Gospel's Joyful Sound," "God Be with You till We Meet Again," and "Go, Tell It on the Mountain." The JHC added three more to the master list: "To God Be the Glory," "Leaning on the Everlasting Arms," and "Take the World, but Give Me Jesus."[81] Later "Come, Sing the Gospel's Joyful Sound" and "Leaning on the Everlasting Arms" were deleted, but "Precious Lord, Take My Hand" was added.

Revision of hymn texts

Once the master hymn list had been established, it was necessary to review the texts of all the selections for possible language revision. Two basic guidelines were to eliminate Elizabethan English as much as possible and to use inclusive language. However, because of the nature of the English poetry, the familiarity of the hymn, or the difficulty of finding suitable substitute words, exceptions had to be made to these guidelines. It was especially difficult to replace the word *thee* when it occurred at the end of lines. An example of this is *Christian Worship* hymn 402: "My faith looks up to thee, / Thou Lamb of Calvary." The JHC did not revise this line; *Lutheran Worship* hymn 378 has this revision: "My faith looks trustingly / To Christ of Calvary." Generally the JHC was more likely to retain the language of an original English hymn than one that had been translated from a foreign language.

When considering and accepting hymns for the new book, the JHC followed this procedure: (1) the hymn texts, tunes, and settings were recommended to the JHC for adoption by the Hymn Committee, which had previously studied them; (2) each text, tune, and setting was reviewed by the JHC; (3) the JHC voted on motions to amend a pro-

---

[78]JHC minutes, August 9, 1988, p. 4.
[79]Prange diary, August 9, 1988.
[80]JHC minutes, August 10, 1988, p. 4.
[81]JHC minutes, August 11, 1988, p. 5.

posed text, tune, or setting; (4) some changes were made by common consent with no vote taken; (5) some texts, tunes, or settings were referred back to the Hymn Committee for further study; (6) finally, a vote was taken to accept the text, tune, and setting of the hymn.

The JHC began the review process with the Advent hymns in February 1989. Hymns for the following sections were taken up in August 1989: Christmas, New Year, Name of Jesus, Epiphany, Transfiguration, and Lent. The following sections were reviewed in January 1990: Palm Sunday, Maundy Thursday, Good Friday, Easter, Ascension, Pentecost, Trinity, and St. Michael and All Angels. In August 1990 these hymn sections were acted on: Reformation, End Time, Opening of Service, Worship and Praise, Hymns of the Liturgy, Word of God, Baptism, Confession and Absolution, Holy Communion, Close of Service, Invitation, and Redeemer. The process continued in January 1991 with these sections: Justification, Faith, Prayer, Trust, Commitment, Stewardship, Christian Love, and Christian Home. In August 1991 the review was completed with the following: Christian Education, Social Concern, Church, Ministry, Saints and Martyrs, Evangelism, Mission, Morning, Evening, Confirmation, Marriage, Death and Burial, Thanksgiving, Nation, and Church Anniversary.

Here is a sample of the action taken by the committee on hymn 408, "If God Himself Be for Me":

> RESOLVED: in #408, stanza 4, line 6, change "Rejoicing" to "Courageous" and in stanza 6, line 3, change "mighty prince's" to "earthly tyrant's"
> RESOLVED: in #408, stanza 7 should read: "My heart for joy is springing, / And can no more be sad, / 'Tis full of joy and singing, / Sees only sunshine glad . . . "
> RESOLVED: in #408 add TLH stanza 2 as is
> MOTION FAILED: in #408 to delete stanza 6, "No danger . . . " (Note: in #408, stanza 6, rearrange by putting lines 5-8 before lines 1-4)
> RESOLVED: in #408 use the order as follows: TLH 1, 2, 3, 5, 6, 13, 15
> MOTION FAILED: in #408 delete stanza 4, "He canceled . . ."[82]

These actions resulted in cutting back the 15 stanzas of the hymn in *The Lutheran Hymnal* (No. 528) to seven stanzas in *Christian Worship*

---

[82]JHC minutes, January 4, 1991, p. 6.

(No. 419). Some of the TLH language was revised, and lines in one stanza were reversed. Some JHC members wished to cut back the number of stanzas even more. It was not unusual to have disagreements on the ideal number of stanzas in a hymn. The point was made repeatedly that though seven stanzas of a hymn might be printed, the presiding minister can pick from these the ones that are most appropriate for the particular service.

Some hymns were given a second tune. One example is "O Little Town of Bethlehem" (JHC #49). *The Lutheran Hymnal* had the melody ST. LOUIS. The JHC resolved to include FOREST GREEN as a second tune.[83] The motion was defeated to substitute FOREST GREEN for ST. LOUIS. The motion was defeated to use "block harmony" for the first line of ST. LOUIS. *The Hymnal* setting of FOREST GREEN (originally from *The English Hymnal*) was approved. Later an attempt was made to delete one or the other of these melodies, but both motions were defeated.[84]

At times there was disagreement as to the best tune to use for a particular text. The Advent text "Lo, He Comes with Clouds Descending" had appeared in the *Sampler* with the tune PICARDY.[85] The *Lutheran Book of Worship* and other hymnals use the tune HELMSLEY. The motion was made to substitute HELMSLEY for PICARDY in the new hymnal, but this was defeated.[86]

Some texts received new tunes. One example of this is "Arise and Shine in Splendor," which in *The Lutheran Hymnal* (No. 126) had the tune O WELT, ICH MUSS DICH LASSEN. This tune is closely wedded to Paul Gerhardt's evening hymn "Now Rest Beneath Night's Shadow" (CW 587). It is a marvelous tune for that hymn. But it does not really fit the mood of "Arise and Shine in Splendor." The JHC resolved by a close vote of 7 to 6 to find another tune for this text.[87] The outcome of this resolution was a new tune by committee member Bruce Backer that was named EPIPHANY (CW 81).

In one case a new hymn was created from the stanza of an existing hymn. The Hymn Committee had recommended that the last stanza of "A Lamb Goes Uncomplaining Forth" not be included in the new hymnal ("And when Thy glory I shall see"). The JHC first resolved to restore

---

[83] JHC minutes, July 31, 1989, p. 2.
[84] JHC minutes, January 4, 1991, p. 5.
[85] Used also in *Lutheran Worship* hymn 15.
[86] JHC minutes, July 31, 1989, p. 2.
[87] JHC minutes, August 2, 1989, p. 4.

this stanza. But a second resolution called for the creation of "a one-verse new hymn, to be placed in the 'End Time' section, titled, 'Lord, When Your Glory I Shall See.'"[88] Project director Eggert wrote a new tune for this stanza, which he named WEDDING GLORY (CW 219), and this hymn was one of those sung at his funeral.

Sometimes there were motions to include familiar hymns from *The Lutheran Hymnal* word for word in the new hymnal. The motion "to adopt TLH 172 (O Sacred Head, Now Wounded) as is" was lost.[89] But in another case this was the only solution when language revision proved to be too difficult. At one of its last meetings, the JHC debated the merits of a proposed revision of the text for the hymn "Jesus, Priceless Treasure." Finally Eggert made a strong case for simply using the translation from *The Lutheran Hymnal,* and this was adopted.[90]

One popular hymn included in *The Lutheran Hymnal*, "Nearer, My God, to Thee," was not included on the original master list. Twice attempts were made to add it to the new book. The first motion in August 1988 was defeated 8 to 3.[91] Near the end of the project, the question was raised again when the Hymn Committee proposed that it be added to the new hymnal. The result was this JHC motion: "RESOLVED: to not add 'Nearer, My God, to Thee' to the master list."[92]

One hymn barely made it into the new hymnal: "Before the Ending of the Day." This hymn was not on the original master list but was added at the September 1991 JHC meeting.[93] At the January 1992 JHC meeting, the motion was defeated to remove this hymn from the master list.[94] Prange reports: "Had a struggle to keep 'Before the Ending of the Day' in the book."[95] This was a hymn high on the list of possible deletions should this became necessary. Fortunately this beautiful evening hymn found new life in *Christian Worship.*

Several generally unpopular decisions were made by the JHC with respect to publishing the hymns. One was to omit Scripture references

---

[88] JHC minutes, August 3, 1989, p. 4.
[89] JHC minutes, August 3, 1989, p. 4.
[90] JHC minutes, January 6, 1992, p. 8.
[91] JHC minutes, August 8, 1988, p. 2.
[92] JHC minutes, January 5, 1991, p. 7.
[93] JHC minutes, September 27, 1991, p. 3.
[94] JHC minutes, January 6, 1992, p. 7.
[95] Prange diary, January 6, 1992.

on the page.⁹⁶ People were familiar with having the references in *The Lutheran Hymnal*. The problem is that some hymns have a multitude of biblical allusions, and to print only one of them is not really accurate. And to print a reference for only those hymns that are clearly a paraphrase of some Scripture text is to give the impression that those hymns without such a reference are not biblical. A very complete listing of Scripture text references in hymns is included in *Christian Worship: Handbook*.⁹⁷

A second unpopular decision was to exclude *Amen* at the end of hymns. Initially the JHC resolved "to use *Amens* after all hymns in the hymnal except those which end with 'Alleluia,' 'Amen,' or 'Lord, have mercy,' or perhaps some form of strong doxological statement which would make an *Amen* undesirable."⁹⁸ This resolution proved to be somewhat unworkable, and later the JHC decided "to delete *Amens* from hymns."⁹⁹ The suggestion was made for Northwestern Publishing House to print a card with *Amens* in all keys for the organist. *Christian Worship: Manual* includes a chapter that provides the rationale for the decision to omit *Amens*.¹⁰⁰

There was much divided opinion among members of the JHC as to the wisdom of some of the decisions made by majority vote. Certainly Kurt Eggert did not always find himself on the side of those urging change. Many of the votes were very close. Some ended in a tie that the chairman had to break. But the entire process was most beneficial for the members of the JHC in broadening their understanding of the wonderful treasury we have in our hymns. Worshipers confronted with new wordings, tunes, and settings were often upset. But they were also challenged to think about how the church can best express its faith now and in the future.

"A Mighty Fortress Is Our God"

The text revision that provoked the most criticism was the fourth stanza of the great Reformation hymn "A Mighty Fortress Is Our God." Many letters and critical comments were received about the final translation adopted by the JHC.

---

[96] JHC minutes, September 28, 1991, p. 5.
[97] Aufdemberge, *Christian Worship: Handbook*, pp. 939-971.
[98] JHC minutes, July 31, 1989, p. 3.
[99] JHC minutes, August 2, 1991, p. 12.
[100] *Christian Worship: Manual* (Milwaukee: Northwestern Publishing House, 1993), pp. 307-309.

In the fourth stanza of this hymn, Luther's German says: "Nehmen sie den Leib, / Gut, Ehr', Kind und Weib." The TLH translation was very literal: "And take they our life, / Goods, fame, child, and wife." Many worshipers knew these words by heart. They were upset when they discovered the text of *Christian Worship*: "And do what they will— / Hate, steal, hurt, or kill." This was obviously not a literal translation of Luther's German text. How did this text come to be?

The first time the Hymn Committee presented "A Mighty Fortress Is Our God" to the JHC was in August 1990 (hymn 192 during our committee work). Nine changes from *The Lutheran Hymnal* were suggested, including the following wording of verse 4: "And take they our house / Goods, fame, child, and spouse" (the house/spouse rhyme is used by both *Lutheran Worship* and *Lutheran Book of Worship*). The minutes show that various motions were made.[101] Prange reports: "One of longest debates was over 'A Mighty Fortress.' Some wanted no revision in the hymn. I spoke strongly for some revision. Vote on motion to keep TLH wording was 7 to 7, which I broke [as chairman]."[102] But overnight a member of the Hymn Committee changed his mind on the question, and a motion to keep the TLH wording without change was reintroduced and approved by a vote of 8 to 5.[103] The Hymn Committee was also instructed "to prepare a new text version to be used with the second (isometric) tune/setting."

In January 1991 the Hymn Committee came back to the JHC with a recommendation that there not be two different wordings of the text for the two tunes/settings (as *Lutheran Worship* does in hymns 297 and 298) and that four slight changes be made in the TLH text. This was accepted by the JHC. Three motions to further amend the TLH text failed.[104]

This version with four slight text changes was sent to a group of reviewers for their comments and criticism. At least one of the reviewers was very critical of retaining the TLH wording of "A Mighty Fortress Is Our God," pointing out the desire of the JHC to make language as inclusive as possible. This is lacking when one asks a child or widower or woman to sing about the threat of losing one's "wife." As a result of this criticism, the Hymn Committee reconsidered the text of hymn 192.

---

[101] JHC minutes, August 6, 1990, p. 2.
[102] Prange diary, August 6, 1990.
[103] JHC minutes, August 7, 1990, pp. 3,4.
[104] JHC minutes, January 3, 1991, p. 2.

Jeske, a member of the Hymn Committee, notes some other problems with the TLH version besides the matter of inclusive language: "Another problem is in the antecedent of the word 'they' in the line 'They yet have nothing won.' The closest previous noun or pronoun, grammatically to the antecedent, is the word 'these' from the line 'Let these all be gone.' The word 'these' refers to one's material possessions: the goods, fame, child, and wife. In English this line sounds like losing one's wife is no big deal because she yet has nothing won. . . . There was enough confusion over the antecedent to warrant taking a shot at revising the stanza. The text subcommittee and the Hymn Committee had nothing but scorn for the 'spouse/house' rhyme. A final problem was the archaism in 'remaineth.' The TLH version was quite inconsistent in its use of KJV English. It used 'remaineth,' but 'for us fights,' not 'fighteth.'"[105] At the January 1992 JHC meeting, the Hymn Committee recommended the text of "A Mighty Fortress Is Our God" now printed in *Christian Worship*.

Obviously, members of the JHC were almost evenly divided on the question of which text to use for "A Mighty Fortress Is Our God." But finally, as one of the last orders of business on January 4, the JHC accepted the version proposed by the Hymn Committee with the note: "It was suggested to seek critical review for stanza 4 of #192."[106] One additional slight change in the text was made at that meeting.[107] The last meeting of the JHC was a short day-and-a-half session on April 3–4, 1992. There is no reference to hymn 192 in the minutes of that meeting.

It should be pointed out that many English translations of foreign-language hymns in *Christian Worship* are less than literal. Even though the wording found in stanza 4 of "A Mighty Fortress Is Our God" does not literally say what Luther wrote, it does express the truth he wanted to express: even though the enemies of Jesus Christ "hate, steal, hurt, or kill" and we lose everything, still "our victory is won" and "the kingdom's ours forever." These are words that every Christian can sing with conviction.

Hymn settings and altered tunes

One of the questions Eggert asked at the second meeting of the JHC was, "Which factors need to be considered in deciding on the basic type

---

[105] Private communication, Jeske to Prange.
[106] JHC minutes, January 4, 1992, p. 6; the vote on the motion was not reported.
[107] JHC minutes, January 6, 1992, p. 8.

of hymn harmonization? Different types of harmonization for different type hymns?"[108] The Hymn Committee discussed these questions, and their report to the JHC provoked "vigorous debate on the ideal degree of complexity of hymn harmonizations."[109] This debate resumed at the next meeting concerning "the comparative merits of 'organ' settings versus 'choral' settings for hymn harmonizations."[110]

The hymn settings in *The Lutheran Hymnal* are chordal, and the four voices can be readily sung by choirs and even by worshipers in the pew. Many of the settings in *Lutheran Book of Worship* and *Lutheran Worship* depart from this style and don't work well for four-part singing. They are referred to in the above resolution as "organ settings." Some tunes, notably plainsong melodies like "Oh, Come, Oh, Come, Emmanuel," are better harmonized with what has been called a linear setting.

The JHC, especially the Hymn Committee, struggled with how to best set each individual melody. Backer presented a study to that committee titled "The Texture of Hymns in the New/Revised Hymnal of WELS." The Hymn Committee report states that "by consensus it was agreed that settings should be simple, chordal, choral rather than in organ style."[111] Yet this was not followed in all cases, and concern continued to be expressed about how difficult some settings were. Prange reports that at a meeting of the District Worship Coordinators, "we got into the matter of hymn tune settings with much discussion of how difficult they should be."[112] This concern prompted the Hymn Committee to review all settings that had been approved up to that time.

When a certain tune is used for more than one hymn in *Christian Worship*, the JHC decided to provide alternate settings. There is a note at the bottom of the hymn where these alternates are offered. Near the end of the project, music editor Moldenhauer reviewed the use of multiple tunes and settings.[113] It was also decided to provide 16 hymns with descants and 12 with guitar chords.[114]

---

[108] Eggert, "Questions and Areas of Concern," February 21, 1985, p. 1.
[109] JHC minutes, January 2, 1986, p. 1.
[110] JHC minutes, May 30, 1986, p. 1.
[111] Hymn Committee progress report, August 13, 1987.
[112] Prange diary, October 21, 1989.
[113] JHC minutes, July 31, 1991, p. 7.
[114] The list of these hymns is given in *Christian Worship*, p. 937.

The rhythm and even notes of some familiar melodies were changed. One example is the tune ES IST EIN ROS ("Behold, a Branch Is Growing"). There are 14 changes in the rhythm of this hymn in *Christian Worship* compared with *The Lutheran Hymnal*. Why? Rhythmic changes were often made because of the original character of certain tunes. Almost all new hymnals have followed a general editorial guideline of preferring earlier forms of hymn melodies. The JHC generally sought to follow the same rhythm and notes in melodies found in other hymnals, especially Lutheran ones, because these would be the basis for choir and organ music published in the future. The setting of ES IST EIN ROS in *Christian Worship* (No. 47) is nearly identical with that in *Lutheran Book of Worship* (No. 58) and *Lutheran Worship* (No. 67).

In time worshipers will become familiar with these new rhythms as they did with those of the past.

Service of Word and Sacrament

At each meeting of the Joint Hymnal Committee, items from both the Hymn and Liturgy Committees were acted on. After the Liturgy Committee had completed its long struggle to revise the pages 5 and 15 services of *The Lutheran Hymnal,* it took up the task of revising other services and creating some new ones. The most ambitious of these was the Service of Word and Sacrament.

It had been agreed from the beginning of the hymnal project that another Word and sacrament service was needed in addition to the revised pages 5 and 15. When the Liturgy Committee began discussing what form this service should take, it was decided not to provide an alternate musical setting for the text of the Common Service, the traditional western rite.[115] The service would have new text and music but would follow the basic structure of the western rite.

Schulz describes this service in a report that he made on Liturgy Committee progress:

> Liturgy Committee 3 has produced an entirely new service in which the Lord's Supper will be celebrated. At the present time this service is called "A Service of Word and Sacrament," although some committee members would like to call it "An American Service." It has many elements

---

[115]Both *Lutheran Book of Worship* and *Lutheran Worship* provided alternate musical settings for the western rite.

that tie it to the past and make it unmistakably Lutheran. But it also has some features that will lead the worshiper to reflect deeply and positively on his/her Christianity when leaving church. It has the following major divisions:

FORGIVE US, LORD (Greeting, Confession, Absolution)
HEAR US, LORD (a *Kyrie, Gloria,* and Prayer for the Day)
TEACH US, LORD (Lesson, Gospel, Sermon)
FEED US, LORD (Sacrament)
USE US, LORD (Response to the Word and Sacrament, Offering, and Prayer of the Church)
BLESS US, LORD (Final exhortation to the worshiper going out into the world, followed by the traditional blessing)

The Liturgy Committee has approved the text. No liturgical music has been prepared for this or any service (except for that of the *Sampler,* which was prepared by James Engel). We have had many discussions on this subject and wish to pursue the topic again this week.[116]

In August 1987 the JHC gave "preliminary acceptance to the text of the Service of Word and Sacrament."[117] There were questions raised, however, about the way the service was structured. The service was discussed again at the August 1988 JHC meeting.[118] The motion to strike the sit/stand rubrics was lost. Although several spoke in favor of having liturgical dialogue either all spoken or all sung, the reluctant consensus was to go with WELS tradition and use spoken versicles with sung responses. The motion was approved to "send the Service of Word and Sacrament to composers."[119]

Finding the right musical setting for the text proved to be a big problem. Prange reports on an earlier meeting of the Liturgy Committee: "Jim Engel there for entire meeting. We went through items related to . . . Word and Sacrament. In the afternoon we listened to and sang the various compositions we had received. All agreed that only about

---

[116]Schulz, "Goal and Implementation," August 11, 1987; this version of the Service of Word and Sacrament had no opening hymn but included an "entrance hymn" after the absolution.

[117]JHC minutes, August 14, 1987, p. 2.

[118]JHC minutes, August 8, 1988, p. 2.

[119]JHC minutes, August 11, 1988, p. 6.

three were worthy of further consideration."[120] At the October 1988 meeting of the Liturgy Committee, there was more discussion on musical settings. Prange reports: "Engel presented some examples of work done. Tough struggle."[121] There was also discussion about reconsidering the entire text of the service, but a motion to do so resulted in a tie vote.[122] The committee did, however, make some changes in the service, including dropping the designations for the major divisions and other revisions that brought it more in line with other services being developed.

With Engel's death in April 1989, the Liturgy Committee lost its consultant in the matter of musical settings. Eggert and Moldenhauer stepped into the breech. At its September 1989 meeting, the committee heard a setting for the Service of Word and Sacrament that Eggert had prepared. Originally it was hoped that one composer would produce a setting for the entire text that would be acceptable. But in the end the Liturgy Committee had to select settings from four different composers: Eggert—*Kyrie,* Song of Praise, Preface; Moldenhauer—General Verse; David Schack—*Sanctus, Agnus Dei;* Richard Hillert—Thank the Lord (used by permission from *Lutheran Book of Worship*).[123] The setting for the Service of Word and Sacrament was presented to the JHC in August 1990 and approved for critical review.[124]

The service was presented to the District Worship Coordinators at their October 1990 meeting. Initially the Commission on Worship planned to field-test this service in 100 congregations during the 1991 Easter season,[125] but this was later revised to authorize a "field test in volunteer congregations."[126] One reason for this change was the fact that the service was extensively tested in 12 district seminars conducted in early 1991 by the committee for "Revitalizing Parish Ministry," part of the spiritual renewal effort of the synod. One of the members of this committee, James Huebner, also provided an introduction and explanation of the service. The Service of Word and Sacrament was used as the opening service of the WELS

---

[120]Prange diary, March 18, 1988.
[121]Prange diary, October 14, 1988.
[122]Prange diary, December 10, 1988.
[123]See *Christian Worship,* p. 926, for this information.
[124]JHC minutes, August 8, 1990, p. 6.
[125]CW minutes, November 16–17, 1990, p. 2.
[126]CW minutes, March 15–16, 1991, p. 3.

National Convention in August 1991, where Prange reports it "sang very well."[127]

Not everyone was pleased, however, with the service. Congregations that field-tested the service asked members to fill out questionnaires. One person wrote: "I hate to sound so negative, but I have never been hit by something so repulsive and unappealing as this pretense of being a version of the historic liturgy of the Christian church. It shows that those who concocted it don't know the historic liturgy of Christendom. . . . If J. S. Bach were to worship in _____, he'd be lost in the shuffle just like me. . . . I am truly saddened by what's been happening in my lifetime as it has affected my worship. . . . How much longer will sound doctrine stand in our midst if we let our precious liturgical heritage slip away?" There were, no doubt, also many positive responses to this service, but one tends to hear more often from those who have negative feelings about a certain item.

The Service of Word and Sacrament is different. But it does not compromise in any way the truth of God's Word; in fact, much of its wording comes straight from Scripture. And it has proved to be very popular in the congregations using *Christian Worship*.

Service of the Word

Along with a new service in which Holy Communion would be celebrated, the Liturgy Committee also prepared a service that emphasized the reading and preaching of the Word of God. Several members of the JHC urged that a service be constructed that gave variety. The proposed service was presented to the JHC in January 1987. The minutes report that Johnson presented the proposed Service of the Word. Its most prominent feature would be four basic services—Christ our Servant, King, Shepherd, and Lord—to be used at different times in the church year. Following are some points noted during the discussion:

1. There is no regular psalmody for the day.
2. If the amount of liturgical music were kept to a minimum, this service could be very helpful to missions, exploratory services, and churches with slender musical resources.
3. The offertory sentences came in for some criticism.

---
[127] Prange diary, August 5, 1991.

4. It was suggested that the relationship of the four themes to the seasons of the church year might be more clearly spelled out.[128]

The Liturgy Committee continued to work on this service, and a revised version was presented to the JHC in January 1988 with the request for reactions and suggestions from committee members.[129] One of the things creating a problem was how best to print these four services: all four in columns side by side, two separate services in two columns to a page, or all four services printed separately. The JHC chose the first of these options and approved the Service of the Word for critical review in August 1988.[130] This review resulted in further revisions of the text and the authorization to request composition of liturgical music.[131] The musical setting was ready for the January 1990 JHC meeting and was approved for field-testing that was carried out in the fall of 1990.[132]

The results of this field test by various congregations showed that a major revision of the service was needed. Among the major criticisms was the fact that the format created confusion for the worshiper. As a result, the Liturgy Committee decided to rework the service completely. Prange reports his sentiment: "Meeting of Liturgy Committee. Went through Service of the Word. I pushed for one rather simple service with propers giving the variation. This view seems to be prevailing."[133] The Liturgy Committee was feeling some pressure to complete work on this service because the hymnal project was nearing completion.

A major revision was offered to the JHC at its summer 1991 meeting. Liturgy Committee chairman Hartwig reports: "The Service of the Word was most drastically revised in consequence of criticism which came from the field-testing."[134] The JHC approved the service for field-testing "as soon as possible at the discretion of the project director and music editor." But a revision of the absolution was requested.[135] Some

---

[128]JHC minutes, January 2, 1987, pp. 2,3.
[129]JHC minutes, January 22, 1988, p. 3.
[130]JHC minutes, August 9, 1988, pp. 2,3.
[131]JHC minutes, July 31 and August 4, 1989, pp. 2,5.
[132]JHC minutes, January 4, 1990, p. 5.
[133]Prange diary, May 10, 1991.
[134]Report of the Liturgy Committee, July 29, 1991.
[135]JHC minutes, August 2, 1991, pp. 11,12.

slight alterations were again made in this service at the last two meetings of the JHC. Many hours were spent in working on earlier versions of this service, but in the end, time ran out and the resulting service is indeed "rather simple."

The Common Service

The *Sampler* had included a revision of the TLH page 5/15 services. This service had been thoroughly field-tested by synod congregations and met a generally favorable response. But there were some valid criticisms of the revised service which needed to be addressed.

Two of the major points of disagreement within the Liturgy Committee and the JHC were a replay of previous discussions: the role of the *Kyrie* and the placement of the Psalm. Tiefel and Prange, both members of the Liturgy Committee, found themselves at odds on these two issues. They decided to have dinner together and try to come to an agreement that both could support. Prange reports this meeting: "I had 6:00 P.M. dinner with Tiefel at Alioto's. We went through the *Sampler* service. I will not budge on *Kyrie* but will on placement of the Psalm (response to first lesson)."[136] Tiefel agreed to support this compromise.

This broke the deadlock in the Liturgy Committee, which presented a revised version of what came to be called The Common Service at the August 1990 meeting of the JHC. The *Kyrie* remained as part of the Confession of Sins; the Psalm was placed after the First Lesson. Discussion on The Common Service continued at the January 1991 meeting. Some members of the JHC did not want to make any changes in the *Sampler* service. A motion was defeated "to follow the *Sampler* order in the Lessons and Psalm placement."[137]

There was also considerable debate about the placement of the Lord's Prayer and singing of the Doxology. The motion prevailed to "print the *Sampler* version of the Lord's Prayer and the Doxology with 'yours.'"[138] This had the effect of retaining the familiar form of the Lord's Prayer in the TLH communion order, where the presiding minister prayed the petitions and the congregation sang the Doxology. The JHC met again in the summer of 1991, and the previous decision was reversed. The Lord's Prayer was removed completely from the Communion order

---

[136] Prange diary, January 19, 1989.
[137] JHC minutes, January 3, 1991, p. 2.
[138] JHC minutes, January 7, 1991, p. 10.

and placed after the Prayer of the Church, to be spoken entirely by the people. It was also resolved "to distribute The Common Service synod-wide to all pastors, at a time to be determined."[139]

There was some sentiment in the synod to print the complete pages 5 and 15 services of *The Lutheran Hymnal* unrevised in the new hymnal. A memorial to the 1991 convention of the synod asked "that the new hymnal retain the page 5 and page 15 liturgies of *The Lutheran Hymnal* as additional worship choices."[140] The JHC went on record as opposing this course of action: "RESOLVED: that the sentiments expressed by the chairman be those of the JHC regarding not printing TLH pages 5 and 15 in *Christian Worship* (unanimous vote)."[141] The convention resolved "that the page 5 and page 15 liturgies of *The Lutheran Hymnal* be printed in 'new hymnal' format" but left it up to the JHC as to how this should be done.[142] The JHC decided to ask Northwestern Publishing House to reprint pages 5 to 31 of *The Lutheran Hymnal* in a booklet form that could be glued into the front cover of the new hymnal.[143]

The introductory note in *Christian Worship* says of The Common Service: "[This] is a version of the historic liturgy of the Christian church. It became the service commonly used by English-speaking Lutherans in America and appeared as 'The Order of the Holy Communion' in *The Lutheran Hymnal*." Because of its long and wide use among American Lutherans and its close association with the historic Christian rite, a form of The Common Service similar to that in *Christian Worship* will no doubt remain a standard in our congregations.

Nicene Creed

The most public controversy that erupted during the entire hymnal project was over the wording of the Nicene Creed, specifically two phrases: to confess that Jesus came down from heaven "for us and for our salvation," leaving out the word "men" after "us," and that Jesus "became fully human," replacing the word "man." Both these changes were the result of the JHC's endeavor to use inclusive language wherever possible.

---

[139] JHC minutes, July 29–August 2, 1991, pp. 9,10,12.
[140] 1991 BORAM, p. 342.
[141] JHC minutes, August 1, 1991, p. 10.
[142] 1991 *Proceedings*, p. 96.
[143] JHC minutes, September 27, 1991, p. 4.

The JHC began the lengthy discussion of this matter at the January 1988 meeting. The report in the minutes is quite detailed: "Hartwig presented the Liturgy Committee's versions of the Apostles' Creed, Nicene Creed, and Lord's Prayer. Preliminary discussion centered around the principles which would govern any text revisions. The influences most frequently mentioned: the ICET text [which the LBW has used almost verbatim]; TLH's version, which is what people are used to; the Latin or Greek original text; LW's version; the need for clarity and consistency; scriptural considerations. Various members of the Liturgy Committee made the point that our only real alternative was an eclectic text, that none of the above influences or principles were absolutely determinative. And yet many speakers urged that the ICET text be given the greatest weight in order to bring the WELS into the mainstream of liturgical usage."[144]

The acronym ICET refers to the International Consultation on English Texts, a group that had published English translations of some of the most basic texts used in Christian worship, whatever the denomination. This group later took the name English Language Liturgical Consultation (ELLC).

Several wording changes were made in the Nicene Creed at that meeting. "We" was substituted for "I." This reflects the original Greek and makes the Nicene Creed a confession of the whole church. The Apostles' Creed is more of a personal confession related to its roots as a baptismal profession of faith and retains "I." At the beginning of the Second Article, "we believe" replaced "and." The word "men" was dropped from the phrase "for us men and for our salvation." The minutes give this rationale for the change: "the word is unnecessary and too easily perceived as sexist." There was one "no" vote on this change. A number of other wording changes were approved at this meeting, none of which produced much controversy. The Liturgy Committee was asked to proceed with critical review and field-testing of these changes.

At the next meeting of the JHC, there was further action on the wording of the Nicene Creed. This resulted from the resolution approved by a vote of 7 to 2 (obviously a number of abstentions) "that the ICET text be used for the Nicene Creed, except when textual, confessional, or stylistic considerations are stronger."[145] The effect of this resolution was to

---

[144] JHC minutes, January 22, 1988, p. 1; other references to this meeting are from these minutes.

[145] JHC minutes, August 11, 1988, p. 6.

substitute the words "fully human" for "man" when confessing the incarnate Son of God.[146]

Hartwig was asked by the JHC to "write up a detailed rationale for all changes in the two creeds."[147] His essay "The Creeds in Contemporary English" appeared in the Summer 1989 *Wisconsin Lutheran Quarterly,* and a shorter version was included in the Summer 1989 *Focus on Worship.* Hartwig also prepared an article for the *Northwestern Lutheran* titled "The Creeds for a New Day."[148] In this way the revised texts of the Apostles' Creed and Nicene Creed appeared in print for the general public.

Hartwig explained the reasons for the major changes in the creeds. Concerning the term "fully human," he writes: "This revision is one of the finest in the creed. It gives the sense of the original text precisely. More important, it states the whole Bible truth. Our Savior was in all points made like us; he was a human being in the full sense of the word; he was a perfect man with rational soul and human flesh. And as we become accustomed to this new form of expression, we may also be reminded that sinful humans are no longer fully human in the perfection that God made us. We are 'bent people.'"

It was not long after the appearance of this article that questions and criticism began to be heard. It was charged that because ICET was a "liberal group," the JHC should not use their wording for the Nicene Creed. One layman wrote President Mischke: "The point I am wondering about now is why in the Nicene Creed we feel we have to make our Lord a neutral human instead of the Son of Man the Bible so clearly states that he is."[149] To the credit of this individual, after he received an answer from JHC chairman Prange, he again wrote Mischke, thanking him and saying that things were explained "very well and removed my concerns."[150]

But the issue was far from settled. Questions continued to be raised. Two memorials were addressed to the 1991 WELS Convention asking the synod to reject the JHC wording of the Nicene Creed. The delegates supported the JHC translation by adopting the following resolution:

---

[146]See JHC minutes, February 10, 1989.
[147]JHC minutes, January 22, 1988, p. 3.
[148]*Northwestern Lutheran,* May 15, 1990, pp. 190-193.
[149]Letter to Mischke, June 16, 1990.
[150]Letter to Mischke, July 24, 1990.

> WHEREAS the JHC has presented the English-speaking church with a historical, readable, recitable, contemporary, yet soundly confessional rendition of the Nicene Creed for use in our worship services; therefore, be it
> RESOLVED, That the committee proceed to incorporate its wording of the same into the liturgies of the "new hymnal."[151]

This resolution quieted the waters for a time, though letters critical of the translation continued to be received. A new and much more public controversy erupted after the last meeting of the JHC had been held in April 1992. William Weinrich, a professor at the LCMS seminary in Fort Wayne, Indiana, published an article in the *Concordia Theological Quarterly* titled "The New WELS Creed."[152] After presenting his reasons for rejecting the translation "fully human" when referring to Christ, he concluded: "Whatever else the new WELS creed may be, it falls seriously short of reasserting the faith of Nicaea and the trinitarian and christological doctrines which the fathers there believed to be necessary to confess and to preach the gospel purely."

Christian News reprinted Weinrich's article and captioned an anonymous letter with the bold heading "Is the WELS still orthodox?"[153] A number of letters were also received from WELS pastors about the wording of the Nicene Creed, including the omission of the word "men" in the phrase "for us and for our salvation." One JHC member suggested that perhaps the wording "for the salvation of all" would be better and would satisfy the critics. But the leaders of the hymnal project stood firm against any change. Tiefel contributed an article to the Winter 1993 issue of the *Wisconsin Lutheran Quarterly* defending the JHC wording of the Nicene Creed against the criticisms of Weinrich and others. Prange reports in a diary entry: "Talked to Kermit [Moldenhauer], Jeb [Schaefer], and Kurt [Eggert] on 'fully human' and other things. Kurt talked to Mischke, who feels we should make no changes."[154]

The work of translating the creeds into contemporary English was theologically beneficial for the members of the JHC. It presented them with the opportunity to grapple with essential doctrines of the Christian

---

[151] 1991 *Proceedings*, p. 97.
[152] *Concordia Theological Quarterly*, Vol. 56, No. 2-3, April–June 1992.
[153] *Christian News*, September 14, 1992, p. 8.
[154] Prange diary, December 4, 1992.

faith. The ensuing controversy forced many people, including pastors and professors, to think through again just what is meant when we confess that Jesus Christ is "fully human."

Morning Praise and Evening Prayer

The Lutheran Hymnal included The Order of Matins and The Order of Vespers. Most WELS congregations were at least familiar with the evening service; at times some congregations used Matins in place of The Order of Morning Service without Communion. What form would these services take in the new hymnal?

The Liturgy Committee began working on a revision of Matins and Vespers in 1986 and presented these to the JHC in January 1987.[155] The language of the texts was updated. Both revisions suggested beginning with an "ordinary" hymn, one sung each time the service was used. Some members of the JHC suggested that the services needed to provide more opportunity for singing hymns. There were questions about the music for the canticles in these services. The Liturgy Committee was asked to revise both services "taking into consideration the suggestions and comments" made.

At the next meeting of the JHC in August 1987, the texts of both services gained preliminary acceptance, and the Liturgy Committee was "given permission to seek liturgical music for the sung responses and canticles."[156] At this time these services were called Morning and Evening Worship, replacing the Latin names Matins and Vespers.

As the Liturgy Committee went about the task of providing music for these services, Eggert came with the proposal that Evening Worship have alternate beginnings: the familiar one from *The Lutheran Hymnal* and one patterned after the Service of Light in *Lutheran Book of Worship* and *Lutheran Worship*.[157] Eggert had been much impressed with this service when he attended a summer music conference at St. Olaf College. The Liturgy Committee accepted his suggestion. Eggert also supplied the music for the two canticles in Evening Worship: "Song of Mary" and "Song of Simeon." Both were included in the service rather than being options as in *The Lutheran Hymnal*. The text for the "Song of Simeon" was slightly different from that in The Common Service to fit

---

[155] JHC minutes, January 2, 1987, pp. 1,2.
[156] JHC minutes, August 14, 1987, p. 2.
[157] Prange diary, April 8, 1989.

the music Eggert had written. Words from Psalm 141, "Let My Prayer Rise before You," were added with a setting from *Lutheran Book of Worship* by David Schack, used by permission. Seasonal Responses to the Lesson, which could be sung or said, were supplied for both the evening and morning services.[158]

The Liturgy Committee had hoped to provide new music also for Morning Worship, but this proved to be especially difficult because of the long hymn of praise, the *Te Deum*. Prange reports on a meeting of the Liturgy Committee held in a motel room during the August 1988 JHC meeting: "Met in Johnson's room. Some revisions in our services. Then we looked through four settings for Morning Worship. The *Te Deum* will be difficult to handle. None were very satisfactory."[159] Later that afternoon the entire JHC heard music editor Engel present the four settings. The minutes report: "The group sang each through twice and then rated them piece by piece and overall. The purpose was only informational and educational: the Liturgy Committee has not committed itself to anything yet regarding the music."[160]

The Liturgy Committee continued to struggle with the problem of what to do about the music in Morning Worship. In April 1989, when meeting in West St. Paul, Minnesota, at Johnson's church, the committee interviewed a local musician and sang through her setting of Morning Worship. This setting was sung by the JHC near the end of their summer 1989 meeting.[161] The minutes report "many favorable comments," that this setting was "good or better than any of those presented at earlier JHC meetings," but "nevertheless there are some compositional weaknesses that would need to be addressed." Several other observations were noted: "writing a *through-composed Te Deum* is a formidable task and might be beyond the ability of anyone available to us," and "the TLH settings for the *Venite* and *Te Deum* are not perceived as being boring or problems. Is it possible to keep them as alternates somewhere?" The JHC took no action on the setting they had heard.

After Moldenhauer became full-time music editor for the project in the summer of 1989, he attended the Liturgy Committee meeting in September. Prange comments on this meeting: "We spent a lot of time

---

[158] The final versions of texts and settings for Evening Worship were approved by the JHC for critical review and field-testing in January 1990.

[159] Prange diary, August 10, 1988.

[160] JHC minutes, August 10, 1988, p. 5.

[161] JHC minutes, August 4, 1989, p. 6.

talking about _____'s Matins setting. Moldenhauer is not enthused about it."[162] The upshot of this continuing uncertainty about the musical setting for Matins led the Liturgy Committee to go back to the setting in *The Lutheran Hymnal*. The revised TLH setting was presented to the JHC in January 1991 and was approved for critical review.[163] At the same meeting, the names for the two services were amended to Morning Praise and Evening Prayer.[164] The attempt to provide a new musical setting for the revised service of Morning Praise had failed, but not for lack of trying.

Among the questions Eggert asked at the first JHC meeting in January 1985 was, "Will chants be provided for the pastor's part in any of the liturgies or portions of them?"[165] This subject came up at the April 1989 meeting of the Liturgy Committee, which "got into a discussion of whether we should include pastor's chant. Resolved to do this in Matins and Vespers."[166] The JHC accepted this proposal, and the minister's chant line is provided in *Christian Worship* for Morning Praise and Evening Prayer but for no other service.[167] This helps to make these two services with monastic origins unique in the new hymnal.

Singing the Psalms

At the initial meeting of the JHC in January 1985, Prange presented an essay that suggested that one improvement in the liturgical section of the new hymnal would be to make greater use of the Psalms.[168] Later that year he made a presentation to the Liturgy Committee that questioned whether it would be "practical to try to get congregations to chant the Psalms."[169] Prange expressed a preference for placing the Psalm "before rather than after the First Lesson." He went on to say, "If the people would be able to sing the psalmody as a musical response to the First Lesson, then it might better come after [the First Lesson]. But as things are, the Psalm between the Prayer of the Day and First Lesson

---

[162]Prange diary, September 15, 1989.
[163]JHC minutes, January 4, 1991, p. 6.
[164]JHC minutes, January 2–7, 1991, pp. 1,6.
[165]Eggert, "Guidelines for the New Hymnal," January 18, 1985, p. 1.
[166]Prange diary, April 8, 1989.
[167]JHC minutes, January 4, 1990, p. 4; January 4, 1991, p. 5.
[168]Prange, "Improving the Liturgical Section for the New Hymnal," p. 2.
[169]Prange, "The Use of the Psalms in Christian Worship," October 17, 1985, p. 2.

would be the linkage between the introductory service and the 'procession' to the place for reading the Lessons; as such it would retain some of the flavor of the Introit."

The placement of the Psalm in the service was a major point of controversy for the JHC as is demonstrated by this report: "There was considerable discussion on the role of the Introit/psalmody/sentence. Some pleaded for its retention in the traditional place before the *Gloria*; some urged that provision be made for greater singing of the psalmody; some . . . pleaded for more encouragement for using full psalms."[170] In the *Sampler* the Psalm was placed after the Prayer of the Day, and 12 psalms were included, taken from *Lutheran Worship* and pointed for singing, but without refrains. This method for singing the Psalm did not prove particularly successful. One synod pastor wrote on his *Sampler* questionnaire: "It is almost certain that the Psalm, when used, will be used almost exclusively as a responsive reading by the congregation." The *Lutheran Book of Worship* pointed the psalms but included no music.

The Liturgy Committee discovered a somewhat different way of singing psalms in the newly published Roman Catholic hymnal *Worship III*.[171] Here the psalms were presented on a single page (or in some cases two pages) with one or more antiphons (refrains) and the option of using either a psalm tone or Gelineau tone for singing the text. This way of doing the psalms appealed to the committee. Prange reports about a meeting of the Liturgy Committee: "Came to agreement on the form psalms should take."[172]

Liturgy subcommittee 3 (Hartwig, Johnson, Tiefel) did extensive work in shaping the psalm section for presentation to the JHC. Psalms were selected based on which would be used as propers; psalm refrains and chanting tones were chosen or composed with the help of Eggert and Moldenhauer; the psalm text was marked for singing. The entire Liturgy Committee sang through the psalm refrains, which in Prange's judgment were "generally very good."[173] The work on the psalms was presented to the JHC at its 1991 summer meeting and approved at the September meeting with some minor amendments.[174]

---

[170] JHC minutes, January 3, 1986, p. 2.

[171] *Worship III* (Chicago: GIA Publications, Inc., 1986); *Christian Worship*, p. 926, acknowledges 11 psalm settings from GIA.

[172] Prange diary, October 15, 1988.

[173] Prange diary, March 1, 1991.

[174] JHC minutes, September 27, 1991, pp. 2,3.

One decision concerning the singing of psalms has been criticized: the fact that in most cases only selected verses were printed and not entire psalms. This process of shortening the psalms continued up to the very end of the hymnal project. Just a month prior to the final JHC meeting, Prange reports that the Liturgy Committee "went through the psalms to shorten."[175] These were presented in April 1992 to the JHC, where the agenda for the meeting notes: "Information will come from Hartwig on the abridging on many of the psalms. Copy of the psalms which you receive will show this abridging. Refrain for Psalm 89 supplied. Refrains changed for Psalms 92 and 103. Drop Psalm 104." These abridgements and other changes were accepted, and the psalms were ready for inclusion in the new hymnal.[176]

Not a few members of the JHC wondered whether congregations would actually learn to sing the psalms. The earlier and latter expressions of doubt that this would ever be possible have been laid to rest. Singing psalms has become one of the significant improvements made in worship where *Christian Worship* is used. In fact, the form of psalm singing in *Christian Worship* has been adopted in the *Hymnal Supplement* of the Lutheran Church—Missouri Synod.

Holy Baptism

Another of Eggert's questions asked at the first meeting of the JHC was, "Which rites should be included in the hymnal: Baptism? Confirmation? Marriage? Burial?"[177] There was little disagreement within the JHC that services for baptism, marriage, and burial should be included. Crafting at least the first two proved to be a major challenge for the Liturgy Committee.

Subcommittee 3 was assigned the task of supplying the text for Holy Baptism. The philosophy with which the committee worked is described as follows: "The order of Holy Baptism . . . was designed to join the baptism with the regular order of service in a manner that would achieve a satisfactory integration of the baptism with the liturgies of corporate worship."[178] This rite was to replace the usual Confession of Sins and Absolution at the beginning of the service because of Luther's insight

---

[175] Prange diary, March 9, 1992.
[176] JHC minutes, April 3, 1992, p. 2.
[177] Eggert, "Guidelines for the New Hymnal," January 18, 1985, p. 2.
[178] *Christian Worship: Manual*, p. 165.

that "confessing sins and receiving forgiveness is nothing else than a reliving of baptism. Thus this order provides opportunity not only to baptize but also to recall the lasting blessings of baptism."[179]

This new order for Holy Baptism was presented to the JHC for the first time in January 1990. The minutes note that "comments were given on both sides on whether to build the rite around the Creed or Confession of Sins."[180] Prange reports: "Went through baptism service with many questions."[181] Some felt that the service should be more closely related to the Apostles' Creed, the baptismal confession of the church. The creed was not part of the rite of Holy Baptism. The JHC referred the service back to the Liturgy Committee for further study.

A revised version of the rite, but with no substantial changes, came back to the JHC in January 1991, which in Prange's words was "not really well accepted."[182] The text was amended at a number of places. Questions were raised about the diminished role of sponsors in this rite and the fact that the baptismal emphasis was somewhat overshadowed by its place within the Confession of Sins. Nevertheless, the JHC did resolve "to give tentative approval of Holy Baptism for critical review with exceptions noted."[183] Some additional revisions were made at the next meeting of the JHC when it was approved for use.[184] In *Christian Worship* this service is placed before any of the others, and its use in The Common Service, Service of Word and Sacrament, and Service of the Word is noted. A form for an emergency baptism is also included.[185]

Time will tell whether this effort to integrate the rite of Holy Baptism into the Confession of Sins part of the liturgy will have a lasting effect on future worship forms. It does emphasize an important teaching about Baptism that this sacrament ought to have lasting consequences throughout the life of a believer.

Christian Marriage

Those shaping the new hymnal considered it important to include a rite for Christian marriage in order to help set a standard for weddings

---

[179] *Christian Worship*, p. 12.
[180] JHC minutes, January 6, 1990, p. 7.
[181] Prange diary, January 6, 1990.
[182] Prange diary, January 5, 1991.
[183] JHC minutes, January 5, 1991, p. 7.
[184] JHC minutes, August 1–2, 1991, pp. 8,11.
[185] *Christian Worship*, p. 14.

in congregations of the synod. Eggert suggests that the "inclusion of the marriage rite in the hymnal might effect some stabilizing influence and help congregations and couples to keep a spiritual viewpoint of the ceremony rather than a concentration on the secular or sentimental."[186]

Though having such a service was desirable, it was no easy task to craft a rite that would satisfy everyone. Preparing a service for Christian marriage went on just as the Wisconsin Synod was dealing with the wider issue of the roles of man and woman in God's world. Discussions about this issue were taking place literally in every corner of the synod. As there were various opinions about this subject in the synod at large, so there were various opinions within the JHC.

Liturgy subcommittee 4 was assigned the initial responsibility for preparing this service for Christian marriage. As with other services being prepared for the hymnal, the committee took a look at previous marriage rites. In 1529 Luther proposed a three-step procedure to deal with "the bridegroom and bride (if they desire and ask it)."[187] The first step was to publish the banns from the pulpit. The second step was "marrying them at the entrance to the church with words such as these: 'Hans, dost thou desire Greta to be thy wedded wife?' *He shall say:* 'Yes.' 'Greta, dost thou desire Hans to be thy wedded husband?' *She shall say:* 'Yes.'" This step concluded with an exchange of rings and the wedding blessing.

The third step was before the altar, where the pastor read portions of Genesis chapters 1, 2, and 3 and Ephesians chapter 5. It is noteworthy that Luther suggests reading the words addressed to the husband ("love your wives") before those addressed to wives ("submit yourselves unto your own husbands"). Notice also that these words come after the vows and not before. Luther concludes this step by quoting Proverbs 18:22 and saying a prayer. The entire service was very simple.

Luther did not ask the bride to promise to *obey* her husband. The word *obey* was added to the vows by John Calvin for the marriage service in Geneva.[188] The bride's promise to obey became a traditional part of the marriage ritual. It is included in *The Pastor's Agenda* prepared by the WELS Commission on Worship and published by Northwestern Publishing House in 1978: "N., will you have N., here present to be your husband? Will you love him, honor and obey him. . . ."[189] However, an

---

[186]Eggert, "Enriching Our Worship Heritage," June 1986, p. 14.

[187]*Luther's Works*, Vol. 53, "The Order of Marriage for Common Pastors," pp. 110-115.

[188]Stevenson, *To Join Together* (New York: Pueblo Publishing Company, 1987), p. 89.

[189]*Pastor's Agenda*, p. 23.

earlier agenda published by our synod did not include the promise to obey. Only words addressed to wives and husbands from Ephesians 5 were spoken.[190]

Prange, a member of liturgy subcommittee 4, had written an editorial for the *Northwestern Lutheran* titled "Domestic Violence," which touched on the promise to obey in the marriage vow: "Sometimes a husband will justify the abuse of his wife by suggesting that she had it coming: 'She did not obey me.' That is to make a travesty of the word which has often been included in the woman's marriage vow. To say the least, it is a word subject to gross misunderstanding when seeking to describe the proper relationship between husband and wife."[191]

The first draft of the marriage rite prepared by liturgy subcommittee 4 did not include the promise to obey or quote Ephesians chapter 5. Words and thoughts from 1 Corinthians chapter 13 were the basis for the the brief marriage exhortation, which concluded with the question addressed to the couple: "N. and N.: are you ready to bind yourselves together as husband and wife, promising love and faithfulness to each other as long as you both shall live?" Groom and bride were asked to declare together: "We are." This joint declaration of intent was a unique feature of this proposed rite. This was followed by the couple joining their right hands and speaking an identical promise to each other.

This version of the service was presented at the April 1989 meeting of the Liturgy Committee, where it was generally accepted, though questions were raised about the omission of the word *obey*.[192] Additional concerns were expressed about the fact that Ephesians chapter 5 was not quoted. The Liturgy Committee met again in September 1989 and decided to include words from Ephesians chapter 5 (wives to "submit" and husband to "love") in the rite's brief exhortation.

This revised marriage rite was presented to the JHC at the January 1990 meeting.[193] Concern was expressed that there were identical vows for groom and bride. Some members of the JHC expressed a strong desire for this service "to say more about the headship of man and sub-

---

[190] *Agende herausgegeben von der Allgemeinen Evang. Luth. Synode von Wisconsin u. a. Staaten* (Milwaukee: Northwestern Publishing House, 1926), pp. 129-131 (English translation).

[191] *Northwestern Lutheran*, May 1, 1988, p. 164.

[192] Prange diary, April 8, 1989.

[193] JHC minutes, January 4, 1990, p. 4.

mission of woman."[194] The service was referred to the Liturgy Committee for further study.

At the March meeting of this committee, much time was spent discussing the marriage service. Emotions ran high. Finally one member of the committee suggested a vow for groom and wife with slightly varied wording, and this was agreed to.[195] The committee met next in May, and again there was a major discussion on the wording of the marriage rite.[196] This time the issue centered on whether to include the words of Ephesians 5:21 in the exhortation: "Submit to one another out of reverence for Christ." Then would follow the words of verse 22: "Wives, submit to your husbands as to the Lord." Those who supported including verse 21 pointed out that in the Greek text, the word for "submit" is not found in verse 22 but only inferred. The service as revised by the Liturgy Committee was approved for critical review by the JHC at its August 1990 meeting, though the promises of groom and bride were referred once again to the Liturgy Committee.[197]

Finding suitable wording for the promises acceptable to all members of the Liturgy Committee continued into the summer of 1991. Members exchanged letters and telephone calls expressing their various positions. Finally in July 1991, during a meeting of the JHC, Prange reports that "the Liturgy Committee met and approved the marriage services with no changes from what Wayne [Schulz] and I had done."[198] This final revision of the rite for Christian marriage was approved by the JHC for distribution,[199] with final approval given in January 1992.[200]

The text approved for Christian marriage by the JHC includes a portion of Ephesians 5:21 followed by specific application for wives and husbands. The groom is asked to promise that he will "be guided by the counsel and direction God has given in his Word and love [his] wife as Christ loved the Church." The bride is asked to promise that she will "be guided by the counsel and direction God has given in his Word and submit to [her] husband as the Church submits to Christ." This word-

---

[194]Prange diary, January 4, 1990.
[195]Prange diary, March 16, 1990.
[196]Prange diary, May 4, 1990.
[197]JHC minutes, August 6-10, pp. 5,8.
[198]Prange diary, July 29, 1991.
[199]JHC minutes, August 2, 1991, p. 12.
[200]JHC minutes, January 4, 1992, p. 4.

ing brings out the truth that "it is reverence for Christ on the part of husband and wife that lays the foundation for Christian marriage."[201]

The rite of Christian Marriage in *Christian Worship* has been generally well received by pastors and congregations of the synod. It has served its original intent of being a stabilizing influence and helping couples to keep a spiritual viewpoint of the ceremony rather than a concentration on the secular or sentimental.

Church year calendar and propers

Both the *Lutheran Book of Worship* and *Lutheran Worship* had adopted a revised calendar for the church year. The three pre-Lent Sundays of Septuagesima, Sexagesima, and Quinquagesima had been eliminated by an expansion of the Epiphany season. Sundays in the Easter season were designated as being "of Easter" rather than "after Easter." Sundays were counted "after Pentecost" rather than "after Trinity." *Lutheran Book of Worship* called the last Sunday of the church year "Christ the King"; *Lutheran Worship* called it "Sunday of the Fulfillment." Those shaping the new hymnal had to decide whether to keep the calendar from *The Lutheran Hymnal* or make some revisions.

Both of the new Lutheran hymnals included a three-year selection of Scripture readings for the Sundays and festivals of the church year. This series had been prepared by the Inter-Lutheran Commission on Worship. A special WELS Lectionary Committee had studied these selections and reported to the 1977 convention of the synod that "no doctrinal, pastoral, or liturgical reasons were found to stand in the way of the use of these series of texts." The synod resolved that "the use of these series of texts be left to the discretion of the individual congregations of the synod."[202]

One of the questions raised by Eggert at the second meeting of the JHC was, "Which lectionary should be used for the Sunday service?"[203] The minutes for this meeting report that "there was considerable discussion on whether or not to use the ILCW three-year lectionary. It was recognized that most WELS pastors are using it, but some weaknesses were noted."[204] One of those critical of the three-year lectionary was the

---

[201] *Christian Worship*, p. 141.
[202] 1977 *Proceedings*, p. 158.
[203] Eggert, "Questions and Areas of Concern," February 21, 1985, p. 1.
[204] JHC minutes, March 1, 1985, p. 1.

ELS representative Erling Teigen, who touched on that subject in the essay he delivered at that JHC meeting.

To provide an opportunity for the JHC to study this question in some depth, an essay on the lectionary was presented by Prange in January 1986. He had served as chairman of the synod's Lectionary Committee, which had done the previous study of the ILCW readings. The minutes note that a number of points were made in the discussion expressing concern with the adoption of the three-year cycle of readings.[205]

Not only was it necessary to make decisions about the calendar and lectionary, but the other propers also needed to be considered for possible revision: the Introit (if this was retained), the Collect (Prayer of the Day), the Psalm selections (if longer portions were sung or said), and the Gradual. Eggert urged that the Gradual be replaced by the Verse of the Day, which was meant to introduce the reading of the Gospel.

In August 1986 the Liturgy Committee decided to recommend to the JHC that a listing of the ILCW three-year series, the historic series with possible minor alterations, the traditional collects as previously revised by the Commission on Worship, the verses, and the psalm references be included in the hymnal.[206] Several questions and concerns were raised at the January 1987 JHC meeting: Is the ILCW three-year series officially adopted for our book? Have its weaknesses been discussed? The printing of the propers will use up much space and provide a limited return for all the bulk. Will a three-year set of collects be prepared, or a one-year series, or both? The JHC took no action on this report.[207]

Over the next few years, the Liturgy Committee continued to work on all these items. It was decided not to include an Introit in the services and to replace the Gradual with the Verse of the Day. It was decided to publish the texts of the propers in a separate book with only a lectionary table included in the hymnal itself. The Liturgy Committee was ready with recommendations on the church year and lectionary at the August 1990 JHC meeting. With only slight variations, the calendar found in the other two Lutheran hymnals was proposed with one major exception: the last four Sundays of the year were called the "End Time Season" and given their own special names.[208] Both the three-year and one-year

---

[205] JHC minutes, January 2, 1986, p. 1.
[206] Report of the Liturgy Committee to the JHC, January 2–3, 1987.
[207] JHC minutes, January 2, 1987, p. 1.
[208] *Christian Worship*, p. 159.

series of readings were recommended for the new book. The JHC adopted these proposals.[209]

Liturgy subcommittee 4 had the major task of fleshing out the many details for the propers: slightly revising the ILCW three-year selections, making Psalm selections for Sundays and festivals, preparing revisions of the Prayer of the Day, and selecting the Verse of the Day. Some of this material was reported at the summer 1991 JHC meeting,[210] and additional items were ready for the final JHC meeting.[211] A revision of the traditional one-year series of readings and a selection of the Hymn of the Day was also completed.

One of the requests often heard by those shaping the new hymnal from pastors and others was the need to provide more opportunity for variety in our worship. The propers serve the purpose of offering just such variety, especially when they are utilized to the fullest extent. They also furnish educational resources for instruction in God's Word and its use in worship. Though revising the propers may not have consumed a lot of time on the JHC's agenda, this was an important and time-consuming process in preparing a new hymnal.

Other liturgical items

Several other items were included in the new hymnal whose development will be described in lesser detail. For the most part, these items did not evoke strong disagreements within the JHC, and relatively little time was spent on them in plenary sessions. However, in many cases individual members on the Liturgy Committee spent many hours preparing these items for the new book.

The most important item was the service for Christian funeral. As with Christian marriage, this service provided congregations with a model for corporate worship at this critical time in the lives of Christian families. Eggert suggested the need for such a service in the hymnal with the comment he made in an essay: "The [funeral] rite should provide for and encourage some participation by the congregation. Liturgically speaking, our synodical practice is quite barren."[212]

Most of the initial work on this service was done by Schulz and liturgy subcommittee 4. After being approved by the entire Liturgy

---

[209] JHC minutes, August 6–10, 1990, pp. 4,8.
[210] JHC minutes, July 29, 1991, p. 2.
[211] Agenda notes from JHC meeting, April 3–4, 1992, p. 2.
[212] Eggert, "Enriching Our Worship Heritage," June 1986, p. 15.

Committee, it was presented for the first time to the JHC in August 1988.[213] After further revision, the service was approved for critical review in August 1989,[214] which resulted in a few minor changes to the service. The JHC gave this service final approval in September 1991.[215] This rite in the new hymnal did much to remedy the "barren" practice that Eggert bemoaned.

The Lutheran Hymnal contained three litany-type prayers called Suffrages, which were not often used. The Liturgy Committee decided to replace these with three devotions: morning, evening, and general. These were presented to the JHC in February 1989, when they were reviewed and then referred back to the committee for some revisions.[216] The devotions were later approved for critical review and then given a final okay in September 1991.[217] They have served well their intended purpose of providing a brief order of worship for organizations and committees as well as schools, classes, and homes.

One unique addition to the new hymnal was a set of personal prayers. *The Lutheran Hymnal* did include four short prayers on page 4 for the worshiper and a set of collects on pages 102-109, which were used primarily in corporate worship rather than by individuals. The intention of the Liturgy Committee was to provide a set of very personal prayers that worshipers might use prior to the service.

A number of synod pastors were asked to write the personal prayers, which were then edited by the Liturgy Committee. This proved to be a very lengthy process and required much rewriting. The personal prayers were finally presented to the JHC in the summer of 1991, when the committee acted on 39 of them, the remainder being taken up in September.[218]

At that September meeting, there was a long discussion about the personal prayers. Prange reports on this debate: "Division as to whether they [personal prayers] are appropriate in hymnal. I was grieved that this came to floor now. Left all in confusion."[219] The next day the JHC referred the entire matter of personal prayers back to the Liturgy Com-

---

[213]JHC minutes, August 9, 1988, p. 3.
[214]JHC minutes, August 4, 1989, p. 6.
[215]JHC minutes, September 28, 1991, p. 6.
[216]JHC minutes, February 10, 1989, p. 2.
[217]JHC minutes, September 28, 1991, p. 6.
[218]JHC minutes, July 30, 1991, pp. 4,5; September 27, 1991, pp. 2,4.
[219]Prange diary, September 26, 1991.

mittee. When the order for items in the liturgical section of the hymnal came up, the personal prayers related to worship were placed right after the introduction to the hymnal, but the rest of the prayers were situated near the back of the section.[220] This disappointed some who felt that the worshiper would not as likely use these personal prayers unless they were at the very beginning of the hymnal.

In January 1992 the JHC spent more time on the personal prayers. Prange reports that one night the committee "met till 9:00 P.M. on the personal prayers. We have a ways to go yet on that. I was tired."[221] The next morning it was "resolved to give final approval to the personal prayers with the exceptions noted."[222] Work on revising the prayers continued after the plenary sessions of the JHC had concluded when liturgy subcommittee 4 met with Moldenhauer "to revise personal prayers. We cut out quite a few of them."[223] The agenda notes for the final JHC meeting in April report: "the personal prayers have been extensively revised with many deletions and some additions." These further revisions were accepted by the JHC and became part of the new hymnal as aids for the prayer life of individual Christians.

The new hymnal also included another item not found in *The Lutheran Hymnal*, 11 responsive Prayers of the Church—two in major services and the following on pages 123-131 of *Christian Worship:* Advent, Epiphany, Lent, Easter, Sundays after Pentecost, General Thanksgiving, Mission of the Church, The Nation, and Prayer of Intercession (Bidding Prayer). The texts for these prayers came to the JHC rather late in the project. They were reviewed at the January 1992 meeting[224] and given final approval at the final meeting in April. These responsive prayers have been favorably received in congregations and often used.

The translation of the Athanasian Creed in *The Lutheran Hymnal* needed updating, and this work was done primarily by Hartwig. The JHC reviewed the new version in January 1991,[225] and it was given final approval in September.[226] However, acceptance of the wording of the introductory paragraph intended for the hymnal was deferred in

---

[220]JHC minutes, September 27, 1991, p. 4.
[221]Prange diary, January 3, 1992.
[222]JHC minutes, January 4, 1992, p. 3.
[223]Prange diary, January 7, 1992.
[224]JHC minutes, January 3, 1992, pp. 2,3.
[225]JHC minutes, January, 5, 1991, p. 7.
[226]JHC minutes, September 28, 1991, p. 6.

January 1992 pending further revision,[227] with final approval coming in April.

A new order shaped for *Christian Worship* was Private Confession. This was not intended for corporate worship but for individual use, suggesting words a Christian might use in confessing sins to and being forgiven by a fellow Christian. This order was first presented to the JHC in January 1990, and "discussion included the question of whether it should be included in the hymnal."[228] The JHC concluded that there was a need for it. At their next meeting, they gave approval to send this order out for critical review.[229] After some further revision, this order received final approval in January 1992.[230] It is difficult to know how often it is being used. Its presence in the hymnal does call to the attention of Christians the fact that Martin Luther encouraged the practice of private confession.

Another new item prepared for individual use was Personal Preparation for Holy Communion. The Liturgy Committee at first recommended that a revised translation of Luther's "Christian Questions" be printed in the hymnal along with the Small Catechism. But when it became evident that the Small Catechism would not be included, a new set of questions and answers was prepared. These were not ready for the final JHC meeting and so were referred to the Executive Committee for later action.[231]

Luther's Small Catechism

From the beginning of the project, the JHC was committed to including the text of the Small Catechism in the hymnal. The committee was also aware that certain portions of the Small Catechism would be included in services and other rites. So it was necessary to decide just who would be responsible for these wordings. For that purpose Eggert, Prange, and Tiefel met with William Fischer, representing the Board for Parish Education (BPE), on May 4, 1987. Three agreements were reached at that meeting:

---

[227] JHC minutes, January 4, 1992, p. 5.
[228] JHC minutes, January 6, 1990, p. 7.
[229] JHC minutes, August 8, 1990, p. 6.
[230] JHC minutes, January 4, 1992, p. 4.
[231] JHC minutes, April 4, 1992, p. 4.

1. The texts in the liturgical portions of the services should be fixed by the JHC (Apostles' Creed; Nicene Creed; Lord's Prayer; Baptism, Fourth; Words of Institution; Luther's Morning and Evening Prayers).
2. The BPE should fix the texts for the remaining portions of the Small Catechism to be printed in the hymnal.
3. The reprinting of the Small Catechism is a matter for Northwestern Publishing House to resolve but should be no problem.[232]

This agreement was tested when in May 1990 Fischer called Eggert's attention to the fact that the wording of Luther's Morning and Evening Prayers in the devotions being considered for the hymnal differed from that of the current version of the Small Catechism printed by Northwestern Publishing House.[233] The JHC made some slight revisions in the wording of these prayers.[234] But further consultation was necessary to come to a better understanding on the catechism wording.

Prange contacted Daniel Schmeling, administrator for the Commission on Parish Schools. A meeting of JHC and BPE representatives was set for May 23, 1991.[235] The wording recommended by the JHC of catechism items was reviewed. An okay was given to the text of the Words of Institution that the Liturgy Committee had carefully prepared. The wordings of the Lord's Prayer, Apostles' Creed, Nicene Creed, and Luther's Morning and Evening Prayers were also approved. But there was disagreement on the wording for Baptism, Fourth. This matter was referred to the Liturgy Committee for review[236]. The report of this meeting was presented to the JHC, and a slight wording change was made in Baptism, Fourth.[237]

Nothing, however, had been done about revising those portions of the Small Catechism not included in any worship form but proposed for inclusion in the hymnal. Prange called this to the attention of the Board for Parish Services, which appointed a committee to prepare a revised

---

[232] From Prange's notes of this meeting.
[233] Fischer's letter to Eggert, May 8, 1990.
[234] JHC minutes, January 5, 1991, p. 7.
[235] Kurt Eggert, Victor Prange, Wayne Schulz from JHC; William Fischer, David Kuske, and Daniel Schmeling from BPE.
[236] Based on Prange notes from this meeting.
[237] JHC minutes, August 1, 1991, p. 10.

wording of the Small Catechism.[238] In the summer of 1992, this committee's revision was sent to all pastors of the synod, asking them to share the material with their teachers. In Schmeling's words, this opened a "Pandora's Box" of comments, criticisms, and suggestions.[239] Prange met with the revision committee on September 10, 1992, and concluded that "it is almost certain that Catechism won't go in hymnal."[240] In September the Board for Parish Services resolved to appoint a committee to study the Small Catechism and recommend a standardized version to be used in all WELS publications.[241] The work of this new committee was not completed until after the hymnal had been published. The text of the entire Small Catechism would not be included in the new hymnal.

There is one footnote to the story of the Small Catechism. The revision committee accepted all of the *Christian Worship* wordings except for one, that in Baptism, Fourth. The text in the hymnal reads, "Baptism means that the *sinful nature* in us . . ."[242] The revision committee recommended, "Baptism means that the *old Adam* in us . . ." Since the people recite these words in the baptism service, members of the JHC and others strongly advised against adopting the committee's wording. But it was to no avail, since the 1995 synod convention approved the committee's wording, which had also been endorsed by the Conference of Presidents.[243] As a result, WELS publications have different wordings of Baptism, Fourth.

Hymnal name

Question 32 on the list that Eggert presented at the initial meeting of the JHC asked, "What will be the name for the new hymnal and the color of its cover?"[244] That was hardly a pressing matter at the time, but as the project moved further along, it became a matter for more and more discussion. The working name that Prange used when presenting a hymnal flow chart to the Commission on Worship in November 1989

---

[238]Members of this committee were Daniel Schmeling (chairman), Gary Baumler, John Jeske, Gerald Kastens, David Kuske, and Kermit Moldenhauer.

[239]Schmeling's letter to committee, August 25, 1992.

[240]Prange diary, September 10, 1992.

[241]Members of this committee were Daniel Schmeling (chairman), John Isch, James Fricke, Bruce McKenney, Roger Klockzeim, and Dorothy Sonntag.

[242]*Christian Worship*, p. 12.

[243]This difference is noted in the 1995 *Proceedings*, pp. 62-63.

[244]Eggert, "Guidelines for the New Hymnal," January 18, 1985, p. 2.

was *Lutheran Hymnal II*. This was one of three titles proposed to the JHC for discussion in January 1990. The other two were *Lutheran Hymnal* (without *The*) and *Book of Worship*.[245]

When the JHC met, a secret ballot was taken that showed the majority preferred that *Lutheran* should be in the title. The JHC added a number of other suggestions to the list: *Lutheran Worship and Praise, Christian Worship, Book of Lutheran Worship, Christian Book of Worship, Book of Christian Worship, Christian Worship: A Lutheran Hymnal, Lutheran Hymnbook,* and *Worship for the Lutheran Church*.[246] Prange commented in his diary: "The secret will be to find the least objectionable."[247] A decision on the name was put off till the next meeting.

In June 1990 Tiefel and Prange met with Eggert to discuss a number of matters related to the hymnal project. Among the topics that came up was what the name of the hymnal should be. Eggert was leaning toward something like *Lutheran Worship and Praise*. Tiefel and Prange favored something like *Christian Worship: A Hymnal for the Lutheran Church* (or *A Lutheran Hymnal*).[248]

When the JHC met in August, more suggestions were added to the list of possible names.[249] As the last order of business on Thursday of that week, the decision on a hymnal name was scheduled. The list of suggestions had now grown to 31. It was decided to have five ballots, each person voting for five names down to one. On the first ballot, *Book of Lutheran Worship, Lutheran Hymnal II,* and *Lutheran Worship and Praise* each received 7 votes. On the second ballot, *Lutheran Hymnal II* received 10 votes. On the next ballot, it dropped back to 5 votes, with *Lutheran Worship and Praise* continuing at 7. But *Christian Worship: A Lutheran Hymnal* suddenly surged to 12 votes. On the fourth ballot, this name was chosen by 11; 7 continued to vote for *Lutheran Worship and Praise*. On the final ballot, when each person had but one vote, a decisive majority chose *Christian Worship: A Lutheran Hymnal* with 10 votes; *Lutheran Hymnal II* had 4 votes; *Lutheran Worship and Praise* had 1. A motion followed "to make unanimous the vote for the title of *Christian Worship: A Lutheran Hymnal* as the title of the new/revised hymnal."[250]

---

[245]CW minutes, November 17–18, 1989, p. 3.
[246]JHC minutes, January 2–6, 1990, pp. 3,7.
[247]Prange diary, January 6, 1990.
[248]Notes on meeting with Eggert, Tiefel, and Prange held on June 25, 1990.
[249]JHC minutes (August 6, 1990, p. 2) list some additional names.
[250]JHC minutes, August 9, 1990, p. 9.

Prange reported that he did not push this name but "others did being opposed to the other two."[251]

At the March 1992 meeting of the Commission on Worship, music editor Moldenhauer reported that "the name *Christian Worship* has been researched and found acceptable."[252] There was a hymnal published in 1976 in England with the name *Christian Worship,* but the copyrighted name for our book includes the full title. There was also an American publication by Bethany Press, St. Louis (Christian Board of Publication), with the title *Christian Worship: A Hymnal.* It is interesting that this was one of two hymnals used in the Dexter Avenue Baptist Church, Montgomery, Alabama, where Martin Luther King was once pastor. The name chosen by the JHC for the hymnal reflects the desire of the synod that this book be "in harmony with the character and heritage of our church body" and yet reflect "the larger perspective and mainstream of the worship of the Christian church."[253]

Hymnal logo

The *American Heritage Dictionary* defines the word *logo* as "a name, symbol, or trademark designed for easy and definite recognition." Kurt Eggert was probably more interested than anyone else on the JHC in finding the right logo for the new book. His "WELS Hymnal Project" stationery had the distinctive logo of a treble clef on an open book.

At the same meeting in which the JHC began discussion of the hymnal name, Eggert presented four drawings of a suggested logo that the NPH art department had worked with him in developing.[254] All four of them showed a large treble clef and a cross in various sizes; three of the four also included an open book.

After the JHC had adopted the name *Christian Worship* for the new book in August 1990, several on the committee suggested that the logo should be some kind of symbol for Christ.[255] At the January 1991 meeting, it was requested "that NPH recommend a design which had as its main focus Christ." At the summer meeting, music editor Moldenhauer discussed with the JHC several matters relating to the page and cover

---

[251]Prange diary, August 9, 1990.
[252]CW minutes, March 20–21, 1992, p. 1.
[253]Introduction to *Christian Worship,* p. 8.
[254]JHC minutes, January 3, 1990, p. 3.
[255]JHC minutes, January 2, 1991, p. 2.

design of the new book. He also presented various logo designs that had been prepared: a simple block cross, Trinity symbols, a cross set on a series of circles, and a Trinity symbol on an embossed cross. After a long discussion, "the committee stated a preference for a stamped symbol on an embossed cross with the full title on the cover and shortened title on the spine."[256] At the September meeting, the JHC resolved "to use a cross on the cover without another symbol superimposed on it." The project director was also asked to come with a recommendation for the color of the hymnal cover at the January 1992 meeting.[257]

Work continued on various designs in preparation for the January JHC meeting. Members of the JHC were also discussing informally what would be the best design. Though the JHC had by resolution opted for a cross design, some questioned the wisdom of this decision since the cover of *Lutheran Worship* used the cross logo. Prange expressed his strong feelings to Gary Baumler, editorial chief at Northwestern Publishing House: "I strongly favor simplicity with emphasis on a symbol for Christ. The name of this hymnal is *Christian Worship*. Let's put the emphasis also in our symbol on *Christ*."[258]

Baumler was present at the January 1992 JHC meeting to discuss the hymnal cover. Red was being considered as the color, something Eggert favored from the beginning. Various logo designs were presented, the majority of which were cross and Trinity symbols. Two resolutions were approved: "to use the Chi-Rho symbol on the cover of *Christian Worship*" and "that NPH, the project director, and the music editor (having heard the opinions of the JHC) should choose the cover symbol and design (that is, with or without text)."[259] Prange added a bit of detail in his diary: "The resolution was adopted 5 to 4 with 4 abstentions to use Chi-Rho on cover. Saw only one design with this and not impressed."[260] At the final meeting of the JHC in April, there was no new information on the logo design.[261]

The Commission on Worship met September 4–5, and Moldenhauer reported on various items related to the hymnal project. The minutes note that "the cover design and color will be decided soon" and that "the

---

[256] JHC minutes, July 31, 1991, p. 7.
[257] JHC minutes, September 27, 1991, pp. 4,5.
[258] Prange's letter to Baumler, December 23, 1991.
[259] JHC minutes, January 2, 1992, p. 2.
[260] Prange diary, January 2, 1992.
[261] JHC minutes, April 4, 1992, p. 4.

logo will be a stylized version of the Chi-Rho."[262] Several commission members were not pleased with the design of the logo subsequently proposed by Northwestern Publishing House and communicated their feelings to Baumler and Moldenhauer. The suggested design was also presented to the District Worship Coordinators (DWC) meeting in October for their reaction. By a vote of 14 to 3, the Commission on Worship and District Worship Coordinators approved a motion to "express uneasiness with the style of the proposed *Christian Worship* logo."[263]

This resolution of the District Worship Coordinators was conveyed to Mark Brunner of Northwestern Publishing House, who was serving as chairman of the cover committee. This resulted in a decision to seek designs from an outside art firm and then convene a meeting of NPH representatives with the JHC executive committee. At this meeting in November, a large number of Chi-Rho designs were presented. The selections were narrowed down to three, and each person was asked to rank them: 3, 2, 1. There were 16 total points for the design that is on the hymnal cover, 13 points for the previously proposed logo, and 10 for a third design. Prange reports: "Kurt [Eggert] favored the first, and I supported him. I think it will be better."[264]

A unique feature of *Christian Worship* is the fact that the logo is explained on the back side of the title page: "The logo for this hymnal is a version of the Chi-Rho, a symbol for Christ. In the Greek language these are the first letters of the name Christ. He is the center of our faith and worship, our prayers, our praise and thanksgiving. This hymnal reflects in its name, logo, liturgies, and hymns the story of God's love and salvation in Christ."

The last JHC meeting and the executive committee

When the Joint Hymnal Committee gathered in January 1992, it marked the seventh anniversary of their initial meeting. These had been seven years of individual writing, reflection, and review; seven years of travel and face-to-face discussions and decisions; seven years of sharing information and answering critics; seven years of pursuing the task of shaping a new hymnal while continuing to carry on ministries of preaching and teaching. These had been seven good years,

---

[262]CW minutes, September 4–5, 1992, p. 2.
[263]DWC minutes, October 17, 1992, p. 2.
[264]Prange diary, November 11, 1992.

years of growth, but no one regretted that the end was in sight, least of all project director Eggert.

The JHC met for the last time at the Holiday Inn Express motel on Friday and Saturday, April 3–4, 1992. The agenda notes for that meeting show that the Liturgy Committee was recommending a large number of mostly minor revisions, and the JHC went through these item by item. There were also a few matters from the Hymn Committee. Things moved smoothly. Moldenhauer reported that he would review the use of *Hallelujah* and *Alleluia*. The printing of guitar chords was left to the music editor. "Holy Communion" replaced "Lord's Supper" as a section name for hymns. A few items were referred to the Executive Committee for final decisions.[265]

For Friday evening, Eggert had arranged a closing banquet for the JHC and for those wives who were able to attend. Kurt served as the master of ceremonies, telling a few stories and expressing his personal appreciation for the help and support given him as project director. President Mischke addressed the group, thanking them for the work they had done. Prange's brief summation: "It was a nice evening."[266]

Saturday morning the JHC resumed meeting at 8:00 A.M. With all the business completed by 10:00 A.M., there was a motion for adjournment. Prange closed with a devotion based on Hebrews 13:7: "Remember your leaders, who spoke the word of God to you. Consider the outcome of their way of life and imitate their faith." He pointed out how the members of the JHC stood on the shoulders of many who had gone before. They had learned from the great worship leaders of the past, and now they had learned from each other. An observation by Søren Kierkegaard, a Danish Lutheran philosopher, that hymnals don't solve all spiritual problems was quoted, reminding the JHC that there was still work to be done.

Prange concluded: "The future is in God's hands. He has blessed us, and I am convinced he can use this hymnal for great good. As we complete our work, we above all give him the glory. He enabled us to do this work, blessed us with resources, computers, typewriters, copy machines, a variety of talents and gifts. Soli Deo Gloria."

Then the JHC joined in singing Eggert's hymn "Not unto Us":

> Not unto us but to your name be glory, Lord,
> For grace so rich, so wide, so high, so free.

---
[265] JHC minutes, April 3–4, 1992.
[266] Prange diary, April 3, 1992.

> Abide with us till trav'ling days are over and done,
> And pilgrim feet lead us home, Lord, to you.[267]

The Commission on Worship had appointed an Executive Committee consisting of Eggert, Jeske, Moldenhauer, Prange, and Tiefel to tie up any loose ends in preparation for publishing the hymnal.[268] This committee met a total of four times: June 11, September 3, and November 11 in 1992 and February 5, 1993. Several items on which the JHC had not completed work were approved. The Hymn of the Day selections made by Backer were reviewed and slightly revised. There were some minor wording changes and slight alterations in the lectionary selections. The introduction to the hymnal, written by Eggert, was reviewed and revised. Several of the short service introductory notes were reworded.

One problem that surfaced was securing copyrights of some texts and tunes, and the royalties demanded. Several hymns had to be deleted because of this. The committee also found that the tune LITTLE CORNARD could only be used if a 15 percent royalty were paid, which was more than the tune was worth. Moldenhauer ended up writing a new tune for the text "Lord of Our Growing Years."[269] There was some concern that additional hymns might have to be cut to keep the hymnal at the ideal number of 960 pages, but this was not necessary. The fact that the Small Catechism could not be included in the hymnal gave some additional space for hymns.

At their final meeting, the Executive Committee responded to questions raised about some wordings in liturgical texts and hymns by the synod's doctrinal reviewer. A few changes were made as a result; the reason for not changing other items was explained to him. Prange's letter to the reviewer included this paragraph: "We appreciate very much the suggestions and comments which you made. They were very helpful and caused us to reconsider a number of wordings which the JHC had approved. In some cases we did make changes; in some cases we did not. Since you are the doctrinal reviewer for the hymnal, I wanted to inform you as to the decisions which we made. In cases where we did not change the text, I want to give you our reasons. Though we are coming very close to the time when no further changes can be made in the hymnal, if there is some item which you still feel is in doctrinal error, we

---

[267] *Christian Worship* hymn 392:4.
[268] CW minutes, November 22–23, 1991, p. 1.
[269] *Christian Worship* hymn 507.

will want to reconsider our decision."[270] The reviewer was satisfied with the decisions made by the Executive Committee. The hymnal was now in the hands of the publisher.

The publication process

When people open a hymn book, they don't think of the many hours a committee spends shaping it. They see only the final product: the cover, the print size, the page arrangement, the music. People want a book that is easy to follow, pleasing to the eye, and not too heavy. The JHC worked with Northwestern Publishing House in trying to shape a product that would satisfy the user.

Northwestern Publishing House had taken a most important step in moving the hymnal project along when the offer was made to the synod in 1983 to fund the project director's salary and housing and provide office space and secretarial help. Eggert and Moldenhauer both had offices at the publishing house and were provided with secretarial help. Many times hymnal committees availed themselves of the board of director's meeting room at the publishing house. And it was the publishing house that provided the expertise needed to publish the final product.

Already in 1988, representatives from the JHC met with NPH editors to discuss matters related to publishing the hymnal.[271] It was agreed that the JHC would make the final decisions on texts and music, but the style guide of Northwestern Publishing House would be followed in matters of capitalization (as with divine pronouns) and punctuation. The publishing house would decide on the page size, font style and size, paper stock, and cover material. It would take care of securing all copyright permissions.

As the JHC proceeded with the project, questions continued to surface about various publishing details. As a result, the motion was approved "that the chairman of the JHC arrange a meeting with NPH to discuss matters of style, including punctuation, capitalization, and abbreviations."[272] Meetings were held on September 12 and November 21, 1991, at which the NPH style guide was thoroughly reviewed. Agreeing on a guideline for the capitalization of *word* and *church* proved

---

[270]Prange's letter, February 8, 1993.
[271]JHC minutes, August 8, 1988, p. 1.
[272]JHC minutes, July 31, 1991, p. 8.

the most difficult. It was decided to capitalize *word* when it referred to Jesus and when a word like *Bible* could be used as a synonym; otherwise it would be lowercased. *Church* would be capitalized when the word referred to the holy Christian Church or was used as part of a name, but not otherwise. Applying these guidelines was not always easy. The publishing house suggested doing a trial run on some hymns to see how the final product would look.

A significant change in publication plans occurred when the music editor reported to the JHC "that NPH will publish the hymn book in-house using the computer program for layout."[273] The publishing house had purchased a new music engraving program named *Finale*. Music editor Moldenhauer, with the help of several others, was prepared to enter all the final texts and music into the computer. The printout from the computer would serve as the master for the actual printing of the hymnal. This bypassed the long and costly process of having the music engraved. This process also helped in guarding against errors in the final product since once caught and corrected, those errors would not occur again as texts and music were reviewed.

Several decisions were made by the JHC that show up in the final product: the letters *M* and *C* were used in the major services to designate the minister and congregation;[274] the English titles were used with Latin subtitles for major liturgical songs;[275] and the rubrics (instructions) were printed in black, not red.[276]

One slow-moving and at times frustrating part of the publishing process was securing permissions for the use of copyrighted materials. Moldenhauer reported to the Commission on Worship in March 1992 that "copyright permissions have been returned from some of the publishers. Ten percent of the cost of the book will be prorated to each copyright holder."[277] The next month Moldenhauer reported to the JHC that "hymns from Hope Publishing will be used without text changes because of their restrictions."[278] The Executive Committee had to deal with several sticky copyright problems. Hymnal project secretary Joanne Gruber did much of the detailed work of securing permissions.

---

[273]JHC minutes, July 31, 1991, p. 8.
[274]JHC minutes, July 31, 1989, p. 2.
[275]JHC minutes, July 31, 1989, p. 2.
[276]JHC minutes, January 6, 1992, p. 8.
[277]CW minutes, March 20–21, 1992, p. 1.
[278]JHC minutes, April 4, 1992, p. 3.

Eggert and Moldenhauer worked closely with the staff at the publishing house in seeing the hymnal through this final publication process, leading finally to the first printed copies that came off the press in the summer of 1993.

Kurt Eggert's failing health and death

It was no surprise when Eggert was called as project director for the hymnal. No other person was so qualified for this position. He was a respected synodical leader, a member of the Commission on Worship since its creation, and chairman of the synod's Commission on Higher Education for a time. As founding director of the Lutheran Chorale of Milwaukee, he was progressive without being perceived as radical in his musical tastes. He experimented with the new while appreciating the tried and true. He was knowledgeable about worship trends in the Wisconsin Synod and also in the church at large. Over the years he had proven himself to be a kind, patient, and gifted pastor, teacher, musician, and poet, truly a man of God. He conducted himself with quiet dignity with nary a hint of boisterousness. His conversation was spiced with self-effacing humor. He was good at asking searching questions and slow to make decisions that would have major consequences. He had no love of controversy, seeking consensus whenever possible. A member of the JHC characterized him as a "fine even-tempered man."

This writer first came to know Eggert well when we worked together editing *Focus on Worship*. That was the beginning of a long friendship and working relationship. We spent many hours together in meetings and private conversations as the hymnal was being shaped. In the summers of 1988 and 1989, we drove together to St. Olaf College in Northfield, Minnesota, to attend the annual worship conferences. There was nonstop talking on the way up and back about the hymnal project, choirs and music, and WELS history in general. Kurt was a rich reservoir of insights on many different subjects. He was God's special gift to the Wisconsin Synod in shaping a new hymnal.

Eggert did a great job in getting the hymnal project organized. He outlined for the committees what their assignments were. He asked the questions that needed asking as the project got underway. He consulted with other synod leaders in seeking dedicated and gifted persons to bring the project to completion. He was very conscious of the need to keep the congregations of the synod informed about what was going on. He received a tremendous volume of mail, much of which he was unable to answer as thoroughly as he would have liked.[279]

In the early years especially, Kurt served as the JHC's "gofer": he got what was needed to help the committees work. That included supplying fresh baked goods to boost the energy in meetings. And when there were no goodies, it was duly noted in the minutes: "The lack of doughnuts was noticed and acutely missed by some."[280] Again: "Coffee and tea were provided, but the lack of doughnuts was noted with some dismay and contributed to a weakening of concentration later in the morning."[281] In one of the early letters to the JHC, Eggert writes: "As usual, I am available for taxi service from the airport to the motel."[282] Eggert was a model of servanthood for the JHC.

Eggert was at his best during the first couple years of the hymnal project. But then health problems set in, partly from overwork. The first serious physical setback took place in October 1986 just after the exhausting task of preparing the *Sampler* had been completed. Prange reported: "Mary [Prange] called to say that Kurt Eggert suffered heart attack during Chorale practice (about 4:45 P.M.). He had chest pains. They took him to County Hospital. She continued on with the rehearsal. Don't know yet how serious it was."[283] It was determined that Kurt required surgery, but the doctors decided against doing it immediately because the blockage was too close to the heart.

Eggert did bounce back from this attack, writing to the JHC about a month later: "Just a short note to let you know that I am 'functional.' It was just a month ago that I decided to shuck off all responsibilities in favor of a medical sabbatical. Life in the cardiac care unit is interesting but not worth the cost. I am presently feeling fine and getting ready for round 2 on December 8, which will begin with bypass surgery."[284] Eggert came through that surgery okay, but "prior damage

---

[279]NPH secretary Joanne Gruber wrote Prange: "By the time I came on board, he was no longer able to keep up with his correspondence. . . . Because he insisted on responding personally, form letters of acknowledgment were out of the question, and dictation did not suit him. I tried several times to suggest ways we could keep on top of it all, to no avail."

[280]JHC minutes, August 12, 1987, p. 1.

[281]JHC minutes, January 22, 1988, p. 1.

[282]Eggert's letter to JHC, May 24, 1985.

[283]Prange diary, October 26, 1986.

[284]Eggert's letter to JHC, November 25, 1986.

to heart seems more serious."[285] He was back for the January 1987 JHC meetings.

This was only the beginning of health problems, which in time seriously weakened Eggert's physical strength and his work capacity. In December 1987 he underwent hernia surgery. Signs began to appear that he was not feeling well. During the January 1990 JHC meeting, Prange notes in his diary: "Kurt is gone quite a bit of the time from the meetings. Says he is not feeling well."[286] In May of that year he went into intensive care with bleeding ulcers. In November a gall bladder problem required attention.

Eggert was not able to attend the January 1991 JHC meeting because he was in the hospital undergoing various heart tests. There was some concern that he would not be able to continue as hymnal project director. The arrival of Kermit Moldenhauer on the scene as full-time music editor helped immensely to keep the project on track and relieve the burden on Eggert. He continued to attend as many of the various committee meetings as possible. But obviously his physical ills were taking a toll. The variety of medications he required also contributed to his not feeling well.

One of Eggert's last writings was an article that appeared after his death in the August 1993 issue of the *Northwestern Lutheran*. He titled it "Pressing On to the Future and Holding On to Our Past."[287] He concluded by expressing this hope: "May the new book proclaim the power of the Word of God and the foundation doctrine of forgiveness by God's grace through faith in Christ. May its use among us foster and strengthen appreciation of liturgical worship, and enrich and enliven our relationship with God and each other."

Eggert was back in the hospital in June 1993, and he became progressively weaker. Any hope that he could present the first copy of *Christian Worship* to President Mischke at the synod convention in August faded. Instead, on June 17 Mischke presented Eggert with the first bound copy of the hymnal as he lay on his hospital bed.[288]

The Commission on Worship met with the District Worship Coordinators June 21–23 in Brookfield, Wisconsin. On the morning of June

---

[285] Prange diary, December 9, 1986.

[286] Prange diary, January 5, 1990.

[287] *Northwestern Lutheran*, August 1993, pp. 262,263.

[288] A picture of the presentation is given in the August 1993 issue of *Northwestern Lutheran*, p. 274.

23, Tiefel brought the news that Kurt had died the previous evening at 10:10 P.M. It seemed only appropriate that as one of our synod's premier worship leaders lay dying, planning for the work he loved so much was continuing. Eggert's funeral was held on June 26 at Atonement Lutheran Church, Milwaukee. His pastor, Fredric Piepenbrink, preached the sermon stressing that Eggert had done all to the glory of God. Jeske, Moldenhauer, Prange, and Tiefel of the JHC served as pallbearers along with Gordon Snyder, chairman of the NPH board, and Robert Voss, with whom Eggert worked closely on the Commission on Higher Education. A pastor's choir sang the concluding chorale of Bach's "St. John's Passion," which includes these words: "Lord, let at last your angels come; / To Abram's bosom bear me home."[289]

For the JHC and many others, the most disappointing aspect of the entire hymnal project was the fact that Eggert did not live to see the day when *Christian Worship* would be used in the vast majority of WELS congregations. He saw the hymnal's final manuscripts. On his deathbed he was presented with a copy of the first hymnal. But in God's infinite wisdom, Kurt Eggert was not permitted to see how the many small seeds that he had planted over the years produced an abundant harvest. He never dreamed that the project he had initiated would have such a blessed conclusion.

Kurt Eggert did not live to see the success of *Christian Worship*. But he did live to see something far more glorious, described in words for which he composed the melody:

> "Lord, when your glory I shall see
>   And taste your kingdom's pleasure,
> Your blood my royal robe shall be,
>   My joy beyond all measure!
> When I appear before your throne,
>   Your righteousness shall be my crown;
> With these I need not hide me.
>   And there, in garments richly wrought,
> As your own bride I shall be brought
>   To stand in joy beside you."[290]

---

[289]*Christian Worship* hymn 434:3.
[290]*Christian Worship* hymn 219.

Christian Worship presentation at the 1993 synod convention

The 1993 convention of the Wisconsin Evangelical Lutheran Synod was held at Michigan Lutheran Seminary in Saginaw, Michigan, August 2–6. All members of the JHC had been invited to attend the convention and experience the introduction of the new hymnal. At a noon luncheon on Monday, Moldenhauer presented a special gift copy of the hymnal to each committee member. The signatures of all JHC members were printed on the inside front covers.

At the start of sessions on Tuesday morning, JHC chairman Prange presented a copy of *Christian Worship* to synod president Carl Mischke. Prange began by noting the contributions of Eggert: "We are the richer today for having had Kurt as a companion these many years and especially in the preparation of *Christian Worship*." Prange had special thanks for Ruth Eggert, Kermit Moldenhauer, and Joanne Gruber. All the members of the JHC present at the convention were introduced. Prange concluded:

> I've heard President Mischke say several times that he personally did not need this new hymnal. In fact, he's been heard to say that the old German hymnal was good enough for him. For a person who didn't need this new hymnal, President Mischke certainly gave the project his complete support, for which we are deeply appreciative. That same kind of support and cooperation was forthcoming from many other members of our synod, too numerous to mention, whose help was requested in one form or another along the way.
>
> Even though President Mischke said he didn't really need a new hymnal, I'm certain that he will not turn down this copy of *Christian Worship: A Lutheran Hymnal*. It is my privilege to present this hymnal to you, Mr. President, with the prayer that our gracious God will bless its use in the worship of his people for many years to come. To God be the glory!

Mischke accepted the hymnal on behalf of all the members of the Wisconsin Synod. He thanked the committee for the hours of work they had done in shaping this worship book. With deep emotion in his voice, Mischke recounted his presentation of a copy of *Christian Worship* to Eggert as he lay dying. Following the official presentation, hymnals were distributed to all the delegates and used for worship during the remainder of the convention. A project that the synod had authorized in 1983 had come full circle with its completion a decade later.

Hymnal introduction program

The hymnal introduction program began the moment the new/revised hymnal was authorized. From the very beginning, Eggert, the Commission on Worship, and the Joint Hymnal Committee were helping congregations get ready for *Christian Worship*. Already at the 1985 convention of the Organization of WELS Lutheran Seniors (OWLS), Eggert conducted a "Workshop on the New Hymnal." These WELS seniors were introduced to an outline of what was coming in their worship. They were asked how they would construct a new liturgy and what hymns they would like to retain from *The Lutheran Hymnal*. This was hymnal introduction eight years before *Christian Worship* found its way into church hymnal racks.

The five regional meetings in the fall of 1985 not only gave the JHC some input but also served to introduce the hymnal. One pastor participant wrote a very perceptive letter to his district president in which he surmised that the meetings were of more help to those who attended than to the JHC. He wrote: "I did not feel the consultation was so much for their benefit as for ours. And in that sense it was very beneficial. Not only did we learn their thinking and gain confidence in it, we got a much deeper appreciation of how complex the solutions are, to try to satisfy everybody. . . . I would estimate that the outcome on the part of the participants is 99.44 percent positive anticipation for the new book. Now to the point: this spirit needs to be widely disseminated and actively cultivated, especially in view of the all-too-prevalent attitude of suspicion, reluctance, resistance that haunts the land in the wake of other new hymnals." He went on to propose a program of worship education for circuits. The regional meetings sounded the message loud and clear: a new hymnal is coming.

Eggert and other members of the JHC had many opportunities to make local and regional presentations about the hymnal. In June 1986 Eggert presented an essay to the convention of the Northern Wisconsin District titled "Enriching our Worship Heritage." It was all about the new hymnal. The introduction in the *Sampler*, distributed in the fall of that year, was part of the hymnal introduction program. In the summer of 1987, the District Worship Coordinators heard three presentations:

"Gaining a Perspective on the New Hymnal" by Eggert, "Goals and Implementation of the Liturgy Committee" by Schulz, and "Report on the Work of the Hymn Committee: Goals and Implementation" by Jeske. These worship leaders carried the message back into their own districts: a new hymnal is coming. Various items from the new hymnal were introduced at district conventions, giving people a taste of what was coming. Many articles appeared in the *Northwestern Lutheran* on worship subjects in addition to reports on the progress of the hymnal project and its contents. Readers also had the opportunity to air their concerns in the "Letters" section.

At the same time, it was recognized that a comprehensive program of hymnal introduction was necessary after the book was published. In March 1988 the Commission on Worship began the discussion on how to proceed. It was noted at that time that "individual pastors are the 'key' people."[291] Various ideas were kicked around. A year later the Commission discussed the names of people who might be asked to head up the hymnal introduction program.[292] It wasn't until March 1991, however, that the commission actually got around to making some appointments.[293] David Valleskey was named committee chairman. Bryan Gerlach was asked to be the overall coordinator and prepare educational materials. His congregation in Citrus Heights, California, was requested to release him from some of his pastoral duties, which they agreed to do. In addition, Bloedel, Eggert, Moldenhauer, and Prange from the JHC served on the introduction committee, as well as Mark Brunner, representing Northwestern Publishing House.

Over the next two years, the introduction committee met a total of 11 times to put together the introduction plan. The principle that guided the planning of the committee was this: "experience first, then education." Worship is best taught by experiencing it, not talking about it. Experience must precede reflection and discussion. One doesn't get very far telling people what they ought to do and then hoping they will do it. Ten good reasons might be given why people should try singing psalms or use the Service of Light in Evening Prayer. But the uncertain pastor or layman will be more powerfully convinced and encouraged by actually experiencing the service or psalm.

---

[291] CW minutes, March 25–26, 1988, p. 1.
[292] CW minutes, March 10–11, 1989, p. 3.
[293] CW minutes, March 15–16, 1991, p. 4.

The basic component of the program was a booklet prepared by Gerlach to introduce the hymnal to congregations. A high-quality CD of key liturgical items and a few hymns from *Christian Worship* was professionally recorded for distribution to every congregation. The introduction committee said about this recording: "Special care went into the recording and production process so that the music you hear will be powerful as music, not simply instructive for those who aren't sure how something should go. . . . The recording begins with a great new hymn of praise accompanied by a thrilling variety of instruments: 'When in Our Music God Is Glorified.'"[294]

Also helpful for introducing the hymnal to congregations was the Bible class video by Professor James Tiefel titled "The Way Lutherans Worship." This proved to be a very useful tool for worship education. It allowed people to better evaluate the new hymnal on the basis of a deeper awareness of worship history and theology. This video was one of the most widely distributed of NPH Bible class materials. Many parishes reported great interest in the course content. This was not surprising since worship education at the parish level had been rare in the Wisconsin Synod.

The introduction committee selected a number of pastors and musicians to present the hymnal introduction program in the 116 circuits of the synod. A three-day training meeting for these presenters was held at Wisconsin Lutheran College, Milwaukee, following the 1993 synod convention. Those who came together for that meeting not only received information about the hymnal; they also experienced in practice the use of a large variety of worship materials. This meeting was a preview of the subsequent National Conferences on Worship, Music, and the Arts.

The presentations in the fall of 1993 brought together pastors, teachers, organists, choir directors, and other congregational leaders throughout the synod. These congregational leaders in turn introduced the hymnal in their own congregations following the suggestions contained in the booklet prepared by Gerlach. It was suggested that the hymnals be dedicated and used for the first time on the First Sunday in Advent 1993.

The widespread acceptance and use of *Christian Worship* points to the success of the entire hymnal introduction program. Though not every-

---

[294]CD booklet prepared for the hymnal introduction program.

one was pleased with having to use a new worship book, the general reaction on the part of people was very positive. Back in 1987 Schulz had stated the purpose for shaping a new hymnal: "We are serving the people of God of this time in the many places they live so that they can worship the Lord sincerely and joyfully in ways they can understand according to the Word that has nurtured them and invigorated them for service."[295] Under the blessing of God, wherever *Christian Worship* is being used, that goal is being reached.

Manual

For a hymnal to be used well, some directions are necessary. That's what a manual is for, to give some detailed directions. Eggert suggested that one of the failures of those who shaped *The Lutheran Hymnal* was the fact that there was no manual to give some directions for its use. He made that observation in an essay he read in 1986: "Much of the liturgical material in TLH as well as some of the worthiest hymns of early Lutheranism remain unlearned and unused. In retrospect, some of the fault for this was the failure to provide a manual for worship leaders along with the hymnal, explaining particularly the liturgical materials and indicating how they should or might be used in the worship."[296]

Members of the JHC also recognized the need to publish some kind of manual along with the hymnal. The resources contained in the hymnal would not be fully utilized unless this was done. Time and again someone would make the comment that a given suggestion belonged "in the manual." The book became an essential once the decision was made not to include the Sunday and festival propers in the hymnal. Omitting these items saved considerable space in *Christian Worship*, allowing for the inclusion of more hymns and liturgical items. Since the average member does not make use of the propers, their presence in the hymnal was not deemed necessary.

In March 1988 the Commission on Worship began discussing the publication of such a manual.[297] Eggert, Prange, and Tiefel were asked "to propose something more definite for this book at the March [1990] meeting of the CW."[298] The commission accepted the committee's sug-

---

[295]Schulz, "Goals and Implementation of the Liturgy Committee," August 1987, p. 2.
[296]Eggert, "Enriching Our Worship Heritage," June 1986, p. 7; essay delivered to the convention of the Northern Wisconsin District of WELS.
[297]CW minutes, March 25–26, 1988, p. 2.
[298]CW minutes, November 17–18, 1989, p. 3.

gestion for publishing a four-section book of approximately 400 pages and asked the committee to continue to work out details.[299]

This was done, and in January 1991 Prange gave this report to the JHC: "An editorial committee has been appointed to prepare some kind of manual to be published along with the hymnal. This would have four parts: (1) general, historical, theological; (2) liturgical services in detail; (3) propers for Sundays and festivals; (4) music, hymns. Sections three and four were later reversed. General editor appointed by NPH was G. Jerome Albrecht; section editors appointed by CW were James Tiefel, Wayne Schulz, Victor Prange, Harlyn Kuschel."[300] Gary Baumler replaced Jerome Albrecht as NPH editor after the latter's death. Kermit Moldenhauer worked with Baumler in the final editing of *Christian Worship: Manual*.

The editorial committee met for the first time on February 14, 1991, and mapped out the work that needed to be done. Tiefel agreed to write the first section. Schulz and Kuschel enlisted others to help in writing the sections on the various liturgical services and the hymns and music. Prange put together the last part of the book on the church year and propers.

The goal of the editorial committee was to have the manual ready for publication along with the hymnal. At times over the next couple years, this goal seemed unlikely because of the amount of work involved. But the goal was reached when shortly after the introduction of *Christian Worship* at the 1993 synod convention, the *Christian Worship: Manual* also became available. The book ended up being 40 percent longer than originally anticipated. It includes some essential items like the propers, along with a wealth of theological and practical information about doing Lutheran worship.

The manual was favorably reviewed by several Lutheran periodicals. One wrote: "It must be said that the manual does an admirable job of explaining the hymnal. . . . *CW: Manual* far exceeded my initial expectations. It is much more than just a 'how-to' book with relation to its corresponding hymnal. The book displays a solid allegiance to the traditional Lutheran way of worship, yet it also bears witness to a sensitive flexibility in some matters relating to music (for example, pp. 59,347). Although many different men contributed to its writing, *CW: Manual*

---

[299] CW minutes, March 23–24, 1990, p. 3.
[300] Prange, "Summary of CW Meetings"; report presented to the JHC on January 2, 1991.

shows a remarkable unity of thought and purpose. The book covers a vast amount of issues amazingly well. If there can be one criticism of this book, it would be that its designation as a 'manual' is far too modest."[301]

Reception of *Christian Worship*

When the Wisconsin Synod resolved in 1983 to initiate a hymnal project, one of the stated goals was that the hymnal should be "welcomed and judged to be highly satisfactory by a majority of our members."[302] When *Christian Worship* was introduced to congregations of the synod, people were not asked to return a card indicating whether or not they "welcomed" this new book. There would likely have been quite a few "no" votes at that time. No survey has since been taken to determine whether WELS members judge *Christian Worship* to be "highly satisfactory."

Quite a few worshipers had no use for *Christian Worship* when it came out. Some critics were very vocal. Pastors heard complaints from congregation members; letters were fired off to members of the JHC and synod officials. Most often *Christian Worship* was compared unfavorably with *The Lutheran Hymnal*. Some faulted the revision of the texts; others weren't happy with things musical; a few didn't like much of anything in the new book.

One unidentified WELS member distributed a seven-page document that in 21 separate points sought to demonstrate the weaknesses of *Christian Worship*. It was suggested that many biblical doctrines were tampered with because of changes and omissions especially in the hymns. It was charged that the condemnation of sin was eased or removed; that the heavenly bliss or treasure was lessened; that objective justification was changed to subjective justification; that because Scripture references were dropped from hymns, the inspiration of the Word of God was downplayed; that there were possible Romanizing tendencies, for example, chanting; that a number of the hymns in TLH's ministry section were recast to fit the "everyone is a minister" concept; that male terminology was eliminated to please the feminist movement.

Yet those who did not welcome *Christian Worship* appear to have been a small minority. When one considers the widespread use of *Christian Worship*, word-of-mouth evaluations, and impressive sales figures,

---

[301] Wilfred Karsten, *Concordia Journal*, October 1995, pp. 445,446.
[302] Introduction to *Christian Worship*, p. 8.

there seems to be little doubt that the goal of shaping a hymnal that would be "welcomed and judged to be highly satisfactory by a majority of our members" has been reached.

The sales figures are impressive. The 1994 Report to the Twelve Districts informed the synod that "over 200,000 copies of the hymnal have been sold, and it is being used in more than 60 percent of WELS congregations. A third printing of the hymnal is scheduled for 1994."[303] The next year it was reported that "as of January 30, 1995, hymnal sales were nearing 270,000 copies."[304] These were the sales figures after *Christian Worship* had been in circulation only 18 months. In 1996 it was reported that the hymnal "has been ordered by more than 95 percent of our synod's congregations."[305] By early 1999 Northwestern Publishing House reported that 325,711 pew edition copies and 7,209 keepsake edition copies of *Christian Worship* had been sold. Combined sales for these two items came to $5,643,221. These figures suggest that the vast majority of the over 300,000 confirmed WELS members are now using the new hymnal.

Reviewers of *Christian Worship* who wrote for publications outside the Wisconsin Synod had mixed reactions to the book. One of the more positive reviews was that by Leigh Jordahl, though he was not totally pleased with the new book.[306] He comments favorably on the treatment of the psalms, calling them "a good addition." He is not as pleased with some of the tunes chosen for certain hymns and suggests other options. Noteworthy is his plea that the singing of the Lutheran chorales be encouraged and practiced. The liturgical portion of the hymnal he judges to be "conservative; its first setting might even be termed retrogressive." He is "disappointed that the lackluster Anglican chant melodies were retained." One of the biggest problems with *Christian Worship*, in Jordahl's opinion, is the failure to include a eucharistic prayer of thanksgiving in either Communion rite. Though other reviewers are not pleased with the placement of the *Kyrie* in The Common Service, Jordahl comments, "The three-fold *Kyrie* has been made part of the confession (as it was in the Norwegians' *Lutheran Hymnary*). The scholars generally insist that the *Kyrie* is really an acclamation rather than a penitential plea. In English it simply doesn't work that way, and

---

[303] 1994 *Report to the Twelve Districts*, p. 121.
[304] 1995 BORAM, p. 73.
[305] 1996 *Report to the Twelve Districts*, p. 206.
[306] *Logia*, Vol. III, No. 2 (Eastertide/April 1994), pp. 58-62.

CW has shown good judgment." The bottom line, in Jordahl's words, is that "[CW] need not take a back seat to either LBW or LW for quality."

In the same journal, Paul Alliet has an extensive critique of The Common Service, Service of Word and Sacrament, and Holy Baptism.[307] Along the way he remarks that the severe pruning of the psalms "seems hard to defend." But he is most critical (and puzzled) about the placement of the *Kyrie* in The Common Service and the wording of the absolution. He calls the sentence introducing the "Glory Be to God" clumsy, but overall he judges that the "idiosyncrasies" in The Common Service "do no obvious harm but also serve no evident purpose." Alliet is not happy either with the way the *Kyrie* is handled in the Service of Word and Sacrament, saying that "the structure is clumsy and results in the absolution being obscured." His harshest criticism though is leveled at the rite of Holy Baptism, focusing on the omission of the Apostles' Creed and the generally "teachy" nature of the service. This is the verdict: "In summary, the service for Holy Baptism is a major disappointment. . . . It is just barely acceptable, and pastors may want to consider either extensive reworking or use of another rite."

Glenn Schram was also shocked that "the confession and absolution in The Common Service are divided by, of all things, the *Kyrie*. Aside from the fact that the *Kyrie* was never intended for such use, it detracts from both the confession and absolution. It must also be considered that in the WELS it is customary for the congregation to kneel on the floor, facing the back of the church, during the confession and absolution on Communion Sundays. To expect them to sing the *Kyrie* in this position is to expect too much."[308] One wonders how widespread this reviewer's knowledge was of kneeling practices in the Wisconsin Synod. After a number of other comments and criticisms, he concludes his review with this judgment: "It is not a bad book, but it is a lackluster one."

Charles Evanson, once a member of the LCMS Commission on Worship, finds fault already with the word *worship* in the title.[309] He says this word best describes human action, and that's not the most important thing happening when people gather around Word and sacrament. God's service to the people is what really matters, and the word *worship* does not express that concept well. He has no suggestion for a better title. He faults the book for not including the propers but seems

---

[307]*Logia*, Vol. III, No. 2 (Eastertide/April 1994), pp. 54-57.

[308]*Christian News*, September 13, 1993, p. 6.

[309]*Bride of Christ*, Vol. XVIII, No. 3, pp. 25-28.

unaware of *Christian Worship: Manual*. He notes that there is no catechism or litany included. That *Christian Worship* "makes no provision for a prayer over the bread and cup" in the celebration of the Eucharist is seen as a defect. His conclusion is that "CW simply capitulates to the status quo and offers services which clearly do not propel one forward to a greater appreciation of Lutheran heritage."

A review by David Herman regrets "the editors' decision to include only a portion of each of those [56] psalms."[310] He compares this rather meager number of psalms in *Christian Worship* to the 122 included in *Lutheran Book of Worship*. He wonders why The Common Service perpetuates the musical setting of "the so-called 'Old Scottish Chant' as a vehicle for the *Gloria in Excelsis*." His verdict is that "the liturgical components fall short of what might have been, apparently reflecting denominational preference. The editors have been more successful in the hymnic aspect of their endeavor: 'many worthy representatives of contemporary song enliven the collection of chorales and other hymns from the past.'"

Mark Bighley judges that The Common Service "would seem to be the most successful of the settings included."[311] He is less pleased with the Service of Word and Sacrament, especially because the traditional texts were not used for the musical setting. Concerning the form of the *Kyrie* in this service, he comments, "This is a not particularly happy combination of the *Kyrie* style of SBH, LBW, and LW and that of The Common Service." The singular "I" in the text of the *Sanctus* is scored as "jarring and highly unsatisfactory" because of its use "at this point in the Eucharist, a communal act." He regrets that neither the service of Christian Marriage nor Christian Funeral "gives the option of including Communion." In summary he states, "The hymn section of this book should serve the synod well for a long time to come. Time will tell whether or not the service section will be of lasting value or have wider influence."

As people outside of the Wisconsin Synod became more familiar with *Christian Worship*, one did begin to hear some favorable comments, especially about the general makeup of the book and its ease of use. Worship leaders in other church bodies were favorably impressed with the form *Christian Worship* had adopted to encourage the singing of psalms by the people.

---

[310]*The Hymn: A Journal of Congregational Song*, April 1994, pp. 45,46.
[311]*Cross Accent: Journal of the Association of Lutheran Church Musicians*, July 1994, pp. 41,42.

A pastor in the Evangelical Lutheran Church of America, James Culver, wrote an article that was very critical of his church body's hymnal supplement *With One Voice*.[312] He suggested, "If we buy a supplemental worship resource for my parish, my preference for a supplement to LBW would be the Wisconsin Synod's new hymnal, *Christian Worship: A Lutheran Hymnal*, which contains many contemporary English hymns, additional chorales and alternative translations to those in LBW, and some fine new tunes."

A few congregations outside the Wisconsin Synod have adopted *Christian Worship* as their service book. One of these was Faith Lutheran Church, an LCMS congregation in Georgetown, Texas. After a review of the Lutheran hymnals, Pastor John Selle writes that "for more than a dozen reasons . . . the latter was chosen, and it was decided that the time was ripe to take the very positive and important step of making a new beginning. . . . I know you're going to love everything from the prayers; to the newly included baptism, marriage, and funeral services; to the personal preparation for Communion; to the many, many new (really old, in most cases) hymns, which we all love to sing."[313]

How long will *Christian Worship* continue to serve the needs of the Wisconsin Synod? One former member of the JHC suggested that the Commission on Worship should begin thinking about publishing a supplement to *Christian Worship* in the year 2010, with a new hymnal coming out in 2025 (*Christian Worship* would then be 32 years old). But others suggest that with the rapid growth of publishing technology, church bodies will in the future no longer publish worship books like those of the past. That remains to be seen.

Kurt Eggert titled the last article he contributed to the *Northwestern Lutheran* "Pressing On to the Future and Holding On to Our Past."[314] That was his philosophy of worship, and it had a profound effect on the Joint Hymnal Committee as it went about the work of shaping *Christian Worship: A Lutheran Hymnal*. With God's grace and blessing, that book continues to shape the worship lives of many Christians as they press on to the future while holding on to the past.

---

[312]*Lutheran Forum*, Lent 1996, pp. 46-49.
[313]"The Grapevine," April 1997.
[314]*Northwestern Lutheran*, August 1993, pp. 262,263.

Kurt J. Eggert at his installation as pastor of Atonement Lutheran Church, Milwaukee (1970)

Portrait of Kurt Eggert (1990) that hangs in the Eggert Hymnological and Liturgical Memorial Library at Wisconsin Lutheran Seminary Library

Northwestern College Band (1943–1944)

Summer vacation Bible school at Eggert's first parish, St. Paul's Lutheran Church, Valley City, North Dakota (1949)

259

Boys' Chorus, Michigan Lutheran Seminary (1947)

Girls' Chorus, Michigan Lutheran Seminary (1947)

Facsimile of Viva Vox, Eastertime, 1956

261

*Eggert directing the
Atonement Church choir*

Lutheran Guidepost TV

The Lutheran Chorale of Milwaukee (1988)

263

The Joint Hymnal Committee for Christian Worship *(1985)*

The Joint Hymnal Committee for Christian Worship *(1992)*

Kurt Eggert working with Kermit Moldenhauer, music editor for Christian Worship

Presentation of Christian Worship *by Rev. Victor Prange to Mrs. Ruth Eggert, WELS convention, Saginaw, Michigan (1993)*

Hymnals used by WELS (1850–2000)

Christian Worship *supplementary materials*

Kurt and Ruth Eggert (40th wedding anniversary, 1988)